AUTOBIOGRAPHY

OF

EMMA HARDINGE BRITTEN

AUTOBIOGRAPHY

OF

EMMA HARDINGE BRITTEN

AUTHOR OF

"History of Modern American Spiritualism"; "Nineteenth Century Miracles"; "Wildfire Club"; "Faiths, Facts, and Frauds of Religious History"; "The Electric Physician"; "On the Road; or a Manual for Spiritual Investigators"; "The Western Star Magazine"; "The Unseen Universe Magazine"; and numerous Lectures on Religion, Theology, Social Science and Reform.

EDITED AND PUBLISHED BY MRS. MARGARET WILKINSON
(HER SISTER AND SOLE SURVIVING RELATIVE)

WINFIELD TERRACE, OLD TRAFFORD, MANCHESTER

1900

This facsimile edition published in 1996 by
SNU PUBLICATIONS

First published in 1900 by
Mrs. M. Wilkinson

This is a facsimile edition published in 1996 by
SNU Publications
Redwoods
Stansted Hall
Stansted
Essex CM24 8UD

ISBN 978 0 902036 08 6

Reprinted in England by Booksprint

PREFACE.

THE latter half of the century, now almost at its close, has seen the rise and progress of many movements of thought that have had an appreciable influence in moulding the opinions of the world on many important themes. In Art, Science, Philosophy, Religion, and Morals we have seen the old give place to the new, and many an opinion considered as sacrosant has been dismissed as no longer tenable in the new light that has been shed upon the problems that have vexed the souls of men in the past. To-day chattel slavery is abhorrent. Philosophy is no longer perforce harnessed to the Juggernaut Car of Religious Bigotry ; Art and Literature are the possession of the multitude. Political and Industrial Freedom has become a commonplace of thought, and Religion is rapidly escaping from the trammels of orthodox conventions. While Modern Spiritualism, that at one time was a "voice crying in the wilderness," finds its acceptance assured and respectful consideration given to its facts, and their deductions. At the end of another fifty years who shall say what position "this stone rejected of the builders" will occupy ?

Without here raising needlessly debatable matter, it is not too much to say that the progress and freedom of thought above referred to has to no inconsiderable extent been furthered, if not positively initiated, by what is generally to be described as Modern Spiritualism, for admitting its fundamental fact, that of intercourse between the living and the so-called dead, to be true, there must follow a certain revolution of the world's opinions upon the hitherto accepted conceptions of Science, Philosophy, and Religion. A revolution as important, and as far reaching in results as followed the acceptance of the theories of Copernicus concerning the physical universe, and of the Protestant Reformers as to the opinions previously accepted in the religious world. What Copernicus and Newton did for the science of their days, Huss, Ridley, and Knox accomplished in their times, aided by the Wesleys, Whitfield, and their co-workers. But it is not enough that the world should have been enlightened as to the nature of the physical universe on the one hand, or that religious thought should be measurably purified on the other hand ; a still further enlightenment was also required as to that "other world," as well. Without this further illumination there still remained a state of uncertainty, not to say darkness, over that deepest of all problems, as expressed in that old time question, "if a man die shall he live again?"

The curious conjunction of Materialism and Mesmerism of fifty years ago forms to the student an instructive incident, reflecting as it did the despair of Rationalists on the one side, and the hunger of the seekers after a stable basis for man's immortality on the other hand ; the one side being a revolt against unprovable dogmas, as was the other an equal revolt from the cold conclusions of materialistic science, and both incontinently cursed by the very authorities they severally and jointly questioned by the facts they presented. Cahagnet and Alexis in Paris ; Reichenbach in Germany, Ashburner in England, Bovee Dodds in New York, and many others presented personal facts that could not be accounted for by science, but which, nevertheless, demanded answers, if science was to be complete. For such experiences marked the demolition of the old fanciful line between the Natural and so-called Supernatural, while the advent of the Hydesville Rappings still further accentuated the needful mingling of the two sides of Nature, if a satisfactory science was ever to be established, by which the entire of being was to be brought within the range of rational and orderly conception and discussion.

The history of all movements reveals the fact that when the hour comes the man arrives ! The agent arises, from where least expected, at a time when no one realises it ; but that agent, if called by the divine necessities of the case, sweeps triumphantly to the forefront, and irresistibly accomplishes the appointed task.

Youth, age, or sex, matters not; race or colour is immaterial; the Worker appears, and though the path may be strewn with thorns, and the martyr's crown be the halo earned, yet, in spite of all, the task is accomplished, and the world is helped beyond all staying. The present may give but scant recognition, the future will make amends. To find one's name on the world's roll of honour is no mean reward for tears, wounds and death, suffered for the world's well being.

To such honour came the subject of the Autobiography disclosed in the following pages. Unexpectedly—nay, almost unwillingly—called to her high office, as Embassadress to the Unseen World, Emma Hardinge Britten played her part in the world drama, and filled it nobly and well. And in the following pages she speaks to us in her own glowing periods, and tells us something of her life services, trials and triumphs, on behalf of that cause that has surely revolutionised the opinions of the world at large concerning " that bourne from which," in spite of the Swan of Avon, " travellers " do " return," to make glad the hearts of the bereaved and sorrowing ones of earth.

Arduous as were her platform duties, nevertheless she was just as active in the use of her pen. Articles without number were contributed to our Press in all parts of the world, sometimes on questions other than those with which she was most identified. Politics, Social Reform, Music, Education, History, Travel—she wrote with ability and facility on each, while her permanent contributions to the literature of Spiritualism were numerous and valuable. Among these were: " A History of Modern American Spiritualism," " Nineteenth Century Miracles," " The Faiths, Facts, and Frauds of Religious History," " The Wildfire Club," " The Magnetic and Electric Physician," and as the Editor, " Art Magic " and " Ghost Land " must also be credited to her industry. There were also Editorial contributions and direction to American Spiritual journals, including her own magazines, " The Western Star," in America and " The Unseen Universe " in England. Work enough to occupy a less energetic person entirely without the additional duties of exhaustive travel and continuous lecturing.

The] closing scenes of this busy life were passed in her own land, but the same tireless energy characterised her then as ever. For five years her abilities were unstintedly expended in the Editorial chair of "The Two Worlds," which paper rapidly sprang into public favour under her care. Her severance from that connection was admittedly a matter of pain to her, and doubtless was also a cause of continued regret, because of the untoward circumstances] that induced it. She herself summed it up in her memorable phrase that "Spiritualism is Divine, but Spiritualists are human!" It is pleasing to record, however, that the wound was in great part healed before she departed hence. As of the departed, so of misunderstandings that are past, the old proverb *de mortuis nil nisi bonum* may be the epitaph of things to be forgotten.

Whoso peruses the following pages, from her own pen, may now do so the more clearly from what has gone before. The matters related have been culled from the personal diaries of the subject in hand, and so far can be accepted as a faithful, if limited, statement of the career of her whom we all delight to honour. The task committed to the writer has been, truly, a labour of love. Other hands could have done it with greater claims to ability and merit, but none could have done it with worthier motives. It is the tribute of one who knew her for nearly thirty years, who was glad to be her co-worker, and proud to be her friend. One, too, who gladly recalls many an encouraging word spoken in the days when he was unknown and struggling, and who is not ashamed to say he is still grateful for the unswerving friendship of the past. In this he is not singular, for thousands can assuredly say the same, and remember her as a wise counseller and faithful friend.

The curtain falls on the earthly drama, the chief performer has left the stage. The lights are out, and the audience has scattered, but the memory of the scenes remain. It was a noble life, and a useful one, too. Its effect on millions cannot be told in words. Its ringing pleas for Truth, Liberty, and Progress yet sound in our ears, and the inspirations of those tones remain with us as an undying encouragement to go on in the great work her hands never tired in doing. If the modern Spiritual dispensation ever recognises Saints, Heroes, or Prophets she will, without doubt, be canonised, and placed with honour in our Pantheon, for she spared not energy, faithfulness or any service, in aiding the present day to a larger knowledge of that Gospel of Angel ministry that has done so much to banish the fear of death from our minds, and the bitter load of tears and grief from heart and cheek of the sad, the sorrowing and despairing.

Truly we can say that being "dead" she still speaketh. For there can be no question to the Spiritualists that she is as ever a worker from within the veil as she was while this side thereof. We hail thee then still, Emma Hardinge Britten, noble woman, faithful worker, and nobler title than all, faithful friend of mankind and true fellow worker with the unseen Angel hosts, to whom, for our emancipation she gave her all. My loving task is done; accept it, dear friend, "with all its imperfections on its head," for none may esteem you more than he who is still your fellow worker.

J. J. MORSE.

Dedication.

TO THE IMMORTALS WHO HAVE GUIDED

MY FOOTSTEPS ON EARTH

THESE RECORDS OF MY LIFE HISTORY ARE GRATEFULLY

INSCRIBED BY THE AUTHOR,

EMMA HARDINGE BRITTEN.

CONTENTS

AUTOBIOGRAPHICAL SKETCH

OF THE LIFE AND SPIRITUAL EXPERIENCES OF

EMMA HARDINGE BRITTEN,

TRANCE CLAIRVOYANT AND INSPIRATIONAL SPIRIT MEDIUM.

CHAPTER I.

"There's a divinity that shapes our ends,
Rough-hew them how we will."—Shakespeare.

PERHAPS amongst the most devoted and indefatigable of
the Propagandists, included in the ranks of modern
Spiritualism, not one has enjoyed or suffered, as the case
might be, a larger amount of "biographical press" notice,
both from friends and enemies, than the writer of the
following pages.

The truth is, that my own time has been so constantly
occupied, that, whilst it has been a part of my public duty
to answer, and not unfrequently to debate with, my
enemies, I have been compelled to pass by, unnoticed, the
occasional mistakes and not unfrequently the all too lavish
eulogies of my friends, hoping to be able to correct the
same, some day in "the good time coming."

As autobiographical publications sometimes seem to
imply a self-sufficient idea of the writer's own importance,
a sentiment which would be wholly foreign to my mind or
intention, I may preface my experiences by stating, in
the first place, the sources from which my record has been

drawn, and next, the reasons which induce me to think the references I shall have to make to many notable Pioneers of the early Spiritual movement may compensate for any lack of interest, in an otherwise merely personal narrative.

In the desire to cheer the heart of a beloved and lonely mother, from whose dear side my world-wide travels continually called me away, I never failed to send her, at least once a week, written and printed accounts of my whereabouts and doings.

Now that the dear mother has become a watching Angel of the higher life, I have had occasion to examine her piles of literary treasures, and excising from the dramatic records of the past all but such as may serve to beat down waymarks for the information of those that shall come after me, I proceed to comply with the reiterated demands of the many sympathising friends who have cheered my toilsome path, by selecting such portions of my biographical memoranda as may illustrate the life and work of a Pioneer Nineteenth Century " Spirit Medium."

Cornelius Agrippa and other Mediæval Mystics have affirmed, that a Magician to attain to successful achievement " must be born a Magician."

Reviewing my own youthful experiences, I am perfectly convinced that this remark applies as surely to "Spirit Mediums" as to Magicians—indeed to my apprehension the two terms are synonymous.

The Spiritual gifts that are normal to mediumistic individuals from birth may change and alter during earth life, but never wholly depart, and as this was happily my own case, and I was "born a witch," as some of my public opponents have politely informed the world, I have experienced many changes, though no actual loss of mediumistic unfoldment, throughout a long and busy career.

Referring briefly to my early childhood I can now understand those problematical points in my young life which puzzled alike my parents and teachers. Being gifted with a fine voice and a passionate love for music, even as a little child, I was a centre of attraction, and the subject of extravagant prophecies of future distinction.

Looking back upon my own earliest recollections, I fancy that I was never young, joyous or happy, like other children; my delight was to steal away alone and seek the solitude of woods and fields, but above all to wander in churchyards, cathedral cloisters, and old monastic ruins.

Here strange sounds would ring in my ears, sometimes in the form of exquisite music, suggesting new compositions and pathetic songs, sometimes in voices uttering dim prophecies of future events, especially in coming misfortunes. At times forms of rare beauty or appalling ugliness flitted across my path, wearing the human form, and conveying impressions of identity with those who had once lived on earth.

At the time of these unchildlike experiences, no one around understood me, though the servants of the family would often say in low tones amongst themselves, that, *the child had described some of their dead relatives, also that whatever I prophesied was sure to come to pass.*

The happiest period of these immature years was, strange to say, when I was, as frequently happened, laid on a bed of sickness. To pass away in dreams, as I then believed, into lovely green fields amidst strange and most beautiful people, was such rapture to me, that I was wilful enough to try and take cold, so that I might be laid up and go off to my unknown and fascinating fairy land.

Never understood by those around me, it was only in after years and when I became *called* and associated with a secret society of Occultists and attended their sessions in London as one of their clairvoyant and magnetic subjects, that I myself began to comprehend why a young girl fairly educated, and blessed with many advantages, should be branded with such peculiarities of disposition as must inevitably shut her off from all companionship with children of her own age and standing.

The society of Occultists to whom I can now only allude, and who are named in "Ghost-Land" as the "Orphic Circle," obtained knowledge (by means I am not at liberty to mention) of those persons whose associations they desired.

None of the members were known as such outside their circles, the existence of the society was undreamed of, and those whom they *chose* to affiliate with *they knew of and called*. I having been thus favoured obtained a clue to my own exceptional early experiences, which the subsequent developments of Spiritualism stamped as natural Seership.

As the powers so mystical in my own person were thoroughly comprehended by the "Adepts" of the "Orphic Society," as I may venture to call them, I shall sum up this portion of my early life by quoting a few lines of an article written by one of my occult associates, and published in the *Medium* some years ago.

"A ghost seeress, somnambulist, improvisatrice in music, and a prophetess, the strange weird child, 'Emma Floyd,' was the terror of her nursery attendants, and the problem of all who knew her. It seems probable that hereditary influences were prevalent in this child's nature. Descended from the renowned 'Welsh wizard,' Owen Glendower, little Emma also partook of the characteristics of her father, a sea captain, and a man of phenomenal powers of prevision, and other qualities of a Spiritualistic order. There were many circumstances in Emma's early life which, as a thoughtful woman, she now considers to have been instrumental in preparing her for her present mission. Being deprived of her good father's care at a very tender age, the young girl, like the rest of her family, was compelled to depend upon her own talents for subsistence. Her phenomenal musical endowments determined her friends to educate her for the operatic profession. The exercise of her musical powers, and other circumstances, threw her into the society of persons far above her in rank and educational culture, and thus, as she herself modestly alleges, she derived certain advantages which she never could have enjoyed as a humble musical student, and which she now finds have been of incalculable value in preparing her as an instrument for the Spiritual rostrum.

It was during the time that the young girl enjoyed the fairest prospects of achieving eminence as an opera singer that she found all those prospects blighted by her irrepressible somnambulic tendencies.

During the progress of her studies at Paris she became impelled to rise from her bed in profound sleep, climb tremendous heights, traverse the wintry streets, preach, recite, and enact fearful scenes ; very often the somnambulist would utter wild cries and screams, the result of which was to create so violent an irritation of the vocal chords that she ultimately lost her fine soprano voice, and was compelled to relinquish her operatic pursuits. . . . . .

It has been a favourite theory with me, and with some others much wiser than myself, that in our one earthly career we may live many lives, and, without ever losing our personal identity, undergo changes analogous to many deaths and new lives. I am quite sure I suffered the bitterness of death when my good father, to whom I was passionately attached, passed away from earth. With a breaking heart, I, a little eleven-years-old child, was sent out to earn my bread as a pupil-teacher of music. Hating my life, and longing to join my father—somewhere, anywhere with him—I resolved to follow him, and thus I stood one dark night by the river's brink, and was only saved from seeking a winding sheet in the Avon's depths at Bristol, by the sound of my dead father's voice bidding me return to school, and leading me back, as I distinctly felt, by the hand. To me it seemed as if I had died then, and shortly afterwards commenced a new life in musical studies in Paris. But here it was that my unconquerable somnambulic tendencies impelled me to midnight wander ings, wild screams, and ultimate loss of my promising voice. At that time, in my grief and blighted prospects, I died to the lyric stage and tried to commence a new life as a pianiste and composer. Dear good Pierre Erard, the venerable founder of the grand pianoforte magasin in Paris, gave me the loan of a lovely instrument on condi- tion of my coming every day to the warehouse and practising there for the behoof of buyers.

Endless were the great and notable personages who came to Erard's to hear the child pianiste, but when it was found that I was also a *magnetic subject*, and by a wave of the hand above my head, and even an *unspoken* wish on the part of my audience, that I could play any air desired, my poor mother became astonished and frightened at this new and unusual accomplishment, anxiously con- sulting a medical man on the subject—then so rare and ill- understood—she and others of my best friends were assured that I was under some *evil*, perhaps *Satanic*, influence, and that unless I was stopped in this mad career it would either end in permanent lunacy or death. Stopped, of course, my career as a musician was, and thus I returned to England, adopted the stage as my profession, and became an actress. Of some years of strange and varied experiences at the Adelphi and other London theatres I do not propose to speak in detail; as a curious indication, however, of how the web of human life destiny may be spun out without either the volition or agency of the individuals most concerned, I will come to the closing chapter of my English theatrical experiences, only pre- mising, in justice to others, what more than one living witness *could, if they would*, confirm, and that is that perhaps few young girls in narrow circumstances, leading a busy struggling life, were ever subject to more sore temptations from a vicious aristocracy than myself. With a few good steady friends, and an angel mother ever by my side, I steered my way through the Scylla and Charybdis of London stage life *for a time*, but with a closing story to tell, all too well known to many of my companions of that period, but one which has never before been made public, and one, it may be hoped, as rarely enacted as it may seem strange and incredible. By one cruel and remorseless persecutor, in the person of a baffled sensualist, several of the theatrical *entrepreneurs* by whom I was engaged or in treaty with, were induced by *specially prepared golden arguments* to cancel any engagements with me, so that I might be driven to the last necessity of placing myself under my millionaire enemy's *kind* protection. Burning with rage rather than the despair so coolly relied upon; buoyed up, too, by youth and the ever-present unseen powers that I now so well know shaped my destiny, I endured this terrible taboo for a time, but under my good and beloved mother's counsel I determined at length to baffle it. Having at that time in a great measure recovered my vocal powers, and having also been at one time strongly urged to pursue an Italian operatic career by Sir Michael Costa, I formed the sudden resolution of calling on him, telling him the almost incredible history which was aiming to drive me from the London histrionic stage, and, under another name, offering to adopt an Italian operatic career. On calling at Sir Michael's former residence, I found he had left it, and I could only learn that he had gone to reside in some one of the roads leading out of St. John's Wood. Proceeding at once in that direction, I became confused by the number of roads which invited attention, and whilst I was considering which path to choose, I noticed a crowd of persons standing around an open garden-gate half way along a quiet street, and I determined in my own mind to

enquire of them, believing that I should there find the
party I sought.   As I neared the throng one of their
number, an actor I well knew—a Mr. G. H.—ran up to me,
shook my hand warmly, and before I could utter a word,
declared he was delighted to see me there, and that I was
just the very person that was wanted.   "Wanted; where,
what, why, and by whom?" I gasped out.   G. H. replied,
all in a breath, that Mr. J. W. Wallack had advertised for
an English company to take to the Imperial Theatre, at
Paris, for high-class Shakesperian drama; that I was
wanted, must come.   Of course, he said *I had come for
that purpose*, and he *was sure* I should be at once engaged.
Before I could utter a word, either of enquiry or remon-
strance, I was led up a long garden walk by my chattering
enthusiastic friend, briefly presented to Mr. and Mrs.
Wallack, who stood on the terrace of their house, shaken
hands with, welcomed, and, in about less time than it has
taken me to write this account, I had signed an engagement for so many weeks to play in the Imperial Theatre,
Paris, with the J. W. Wallack Company, to start in four
days, whilst the only stipulation that I was enabled to
squeeze in, amidst a clamour of voices, explanations, and
no explanations, was that the managers should permit me
to take with me, and pay the passage of, my angel
guardian, my ever faithful mother.   . . . .
   Once again, between the straits of Dover and Calais, I
died to the London stage and arrived in Paris a new being.
We had friends and acquaintances in the gay city, and
though the Wallack Company was a total financial failure,
and paid nobody, we spent many pleasant weeks in Paris
when not busy at the theatre amongst my musical
associates.   I had nothing to regret, but still another new
experience to learn, whilst another note of preparation
rung out, in anticipation of my approaching future—
magnetism and magnetic experiment were just then the

rage in Paris. Again invited to morning séances at Erard's pianoforte rooms, my intense susceptibility to occult powers brought me prominently under the notice of the magnetisers, amongst whom were not a few of the highest personages in the land. Tempting offers of engagements as a magnetic subject were made, but these were determinately rejected by my good mother, whose aversion to my participation in such experiments was equally steadfast and unconquerable. The last night of the English Wallack Company's performances had arrived; on that occasion I played in a little character piece of my own writing, and at its close, our most intimate friend in Paris. being, as was his custom, behind the scenes, introduced me to a gentleman whom I found talking with this friend and my mother, and endeavouring to convince her that the best and most attractive spot on earth for the display of my peculiar talents, etc., etc., was the B—— Theatre, of New York, of which he himself was the manager. He had watched me playing various parts many nights, he alleged, and had determined to engage me, and go to New York I must, and that immediately.

Looking through the dim haze of the future, as I had of late repeatedly done, all seemed impenetrably dark, utterly veiled from mortal sight in the direction of my native city of London—yet still there ever seemed to be looming up before me a *new life,* somewhere and somehow, one that gleamed like a prophetic vision, but the shape or nature of which I could not clearly discern. Was it, I often asked myself, in the magnetic flights to other and far distant worlds of being that these prophetic monitions were to be realised? My good mother's positive veto had closed my chances of being a professional somnambulist. Was it to be in the New World then that I was to find the fresh path of discovery, of which, as yet, distant gleams alone had broken in upon my sight?

Yet I shared the common and at one time vulgar prejudice of my country against America, and coldly tried to crush the enthusiasm of the American manager by promising *to think* of his offer, and let him know what we—that is, my mother and I—thought about it. "That would not do," replied the gentleman, whom I at once mentally stamped as a "presumptuous Yankee."

My mother did favour his offer, and as he was about to embark on his return to New York immediately, my answer must be given at once—*I must come.* He would pay my mother's passage out with my own, and engage me for nine months, at what seemed, to a young struggling girl like me, an excellent salary. An adjournment to an office room, a hastily drawn-up agreement, carefully written out instructions for the voyage, promised settlements for our passage, and final signatures on my part and that of my new manager, with any number of witnesses to documents on both sides ensued, and my future path in life and entrance upon a New World's series of adventures was all concluded before the clocks of Paris struck twelve on that—to me—most momentous night.

Reviewing this hurried panorama of events, the next morning on first awakening, I concluded that the repeated assertion of my occult associates was correct, to wit—I was a good magnetic subject, and my new manager was a good magnetiser. Nevertheless, as I sprang from my bed with the question ringing in my ears "To be or not to be," another and still clearer voice seemed to solve all my doubts and difficulties with the o'ertrue words, "There's a divinity that shapes our ends, rough-hew them how we will."

CHAPTER II.

A MUCH greater and wiser writer than the one that dictates this chapter has said:—

"The foundations of Heaven are laid in Hell."

And another—the renowned Dante—farther illustrates some of the special experiences of which I am about to write by remarking that "Out of the way of darkness cometh the path of light."

It may be that I am destined to illustrate both these renowned sayings even in the humble footprints of her who traces out her own life memoirs in these (at present) unknown pages.

If I have abstained from dwelling upon the details of my early life and education, except in their general features and occupations, it is because I could not do justice to their many sad, strange, and even startling events without recalling names that I should now be reluctant to involve with my own, and mention personages who have played out their parts in life's fitful drama, and passed on to scenes far removed from the paths which I have been called upon to tread.

Since parting with these vanished ones, it must suffice to say that a life history crowded up with joys and sorrows, changes of fortune, and romantic adventure was my lot, and filled up my chequered career even before my twentieth year.

All this would be of little or no interest to the readers of a modern Spiritual biography; yet I am well convinced these vicissitudes were so many stepping stones necessary to the formation of a character destined to become the instrument of a world of being the very existence of which was not even dreamed of in the days of my girlhood. It seemed, too, to be necessary for the future reformer to realise in her own person every emotion of the Soul, before the possibilities of Soul power in others could be understood. Yet thus it was, and thus I learned my varied and often tragic life lesson even before the period when most other girls are only emerging into their first years of womanhood. And now, accompanied by my faithful mother, I recall myself hurriedly embarking on the ocean steamer "Pacific," bound for the Land of the Setting Sun, and for the first time in my life on the vast waste of waters that separated me alike from friend and foe.

Landed at length amidst the ceaseless rush and hurry of New York City, America, escorted by one of our fellow passengers to a quiet lodging tendered as a temporary home in his own house, where my poor mother and I sat down to gaze into each other's faces with pitying glances, then to shed bitter tears as the sound of a street organ wailed out the all-too-familiar notes of "Home, sweet home," and finally to dry our tears and pledge ourselves to act out the new life before us as bravely as if we had indeed died to the cares and struggles of the past, and in a new land and—even if they were unknown—conditions do our best to realise that it was Heaven's inspiration that had sent us to the shores of the New World.

The theatre at which I was engaged was not yet open for the season, and some days of rest were before us.

Though courteously received by the treasurer of the company, and guided to what he considered to be a suitable boarding place, the opening incident of our new life was a most unpropitious one. At my first interview with my American manager—the gentleman who had all too-vehemently urged upon me the acceptance of his pressing offers of an engagement—I found such a wide

divergence in our views of future expectations and relations that if I had only been in possession of the means
to do so, I should have determined on immediate return
to England.

Failing in the ability to accomplish my rash purpose,
my next move on the chequer-board of fate was to sink
down into a severe fit of illness. Both my mother and I
deemed this attack one of a purely mental character,
though the good doctor, who was the medical attendant of
the theatre, assured us it was the effect of a New York
climate during the heat of August, on an unaccustomed
organism. Our boarding place also he deemed objection-
able, and he advised our immediate removal to a more
healthful situation; he kindly assisted us in the change,
the result of which was my rapid recovery and first
appearance at the theatre.

Having found amongst the posthumous papers of my
beloved mother her treasured clippings from different
papers in which my widely-bandied name figures, I am
enabled to recall the fact that I was received most
graciously by my Western audience, and became the
subject of warm complimentary notices from the various
New York papers. All would not do. Despite the fact
that I continued in favour with the public, and appeared
with success in several little character pieces that I had
written for myself, the divergence of views between my
manager and myself increased in bitterness, and finally
provoked the following results. The 'gentleman in question first tried to degrade me by compelling me to appear
in the most insignificant parts, and finding that there was
a strong party of friends raised up in my favour both
amongst the warm-hearted company (who knew him so
well) and some of the outside public, he resorted to the
safer expedient of shelving me—that is, of leaving me out
of the bills almost *in toto*.

Many offers of fresh engagements in other theatres were tendered me, but as my contract was for a nine months' season, I was advised *not to give cause* for offence by breaking my engagement.

Here let me pause to offer a tribute of kind but just praise to the warm hearts of "the poor players." They understood it all—pitied and would have lovingly helped me, if they could; but a higher power than that of earth was about us all, and though the position I was placed in, almost alone in a veritable new world, was indeed a most deplorable one, still I can now see that all these to me unexpected reverses of fortune and bitter trials were but providential means for outworking the path of destiny which was ultimately to open up before me.

In the comparative obscurity to which my *amiable* manager condemned me two noteworthy results ensued. One was the formation of a new acquaintance in the person of Mr. Boaler, an English gentleman, who became informed of my position, and who called upon me as an act of kindness; and the other was my introduction by this same gentleman to a well known New York lady, a Mrs. Jennie Watson, of Great James Street.

The ostensible reason for which Mr. Boaler introduced this lady to me was her strong desire to thrash my manager, an act which, she assured me, she had once performed on a certain party before, and one which she should be very happy to repeat again on my behalf. Although I at once declined this lady's noble offer I accepted her friendship, which from that time forth, together with that of Mr. Boaler, continued throughout many years, and was a source of unspeakable pleasure to my mother and myself in our American experiences. The second result of my manager's policy in condemning me to comparative idleness was, that as I needed occupation and amusement, I sought both in the following way. In the new boarding house to which our kind doctor had recommended us, as we, of course, sat at the table at meals with many other boarders of the house, we met amongst them a married couple who, though nice people, excited my equal surprise and horror by perpetually talking of their intercourse with "*Spirits of the dead,*" whom they represented as being all alive again, and behaving very much as if they were on the most intimate terms with the people of the earth they had quitted. Now, in order to apprehend correctly the horror and aversion with which such language inspired me, it must be understood that whilst I had ever been a "Ghost seer," and accustomed to hear mysterious voices, I never could connect such sights and sounds with the "Spirits of the dead." I did not know what, or who were the apparitions I saw, or from whence came the voices, music, and other sounds I heard. When I became the elected Seeress of a certain Occult society (as before referred to) I was always in a somnambulic condition, the details of which I did not remember on awaking. Besides this I had been taught by my Occultist associates that there were realms of *submundane* or *elementary beings* who appeared on earth as ghosts, spectres, and demons; also that there were supermundane existences, such as angels, planetary and solar spirits, but that the apparitions that were seen in human shape were nothing more or less than *shades, vestiges,* or *emanations from the dead, resulting from the pernicious custom of earthly interments, instead of cremation.* I must add, moreover, that in the total lack of any well proven or reliable knowledge concerning these subjects in my case, as in that of millions of other Christians, the intensely spiritual elements of my nature found expression only in the teachings of orthodoxy, and such faiths as I acquired by being sent as a matter of duty to hear preaching, go to church at stated intervals, or officiate as organist or singer at church services; in a word, I was, and ever had been, a very *pious girl*, and the familiar talk of my new associates about *Spirits!* whom *I knew*, or thought *I knew*, either to be " gone to God," or *to the other party*, or else to be sleeping in the ground until some millions of years hence—resurrection day—was so shocking to me that I felt as if it was desecration to remain under the same roof with people who indulged in such talk. After mentioning these, my scruples on this subject, to my landlady, she assured me the parties complained of, whom she called by the hitherto unknown term of "Spiritualists," were amongst her best and most respectable boarders, and she only wished I would see and talk with them in private, when she was assured I should change my opinion of them. Having at length, as a matter of *duty and conscience*, consented to hold this interview in private, I became so deeply interested in the plain, straightforward account of spirit intercourse, and the wide-spread manifestations of spirit phenomena they related to me, that at length I consented to accompany Mr. Ranney, a worthy Canadian gentleman, who was one of the much dreaded " Spiritualists, " to a place wherein, as I was assured, I could learn the truth. of what he alleged for myself.

Notwithstanding the fascination which this subject of possible Spirit return possessed for me, it required many conversations and much persuasion to induce me to visit the *Spirit depot*, as I contemptuously phrased it, where I was to obtain the promised evidences. When my scruples were at length overcome, I accompanied my new friend to a shabby looking house in Canal Street, and after ascending two or three flights of uncarpeted narrow stairs, I found myself in a dismal ill-furnished room, where a number of commonplace looking people were sitting round a wooden table, watching with seemingly deep interest its heavy and incessant rockings to and fro. Although this

"Circle room," as I was informed, was a public one, and open to any strangers who paid the stipulated fee at the door, my companion whispered to me that the party was in the midst of receiving a communication from "the *Spirits*," and we must wait quietly where we stood until it was completed, when no doubt we should be invited to join the circle. Without the slightest idea of what connection might exist between a Spirit communication and that rocking table, but keeping both eyes and ears carefully on the alert, I heard a thin, sad-faced looking man at one end of the table keep on repeating letters of the alphabet over and over again in a monotonous tone, until he at length stopped, when one of the party who seemed to have been engaged in writing something, said, speaking in a clear loud tone : "The Spirit answers, Immortality would be a mere fiction were there no other evidence of it than Bible teaching." This was enough for me. These horrrid "ghoul" like looking infidels were pitching into the Bible ! Without having the slightest idea of the question which had called forth this answer, or by whom, or in what manner the answer came, it was enough for me to hear the words—"fiction" "Bible"—jumbled up together in a slighting and irreverent way.

Like hundreds of others whom I have since observed running away at the first moment they hear anything concerning their stereotyped faiths that they do not like, instead of stopping to enquire or reason about, I, too, ran away—or rather, I should say fled—rushing precipitately down the stairs into the street, and back to my own room, to fall on my knees and pray for forgiveness for having visited such an infidel place, and been found amongst such infidel people.

It was some time before the shock which my *religious* nature had received subsided, and then, weary of the *ennui* which enforced idleness imposed upon me, a bright idea for beguiling my time occurred to me. I had been accustomed to write both for musical and dramatic papers. I had promised some of my literary associates in London jottings from my American experiences, and what a capital article I might make as above ˙ suggested by exposing this "Yankee humbug" of "Spirits" talking through rocking tables! And now, seeing that my engagement at the theatre would end in a few weeks, how very desirable it was that I should at once improve the occasion, and learn sufficient about the "horrid stuff" to enable me to write a crushing article by and by before my return home on "*American fooleries!*"

In pursuance of this *hospitable*, and highly commendable purpose, I listened with more favour than usual to one of my theatrical friends, Mr. Augustus Fenno, with whom I was often associated in such pieces as I was allowed to appear in, and who, besides being an exceedingly sociable companion, was perpetually talking to all who would listen about Spirits—the wonderful things they could do, and the wonderful intelligence they could and did communicate.

Having in one of my interviews with Mr. Fenno mentioned to him my intense disgust and indignation at the words I had heard at the Canal Street séance, at which, as I claimed, I had heard the *word of "God," the Bible*, spoken slightingly of, Mr. Fenno urged me to visit another medium, an acquaintance of his own, as he said, through whom I should hear and witness nothing less than irrevocable truth.

Bearing in mind my determination of showing up the whole thing in editorial articles to my English compatriots, I consented to visit Mr. Fenno's "*rara avis*," provided he would take me THEN AND THERE AT ONCE. "That is to say," rejoined Mr. Fenno, "before I can have any chance of preparing the medium by a visit, of who you are or what to say to you." "Even so," I briefly replied. " All right," said my friend, laughing. "Better so, then whatever you may get will be genuine and unexpected," and so my friend and I in a few minutes were in the street and *en route* to another house in Canal Street, where I was not to be introduced to the medium, but simply to watch, and form my own conclusions.

What results accrued in this visit I must now reserve for the succeeding chapter.

CHAPTER III.

Dawning Light.

ONCE more ascending the narrow uncarpeted stairs of a
Canal Street lodging-house, and with every sentiment of
prejudice awakened by its mean surroundings, I found
myself in a small, plainly furnished room, to which we
were admitted, after sundry knockings and waiting, by a
young person, whom Mr. Fenno briefly named as the lady,
now known as "Mrs. Ada Foye."

To Mr. Fenno's enquiry if she could give us a sitting,
she answered she could. The said "Medium" (as Mr.
Fenno had called her) looked very young, and presented
nothing either in appearance or address of that weird
nature which one generally associates with the idea of a
"Witch"; still less did she evince any of that subtle and
designing manner which ordinarily characterises an impostor. She seemed to be acquainted with Mr. Fenno,
and without deigning to bestow any notice on me, whom
Mr. Fenno briefly announced as "a young friend of his who
wished for a sitting," she motioned me to a chair at an
uncovered table and commenced an animated conversation
with my friend.

Almost as soon as I was seated, a succession of sounds
like blows on the under side of the table ensued. "Oh!
there they are," said the Medium—"your friend is a great
Medium herself." Here I looked up to the ceiling to see
if it was not going to fall on such an iniquitous being as
the party designated as "*a great Medium.*" "Here,"
she added—pushing a card towards me covered with the
letters of the alphabet—"take this pencil"—giving me
one—"I see you are a sceptic, so point to the letters

yourself and they will rap to those they want to spell out words with."

"*They*," I mentally said. "Who are *they*! I should like to know."

The knocks were now loud and furious. I just waited until the Medium and my friend were deeply engaged in some irrelevant conversation, when, seizing the light wooden table, I turned it up savagely in search of the springs or other machinery with which the sounds were made. Instantly, knockings equally loud left the innocent table, and positively thundered beneath my feet on the floor. In a moment I was on my knees, feeling along the ground for *the springs that were not there*. At once, and as if by magic, the knocks left the floor and resounded along the wall, the mantel-shelf, door, and all parts of the room. Baffled and aghast, I sank into a chair, when violent knockings commenced on the back of my chair, almost displacing me, and coming at the very spot where a moment before I had held my hand. *I knew then* those sounds were neither made by machinery or connected with the young woman whom I had come to see. Pitying my evident confusion, Mrs. Foye said—and this time she spoke most kindly—" You are yourself a great Medium, and the Spirits, as I am impressed to say, have a mighty work to perform through you. Now, be calm. Point with that pencil to the alphabet, and Mr. Fenno will take down the letters rapped at. See! I will sit away from the table, but remain in your sight."

Oh, Heavens! what a scene followed. All the friends I had ever known—nay, the mere acquaintances I had casually met, and long since forgotten the existence of, returned unsought, spelled out by rappings at special letters of the alphabet, their names, ages, places of life and death, and at times wrote rapidly, through the Medium's hand, details of TEST FACTS, events, and sometimes of secret things known only to me of all living beings on earth; secrets buried deep in my heart, and only known to me and "the dead." All this filled up in rapid succession over two hours, in which the panorama of my life and many of those with whom I had walked my life path, and now deemed dead, came with an accuracy of detail, and a disinterment of long-buried facts, that no other record on the face of the earth could have given. Doubt had been annihilated; scepticism crushed out. There we sat—we three—two of them entire strangers to the history, character, or past surroundings of the third one present. Yet in that little room were assembled invisible hosts—friends and foes—all telling their own tale, and bringing conviction of their identity such as no sane being could have rejected. All came save one, and that one the dearest of all to me, my only and most beloved brother, the sailor boy, who had parted from me a few short years ago, and the tidings of whose death in a foreign land had crushed my very youth, and converted the bright, ardent girl into a mourning woman; yet he, my girlhood's second self, came not. I felt as if I must not prolong the séance, for I knew my companions were growing weary and we must close this memorable visit.

Then it was that without hinting even at the name or profession of my brother, I expressed the bitter disappointment I felt that *he* had not come; "Try again," said the patient Medium. Loud rappings responded, I seized the card, pointed to the first letter of his name, but the spelling went off into a sentence I could not make out. The letters taken down however by my now excited friend read thus: "*Darling Emma, find a great sea snake for Tom.*" Oh, merciful powers! These were the last words my sailor brother had ever spoken to me on earth. I had long forgotten and should never have recalled them but for this reminder by the only being in existence who knew of them. This was their meaning : I had been trained as an opera singer and practised little else than Italian or German music. The young sailor boy had often expressed a wish that I would learn certain " beautiful sea songs " he loved, amongst which "Tom Starboard" and "A Great Sea Snake " were his ideals of all musical taste.

I had learned the former to please him, but excused myself from the study of the latter on the ground that I could not procure either the words or music. "Tom" was sure " so popular " a ditty must be procurable, and in taking his last leave of me to go on a voyage from which he never returned in earthly life, he called up to me, as I leaned over the stairs to catch a parting glimpse of his beloved face, those very words recorded above. And now, how could I part from him again. Still lingering, pitifully longing for more, 1 said: " If that is you, Tom, tell me the name of the ship you went away in." No knock responded, but the Medium holding out a slip of paper on which she had been rapidly writing, we read this message, *written before my very question was spoken.*

"*Sailed away in H.M.S. the manifestation of a cross girl.*" "What on earth does that mean?" cried my companions.

"*Sailed away in Her Majesty's Ship Vixen,*" I replied ; "but oh, Tom, why do you speak in such enigmas?"

Again the Medium wrote—"I gave those words only to signify the meaning of my ship's name, Vixen, because in after years no one should say that my answers were *mind reading.* My answers were seemingly too silly, darling, to have been in your mind, yet you know their meaning, and that none but *Tom* could have spelled them out, and now good bye for the present. Go back to mother, and she will tell you she has found something in her old tin box worth its weight in gold."

Parting from the dear Medium, no longer with indifference, but with many a loving kiss, and each with

tears in our eyes, I went forth that day into the streets
an utterly changed being; the world and all things around
me were changed.   Dazed as I had been, I pressed home,
both to the Medium and my friend Fenno, such questions
as " Where do these spirits dwell?   Where do they come
from? Do they see us, and if so, why can we not see them?"
To these and other similar interrogatories they had
given brief answers, emphasised by loud rappings, to the
effect that the spirit world was here the soul world of the
earth, though invisible to us, just as our souls are invisible
to our physical eyes, and only to be apprehended through
the manifestations of material forms.

Whether satisfied with these scraps of philosophy or not
I passed out into the air with the consciousness—nay, the
certainty that it was full of Spirits, full of a new though
invisible world, peopled by living beings of whom mankind
had no knowledge, beings deemed dead, lost to us perhaps
for ever, but in reality all alive and thronging around us,
sometimes if not always watching over us, reading our
secret thoughts, tracing out our secret lives—a world within
a world—filling our streets, cities, earth, air, and skies, and
we living all unconscious of their presence, calling them
dead and deeming them gone for ever.

Truly I may say I returned to my temporary home a
changed being, as changed as the world and all its belongings now seemed around me.   No sooner had I returned
to our boarding house than I was greeted by my mother in
the following words : " Emma, my dear, I am sure you will
be delighted with what I am going to tell you.   I went to
the old tin box to search out that paper I told you of,
when, on opening a package of my dearest boy's letters,
thinking it might have been put in amongst them for
safety—what do you think I found?   *Something worth
its weight in gold,*" she continued without waiting for my
answer.

"See, dear, here is that pencil drawing of our dear Tom taken by Mr. Thomas Thorne, just as the dear fellow was going on his last voyage." Here she held up a little pencil sketch of our lost sailor boy, which though executed by an amateur was still a capital likeness. The one point however which rung in my ears like a voice from Heaven, were the words of promise which I still held in my hand, that on my return, "*Mother should tell me she had been searching in her old tin box, and found something which she would consider worth its weight in gold.*"

Were these spirits then prophetic as well as clairvoyant? After kissing the precious find, still in my possession, and looking down from the wall on me as I write, I quietly informed my mother I had just been visiting another Spirit Medium. To this announcement my mother replied with an emphatic declaration, that although she had followed my footsteps over the wide world and was still ready to accompany me anywhere, yet for this horrible and blasphemous subject she had no spark of sympathy, and should I persist in its investigation, I might prepare to see her depart for England by the next ship, for beneath the roof where such abominations were practised, she never would stay.

Finding that I was more disposed to echo her sentiments than to oppose them, my mother inquired of me the result of the interview I had come from. In answer, I read to her, without comment, the questions and answers that formed the séance, together with my notes in full, and then it was that common sense triumphed over bigotry and prejudice; for my common-sense listener, when she heard of precious little tests too clearly identical with her son, husband, and dearest relatives, to be by any possibility mistaken—and when by straighforward questions she succeeded in eliciting from me a perfect detail of the whole scene—after making me go over and over again the instructions I had received as to sitting at a table for development, she closed this experience by placing a small table before me, herself, and a young lady at that time visiting us, and there, with our three pairs of hands solemnly spread out on its surface, in awful silence we sat, "*waiting for the spirits.*"

It would be equally wearisome to my readers and impossible in my own case to recall all the strange gyrations which our table performed when we three, after nearly every meal, rushed up to our sleeping apartment and spread out our three pairs of hands upon that mysterious little wooden thing formerly yclept a table, but now seemingly endowed with a far more active principle of life than either of the three mortals that sat—not at it, exactly—for the thing was continually running away from us, up into corners, and even on to other tables, pitching over into our laps, endeavouring bird-like to soar away up to the ceiling, and then striving to descend, legs uppermost, on to our heads.

The chief delight of this terribly animated piece of wood, however, appeared to be when I would go to the piano and commenced to play. It would have been patent to any observer, had we dared to admit such an one to our impious rites, that the wooden fiend was not only passionately fond of music but also an excellent judge thereof, for not only would it follow me up to the instrument but lay one of its corners caressingly on my shoulder, and keep time by dancing on the floor in fast or slow accentuations according to every change of the piece and time I played.

Both my mother and I have since seen inanimate bodies moved in presence of certain mediums hundreds and hundreds of times, and that without either surprise or fear, but to witness such a magical series of performances for the *first time,* and that without the presence of any

adept who could interpret such mysteries, was, as might be
well supposed, a trial of nerve almost beyond human
power to support. At times, too, whispering voices would
pronounce well-known names in my ear, and bright faces
would flash before me for an instant and vanish, and these
sounds and sights assured me that the terrible little table
was but a kind of electric battery moved upon by invisible
operators, and compelling us to inquire who could be the
authors of such inexplicable phenomena, unless it was
those very Spirits whom we had commenced by invoking.

We were the more bound to accept this conclusion,
when our table performances ceased as suddenly as they
had commenced. All was still again. Not a sign or
motion could be extracted from our wooden witch. But
in place of these I began spelling out by the alphabet,
which a good friend had procured for us, all sorts of
messages, names, and unexpected sentences. The power
which had formerly resided in the locomotive table seeming to have been suddenly transformed to both my hands
and arms, and obliging me to point to the letters which,
taken down, spelled out intelligence in exactly the same
way as Mrs. Foye's had done. Now and then, indeed, a
few knocks were heard sounding directly under my feet,
but these affected me with such an indescribable sense of
terror that I would rush from the room, sometimes even
downstairs and into the street, and it was only by the
utmost persuasion, and the promise to give up further
sittings, that my mother and our friend could induce me
to re-enter *that "haunted place."*

It was not long, however, before these harassing experiences were exchanged for more orderly and satisfactory
methods. Our circle of Spiritualistic acquaintances was
constantly widening, and amongst the number was a New
York music seller, a Mr. Waters.

This gentleman was an earnest and intelligent Spiritualist, and when we explained to him the difficulties which beset our investigations, he assured me I only required "*developing*" in order to become an admirable Medium. Not being quite certain whether the process of *developing me* did not involve some kind of surgical operation, I enquired into the matter with some trepidation.

Mr. Waters replied that it only meant the infusion of new magnetism into the system through the instrumentality of a powerful and experienced Medium. He added that he knew of just such an one who held public circles, a Mrs. Kellogg, and, if I was willing, he would introduce me to her.

"When?" I queried. "To-morrow evening," he replied. "Why not this evening?" "Oh, well," he said, he had a little business to do at his store before he should be free for the rest of the evening. I knew his store; had bought music there; and would, with his permission, accompany him. I could wait, but I wished to see Mrs. Kellogg *at once* or not at all.

"That is to say, you do not trust me," rejoined Mr. Waters, laughing, "and fear lest I should *prepare* Mrs. Kellogg for your reception. There, there, don't apologise, but rather maintain your cautious attitude all through your Spiritual investigations. By such precautions you will be saved from a thousand follies into which too eager and unthinking people have fallen in dealing with this new and mysterious subject."

In a few minutes my mother and I were attired for the street, joined Mr. Waters in the sitting-room, accompanied him to his store, and very soon were *en route* to the house in which Mrs. Kellogg lodged in the upper part of Broadway. Mrs. Kellogg was at that time a well-known and highly esteemed public medium, and on knocking at the door of the apartments she occupied we were informed she was just about to hold her customary Tuesday evening circle. Mr. Waters, being acquainted with the family, was at once admitted, merely adding that he wished the ladies accompanying him should have the privilege of joining the circle. After the customary fees had been paid we were at once courteously invited to take seats in a room already nearly full of strangers. Whilst awaiting my fate with direful misgivings, I was suddenly addressed by the lady medium to whom, by my own request, I had no introduction, with the words "Come here, and sit by me; you are a great medium." Obedient to her command I seated myself at the *table*, when the lady began rubbing my hands with considerable energy, but complaining all the while that I wore a *silk dress*. Why I should not do so was more than I could divine; but before I could arrange a question to this effect, a strange misty sensation came over me, which so completely obscured my faculties that an endeavour to recall who I was only ended in convincing me that I was a highly respectable old gentleman, in which character I gave, what I was afterwards informed were some remarkable *personating tests of Spirit identity* to several strangers in the room. To recapitulate the events and sensations of that evening—the first of my actual test mediumistic experience—would be simply impossible.

It is enough to record that the touch of Mrs. Kellogg's hand appeared like a magician's wand, illuminating the latent fires of magnetic power, which, once enkindled, ever after burned in the steady light of mediumistic power in myself.

During the three hours' séance of that evening it was found that I could give tests of spirit identity by personations, impressions, writing, and automatic movements of my fingers over the alphabet. All present seemed much more interested in this unexpected development than myself, who, to confess the truth, was so bewildered with my own marvellous performances, besides being under the influence of the spirits who were controlling me, that I was far more disposed to question my own identity than that of any of the spirits I was said to represent.

Notwithstanding all the striking evidences of spirit power and identity I had received through Mrs. Foye— evidences which were convincing to everyone but myself —notwithstanding the daily proofs that had multiplied around me since that memorable séance, *I could* not believe, not because I *would not*—but as I now realise, because my own good and wise spirit counsellors perceived the necessity of my being thoroughly sure of the ground I had to tread, and lead others to share with me, before I could yield up a too ready acceptance to such unprecedented facts.

All this I can now perceive "face to face," though then, I may truly say, I could only " see as in a glass darkly."

CHAPTER IV.

"HE BEING DEAD YET SPEAKETH."

As an aid to my future development I had been advised by Mrs. Kellogg to use the alphabet, and continue to sit at stated periods for practice. This I promised to do, but not finding the requisite leisure, my convictions of the Spiritual origin of my previous performances waxed weaker and weaker with the lapse of every hour.

I mentioned in a former chapter that I had come to America in the steamship "Pacific," one of the Collins line. Ever since my arrival in New York, I had maintained a kindly intercourse with some of the officials of the ship, between whom and myself little acts of friendship were exchanged every time she came into port. The ship "Pacific" was due on the memorable day when I became developed as a medium, to wit, on *Tuesday*, Feb. 19th, 1856.

On Wednesday I went down to the wharf in the hope of receiving a little package that was to be sent me from England, in charge of an officer, between whom and myself the most kindly acquaintance had been kept up ever since our landing.

The ship had not arrived, and no tidings were received of her ; but as she was only due some thirty hours, and the season rendered it likely that wintry storms would occasion the delay, no anxiety was felt in consequence.

That evening, just as my mother and I were about to retire for the night, a sudden and unusual chill crept over me, and an irresistible impression possessed my mind that a spirit had come into our presence. A sensation as if water was streaming over me accompanied the icy

chilliness I experienced, and a feeling of indescribable
terror possessed my whole being. I begged my mother
to light up every lamp we had at hand; then to open the
door, that the proximity of people in the house, outside
our room, might aid to dissipate the horror that seemed to
pervade the very air. At last, at my mother's suggestion,
I consented to sit at the table, with the alphabet we had
provided turned from me and toward her, so that she
could follow the involuntary movements of my finger,
which some power seemed to guide in pointing out the
letters.

In this way was rapidly spelled out, "Philip Smith,
ship 'Pacific.'"

For a few moments this mode of manifestation ceased,
and, to my horror, I distinctly felt an icy cold hand laid
on my arm; then, distinctly and visibly to my mother's
eyes, something pulled my hair, which was hanging in
long curls; all the while the coldness of the air increasing
so painfully that the apartment seemed pervaded by
arctic breezes.

After a while, my own convulsed hand was moved
tremblingly, but very rapidly, to spell out: "My dear
Emma, I have come to tell you I am dead. The ship
'Pacific' is lost, and all on board have perished; she
and her crew will never be heard from more."

There was little or no sleep for me that night, and at
my mother's suggestion, immediately after breakfast the
next morning I set off to consult our good friend Mrs.
Kellogg, as she had herself earnestly requested me to do
in any emergency when I might desire her advice.
Despite the unexpected nature of the message I had
received, and the power with which it came, I still
doubted, and it was in that frame of mind that I hurried
up to Mrs. Kellogg's lodgings.

As I ascended the two flights of stairs that led to the

apartments I sought, I noticed that I was being followed by an old gentleman who seemed to be climbing up after me, though with far less ease and speed. Arrived at the landing, what was my surprise to see Mrs. Kellogg coming out of her own room, her large blue eyes fixed and glazed, as if in the same trance condition in which I had beheld her before. Walking straight up to me, she took my hand, and said in a forced unnatural voice—*" My dear Emma, I have come to tell you I am dead. The ship ' Pacific' is lost,· and all on board have perished. She and her crew will never be heard from more."*

"Great Heaven!" I exclaimed, waking Mrs. Kellogg up by my energetic cry; "look here!" and then holding out the paper I had brought with me, I read in a loud—and I suppose an excited—tone, the message I had received the night before with the *fac simile* of her words, except in respect to the signature. At this moment our interview was interrupted by the old gentleman who had followed me up the stairs, and who now cried, in a loud and angry voice: "You are a pair of impostors. How dare you prophesy the loss of my ship?"

"Oh, Mr. Collins, is that you?" said Mrs. Kellogg, from whom I afterwards learned that the poor old gentleman was none other than Mr. Collins, the proprietor of the line to which the ship "Pacific" belonged. He had been also the proprietor of the ship "Arctic," on which his own hapless wife and child had perished in a fearful wreck occasioned by collision with an iceberg.

Without having learned any of these particulars, 1 simply found I was *de trop* in the scene that was then occurring, so, having quietly whispered to Mrs. Kellogg— "I received this communication through the alphabet last night," and placing my copy of the same in her hand, I at once withdrew.

I have since heard that the poor old gentleman, E. K.

Collins, after the loss of his wife and daughter on his ship the " Arctic," had often consulted Mrs. Kellogg as to their fate, and was a firm believer in Spiritualism. Still he was perhaps justly angry, when he heard our predicting the loss of the poor " Pacific," within a few days *only of her expected arrival.*

I need not remind my readers that this statement was strictly verified by subsequent results. The ship " Pacific" and her ill-fated crew were never heard from more ; and despite the indignant threats of prosecution made against " the impostors" who dared to predict her loss on the faith of Spiritual communications, which both myself and others to whom I named the facts did not scruple to repeat ; Philip Smith, and some few of his fellow sufferers, in their messages from the harbour which happily sheltered their enfranchised spirits, were the only revelators that ever lifted the awful veil of doom from their ocean grave. From this time, and during a period of eighteen months, I sat constantly for all who sought my services as a test medium for a great variety of manifestations. These followed in rapid succession, each one affecting my whole frame in a striking and powerful manner. I frequently saw spirits, describing and conversing with them as I did with my fellow mortals. I wrote in various ways, auto-matically, and by impression, spoke in various conditions of trance and semi-consciousness ; became a psychometrist, clairvoyant, and occasionally a physician. In fact, with the exception of boisterous physical manifestations, or that which I coveted beyond all else—a medium for raps— it is impossible to name a phase of mediumship through which I did not pass, and in which I was not exercised.

My experiences during this period were sufficient to fill volumes, and will not in this sketch admit of even a brief description. I visited almost every medium I could hear of ; sat in circles morning, noon, and night ; pursued my investigations in garrets, cellars, saloons, and public halls; was now lifted up in ecstacy, now depressed with misery, harassed by doubts, confused by contradictions and mistakes. But amidst it all there was the one great cardinal fact, that spirits disembodied could communicate to earth, and that spirits still embodied could and do act magnetically upon each other, appear at times in distant places, and frequently *give communications* with as much accuracy as spirits from the other world. No phase of the spiritual phenomena ever more sorely perplexed me than this communication with the spirits of the living. From what source, or by what law such manifestations are made, I cannot now pretend to discuss. My own experience, confirmed by many others, bears ample testimony to this fact. And so frequently did I find that the spirits of persons still on earth were seen by me, described, and gave manifestations as if they were actually in the spirit world, that I was sometimes disposed to attribute the entire phenomena of Spiritualism to the same cause; but in such hours of scepticism some revelations so clearly identical with the departed, and none but them, or some bright and beautiful evidences of true, genuine communication from the angel world invariably reassured me as to the fundamental fact that the disembodied soul of man *can and does communicate from spheres beyond the grave.*

In all my experiences and difficulties, however, I had the advantage of wise, learned, and well experienced Spiritualists to counsel with me. Amongst these I may name with equal affection and reverence the noble gentleman who stood to me in the light of a Spiritual Father— Judge Edmonds—Drs. Gray, Hallock, and Wilson; Messrs. Partridge, Brittan, and many others of the first and most learned and capable investigators. Besides these, I became early and dearly intimate with the three celebrated Fox sisters, Mrs. Kellogg, Ada Foye, J. B. Conklin, and many other professional mediums of a far stronger and more reliable type of power than many of the present day, In addition, I formed one of a band of over twenty New York non-professional mediums, who gave their services free to all comers "without money and without price." It was quite a common thing, in those halcyon days of the great Spiritual outpouring, for investigators to visit one medium, professional or otherwise and, obtaining a communication of a special nature, to go the round of from twenty to thirty accessible mediums, and obtain through all their varied forms of phenomena, the same intelligence, though often rendered in different language and modes of expression.

In my own case remarkable prophetic powers and the disclosure of secrets, sometimes of a most dangerous character, were amongst the specialities of the revelations given. Thus I was frequently visited by detectives, whilst other mediums who were baffled in difficult cases of enquiry generally sent their investigators to me.

One of the most fortunate acquaintances that I was privileged to make, as I then deemed, was with the family of Mrs. E. J. French, a very fine clairvoyant, physician, electrician, and one who from the first days of the modern movement had been gifted with extraordinary powers as a trance, writing, rapping, and physical medium. I had been introduced to this remarkable medium with a view of consulting her professionally as to the possibility of recovering my powers as an opera singer. Whilst giving me absolutely no hope *in that direction*, Mrs. French's spirits, the chief of whom professed to be the great electrical discoverer, Benjamin Franklin, strongly advised that my mother and I should make our home with Mrs. French and her family of three sweet young girls.

Following this advice, we took rooms with Mrs. French, in a new house to which she was removing, and for many years we boarded with her, forming an intimate part of her family, and constantly connected with her life and professional experiences.

I should mention here, as one of the striking features of the early Spiritual outpouring, that the entire cause was chiefly upheld by the learned and professional classes of the community, and although they were often shamefully persecuted, their houses stoned, windows broken, and themselves mobbed and threatened for their peculiar faith, the opposition was always from the least respectable classes, and very seldom exceeded any bounds beyond those of temporary annoyance.

Another noteworthy feature of the cause was, that in the early periods of which I am writing, the least attempt on the part of the Mediums, whether professional or otherwise, to simulate the manifestations, was the exception, not as too often alleged now, a frequent practice. I am under the impression that the Mediums being wholly new to, and unfamiliar with the power of the Spirits, were *afraid*, even if they had been disposed to tamper with Spirit manifestations; hence there was scarcely a case of deception traceable in the ranks.

Returning to my individual experience, the time came of serious import to me and my dear mother, concerning the next move on the chequerboard of fate that we had to make. The period of my engagement at the theatre was within a week of expiration. Through my own, as well as from unnumbered other Mediumistic sources, I was absolutely assured I must give up the stage. With the same wide-spread coincidence of direction I was ordered to go out and *lecture*. Thus whilst I seemed to be irresistibly impelled to refuse all the offers of theatrical engagements that were pressed upon me, I was no less averse to the thoroughly *un-English* idea of becoming a female preacher, as I designated the Spiritual rostrum speakers of my own sex.   What, "I! *a young English lady*, to go out like a bold, strong-minded woman to preach! Oh, shocking!" I cried, and so it appeared to the *weak-minded girl*, still under the influence of tyrant prejudices, and what were at that time old-world opinions. Thus I protested I never would do it, and never could do it.   No! though I might be bidden to the hateful task by the highest Angels of Heaven! I had a certain and somewhat solemn engagement in "the Old Country," as I had learned to call England, and one day, in answer to a letter from the party in question, urging my return, I sat down to write, purposing to inform my correspondent of my intention to be with him again in a month's time.

In place of making this announcement, however, I deliberately wrote, and that whilst in the full possession of my senses, a description of a very rich lady who had herself made my correspondent an offer of marriage.   I told him of some heavy financial difficulties he was then in, and bid him at once marry the lady who had offered herself to him, and think no more of me, for "*I should never return to England for many long years to come.*" Although deeming myself infatuated, if not insane, to write such a letter, write it I did, and sent it.   By the next return post I received an answer, alleging that what I had written was quite true, and though "Heaven alone knew" where I had got the information from, especially the perfect description of the lady in question, it was all true, and since I would not return, he, the writer, had resolved to follow my instructions to the very letter by marriage with an unloved heiress.   And so, that matter settled, what was next to be done?

My dear mother must be provided for in the exile to which I had condemned us both, but how? that was the terrible problem.

Since by the urgent desire of my Spirit friends I found

myself deprived of the only two alternatives which seemed open to me, namely, the stage, or a return to friends and country in England, nothing appeared to me to remain but to endeavour to procure pupils in music—a profession in which I was thoroughly versed. One of my warmest and kindest patrons in the Spiritual ranks was a wealthy merchant—a Mr. Horace H. Day, well known in New York as the founder of large india-rubber works.

Mr. Day had hired an entire building right in the business centre of New York, namely, 553, Broadway. On the steps of this building was placed a large board inscribed with the words SOCIETY FOR THE DIFFUSION OF CHRISTIAN SPIRITUALISM. Though Mr. Day was the entire of "the Society," and the Spiritualism diffused there was not in the slightest degree related to the term "Christian," it had pleased him to adopt that phrase, and to carry it still further by publishing in that very building a weekly newspaper entitled "The Christian Spiritualist." A certain portion of this house was devoted to the sale of the paper and the Spiritual books and pamphlets that, as early as 1850, had then been published. The upper floors were occupied by the printers of the paper, and in the large back drawing-room of the building the generous lessee had placed Miss Kate Fox, who, at a salary of twelve hundred dollars a year, was engaged to sit *free* for the public every morning. When Mr. Day heard of my intention to *give* my services to the public without pay, he kindly placed two handsome rooms, well furnished by his liberality, at my disposal for my séances. Being still too proud to accept of this generous arrangement rent free, I offered to edit his paper, and I continued to do so during the time that I occupied the apartments in question.

Behold me, then, kind reader, leaving my boarding place each morning at ten o'clock with all the punctuality of an official, making my way to the " Spiritual Depôt " of the great city, pausing on the first floor to hear poor patient Kate Fox, in the midst of a captious, grumbling crowd of investigators, repeating hour after hour the letters of the alphabet, whilst the no less *poor, patient* Spirits rapped out names, ages, and dates to suit all-comers.

A few minutes spent in that quarter, with a few words of pitying sympathy from me, and a furious thunder of rapping greetings from the Spirits, and I ascend to the next floor, and halt at a door on which I had hung a large plate inscribed MUSICAL ACADEMY. There I find a very feeble old body, once a humble medium, still a Spiritualist, employed in making my fire. If I scold her for being late, she invariably answers me that she had to *clean down* Miss Fox, *wash up* Mr. Munson (the librarian below), and *wipe out* the printers above, and she had only just then had time to come and *do* me.

The Abigail dismissed with her customary few cents fee, and I am alone, that is to say, as far as the visible world is concerned. Of the invisible hosts around me in that house, charged as it was with magnetic power in every nook and corner, I could write a whole volume and still not detail half the strange phenomena which occurred there, or describe the wondrous evidences of inspiration poured out in that place in various ways, according to the demands of the time. In those rooms from eleven to one, and subsequently, after returning from my dinner, through the afternoon, I sat as a medium for all classes who chose to visit me, winding up during at least three evenings every week by set circles, held for friends or by special appointment.

The musical part in the chambers assigned me consisted of lessons given to such few pupils as I could procure. These were very numerous, though the reputation of the "Spiritual depôt" was sufficient to deter all but the initiated from venturing within the haunted precincts. I had two other occupations to fill up my time in that charmed spot. I had tendered my services to the New York Spiritualists to play the organ for them at their Sunday meetings. My offer of musical assistance was not only eagerly accepted, but a fair salary was—unasked by me—generously paid me, and a volunteer choir of young persons whose musical tastes inclined that way enlisted under my leadership. These dear young singers came regularly to my apartments once a week to practise with me. In a short time, and when I had fully gauged the capacities of my numerous choir, I composed anthems, part-songs, choruses, and solos for them, until at last the reputation of the "Dodworth Hall Choir" became so renowned that crowds of strangers would come to hear the music, even if they were not interested in the lectures. My next engrossing occupation was to write for the paper I had promised to edit ; and thus it was that every moment of my time from early morning to late at night was occupied. And all this time I was happy, for I was surrounded by blessed spirits. By the séances I gave to those who visited me I was enabled to console the mourners, warn the guilty, encourage the good, and teach a true, living religion—namely, the gospel of a good life; and that without book, pulpit, or any other authority than such recitals as good and evil Spirits themselves gave of their real conditions in the life beyond the grave.

I had acquired the reputation of being "a wonderful TEST MEDIUM," and as these tests were in no sense "art or part" of myself or my own knowledge, but were entirely due to the good Spirits who controlled me, I may venture to say they were no more wonderful to my sitters than to myself; for, with each fresh sitting for strangers, I was more and more astonished at the power, genius, and cleverness of the modes in which the Spirits identified themselves, and that by devices that left all possibility of guess work or deception out of the question. In the commencement of these sittings I was as great a sceptic as any of my visitors, but, as time went on and tests multiplied in all sorts of ways, doubt or uncertainty of the powers that influenced me would have been insanity. One of the purposes effected by these curious experiences, therefore, was to bring* indisputable assurance of Spirit presence and identity to myself.

As practical lessons are at all times more effective than dry essays, I shall give an account of one of the singular modes in which the Spirits were at times accustomed to prove their identity through my mediumship.

In my subsequent experience with thousands of mediums in different countries, I can scarcely remember one who was not controlled, or at least assisted, by some *special Spirit friend*, whom the mediums regarded as "Guides" or "Controls." These Spirits I was instructed by my "*guides*" to regard as being analogous to the "familiar Spirit" so often mentioned in the Jewish Scriptures as intervening in human affairs. The functions of these attendant "*Guides*" were still further explained to me by my own Spirit teachers as the fact that there were *Medium Spirits* in the higher world, just as there were medium mortals here on earth. In other words, certain Spirits *only* could effect a magnetic rapport with certain mortals called mediums. In my own case my dear sailor brother, who, passing away at the age of sixteen, had not yet fulfilled all his earth life-work, was, I found, *my* "*Medium Spirit*," and only stood aside—though still present with me—when other *Medium* Spirit friends of my enquirers were able to control me. On a certain occasion one of my friends, who often brought strangers to visit me, called with a lady who wished for a sitting. This lady was a stranger to me, and, in accordance with my arrangements, she was not introduced either by name or place of residence.

"I am a perfect sceptic," she said, haughtily, "though Mrs. Waters, here, wishes me to believe in Spiritualism. What have you to say?"

Inviting her to my table, and my usual method of writing, etc., I gave her two or three tests, which she acknowledged to be correct; but "they might be clever guesses or mind-reading," she added. She wished to communicate with *one special spirit and one only,* and she would *only believe* if he would give his name. I was then, as often before, troubled by the lady's impertinent manner; but without noticing this, I rose, and, advancing to her, I took hold of the ribbon strings of a bonnet she wore, and said, "Pray, madam, tell me what colour is this?" pointing at the same time to a special coloured stripe. "Well," she replied, "that is green." "Aye, but what kind of green?" I asked. "Pea green!" "Good," I cried, "Pea green! then that is me, only there is more than one of us; state the plural of pea."

"Oh," she answered, laughing, "that *is* funny; his name *was* the plural of Pea—it was Pease."

"Once more, then, good," I said. "Now, Madam, what do you call this colour?" pointing to a square check in her dress.

"Well, that is black."

"But what does black signify?"

"Darkness—what then?"

"When does darkness come, Madam?"

"At night, to be sure."

"Hold!" I cried. "THAT IS ME. Knight—PEASE KNIGHT—that is me."

"True; oh, how strangely true," cried the visitor, burying her face in her handkerchief. "His name was *Knight,* and he was christened after his godfather "*Pease.*"

Other tests followed; the stranger left humbled and convinced.

When my visitors were gone, I, who have ever been able to speak to Spirits by a voice, said to those Spirits that I felt were still with me—

"Why could you not give that Spirit's name at once as *Pease Knight,* and why take such round-about methods to convince that woman?"

"In the first place," returned my Spirit guide, "she would never have been convinced unless *the Spirits* had given a name which could not be known to a stranger medium; in the next place, we could not just then find that name in your vocabulary."

"What is my vocabulary?"

"Your brain, on which every thought, word, or deed of conscious being is engraved."

"Is it possible, then, that such words as *Knight* and *Pease* are not to be found on my brain?"

"Certainly they are; but we could not quickly enough arrive at them until the words themselves were spoken, when a chord of association was struck; it was no longer difficult to awaken the names from the vast brain vocabulary, and hence we spoke through your lips words thus recalled."

I make no comments on this strange case, save to say, when impatient and ignorant mortals clamorously ask "Why the Spirits who can give so much of intelligence, do not give so much more?" let us ask back—"Are you quite sure you know why the Spirits *can* give so much and no more? or how, in our present most. imperfect knowledge of Spiritual Science, the Spirits can give anything at all?

"They work BY LAWS, as we do. Do we know those laws? Assuredly not. Then be more patient, more modest, less urgent, and *learn the law* before we arraign the failure which we ourselves make in its working."

CHAPTER V.

"Like warp and woof all destinies
Are woven fast,
Linked in sympathy like the keys
Of an organ vast."　　　　　—WHITTIER.

A TIME came at length in my own career in a foreign land,
and that with my good, trusting, and beloved mother
dependent upon my earnings for support—when a change
in our future plans of life became indispensable.　I felt as
if I had learned all that the good Spirits (at that time)
were able to teach me, by sitting free, as they had
commanded me, for the public of New York as a test
medium, and enduring as I best could the immense
and problematical experiences attending the earlier phases
of the communion between Spirits and mortals.　In
addition to these probationary lessons I had seen far more
of human weaknesses and secret crime than aught but
the wonderful revelations of the Spirit circle could ever
have taught me, and I pined for the change which I felt
was equally necessary and imminent.　The time came at
length when my singular apprenticeship must needs end.
Whilst I was pondering anxiously upon the most prudent
course to pursue in the hope of obtaining some more
remunerative employment than that of a music teacher,
my friends both in the higher life and on earth were
constant and importunate in their demands for me to fill
the position of a Spiritual Rostrum Lecturer.

It was in vain that I protested (in my ignorance of the
progress of public opinion) that I was "not one of the
strong-minded women," and shrank with disgust from the
idea of being "a female preacher."　My earthly friends
declared my trance addresses as given at my circles were

just what was required for the public rostrum, whilst my
Spirit friends by speech and writing alleged that I had
been destined from childhood, and trained by early
education for this special work, whilst my experiences as
a test medium had been simply enjoined upon me to
prepare and qualify me to become a public teacher of the
Spiritual cause. They also added that as they should
make my educational and other abilities minister to their
service, pay for my labours would be just as legitimate as
compensation earned in any direction as a bread winner.

All the conditions they desired to enforce upon me,
however, were that I should not any longer practise as a
test medium, or turn the public platform into a "show,"
or religious services into an "exhibition," by attempting
to give tests from the platform.

My Spirit teachers pointed out that the tests given by
Spirit friends to individuals, called into exercise a totally
different set of organs and brain functions from those
which philosophic teaching spirits employed in giving
scientific or religious addresses, hence the exercise of brain
power in both the above named directions would not only
injure the lucidity of the medium's gifts, but tend to
impair the mental and physical power of the spiritual
control.

Still I shrank from the responsibility of becoming the
teacher of a *new* religion, or of trying to guide human
souls into untried paths of thought on subjects so
momentous as that of life eternal. Realising at length the
utter impossibility of either answering or resisting the
influences, human and spiritual, that were being brought
to bear upon me, this is the expedient that I secretly
resorted to, in order to escape from my painful dilemma.
I put an advertisement into a city paper, offering my
services as a teacher of music or a musical companion in a
family where my mother could be boarded in lieu of any
payment to myself.

The answers I received to this advertisement were more numerous than satisfactory, until I was called on one occasion to meet a gentleman whose proposition and manner were more than ordinarily prepossessing. Presenting me with a card, on which was inscribed, "General Bullard, Troy, N.Y.," this gentleman informed me he desired to find a music teacher and companion for his young wife, who was an invalid, and passionately fond of music. My mother, he added, could be usefully employed as a paid housekeeper. Overjoyed as I was at the prospects thus opening up before me, I had just begun to talk to him about the necessary preliminaries, when Mrs. French, the eminent clairvoyant physician, in whose house we boarded, entered the room with the fixed eyes and stony glare which indicated the deep trance in which she was accustomed to give her medical examinations.

Aghast as I was at this interruption, it at once recalled me to my own grave error in inviting applications to be made at a house where the name and profession of the occupant appeared conspicuously on the door. Disregarding my confused attempts to apologise for this intrusion to my visitor, the entranced medium walked up to him and abruptly said, "You are a great Spiritualist, sir, are you not?" "A devoted Spiritualist, madam," replied the gentleman, "of that I can assure you, though I cannot claim to be a great one. My name is Edward Bullard, and for some time past I have been instrumental in organising public Spiritual meetings at Troy; besides which, my dear wife, Mrs. Margaret Bullard, was one of the earliest mediums of our neighbourhood." Abandoning myself to my now inevitable fate, I sank into a chair, hopeless and speechless.

By this time my mother had joined the party, when Mrs. French, addressing the General as a friend and ally of

the spirit controlling her, whom she announced as
Benjamin Franklin, informed him that he had been sent
there purposely by the spirit world to *compel* me to perform
the duty that world of power demanded of me.   In most
eloquent terms the Spirit then, through Mrs. French,
dwelt on my strange eventful life history, and mediumship;
she declared it had all been providentially ordered, and
every step of my career had been marked out by spirit
guidance.

She spoke enthusiastically of what she called my
spiritual powers, prophesied for me a wonderful future,
and ended by calling on the friend who had been impelled
by the unseen intelligences above to come there that day,
to make arrangements for me to appear immediately
on the Troy platform in the capacity of an inspirational
speaker.

To all this General Bullard assented as enthusiastically
as the demand was made.   He described how, apparently
by mere accident, he had seen the paper in which my
advertisement appeared, but how irresistibly he was
impelled to respond to it.   However, he added, he would
return to Troy at once, and have my name and first
appearance announced as the spirit medium speaker for
the following Sunday.   Turning to my dear mother, who
was scarcely less overwhelmed with the strangeness of the
scene than I was myself, he assured her he would send a
trusty friend and neighbour on next Friday evening to
escort me per Hudson River steamboat up to Troy, and that
he and his wife would meet me, and entertain me at their
own house; make my visit in every way a splendid success,
an epoch in the history of human progress, one that should
go down to all posterity, and be inscribed on the archives
of eternity.   To all this, and much more of the same
kind of what I mentally set down as *insane* talk, I could
not for the life of me find power to make any reply.

Taking my silence. I suppose, as acquiescence, the enthusiastic trio around me completed their arrangements for the future to their own satisfaction at least, leaving me in a state of dull despair.

I am convinced that neither one or other of them entertained the slightest doubt of my entire capacity to meet the requirements of the tremendous task they had assigned me. Both Mrs. French and my mother had repeatedly heard me give long addresses in trance at my circles, and in their confident predictions of the success I was to achieve, made no allowance for the fact of my exchanging a party of admiring friends for a crowd of critical strangers, many of whom might be wholly antagonistic to the doctrines I was likely to preach.

The days that intervened before that awful next Sunday were certainly about the most miserable of my life.

Committed as I was, to do I scarcely knew what, or how, as a sort of preparation for my dreaded task I proceeded to write out a couple of lectures, and spent two days and nights in completing some stuff which I proposed to read when I was *forced*, as I called it, on to the Troy platform. Having from my earliest childhood heard, and of late years conversed with, the voices of invisible beings, it was no surprise to me to hear one of the most familiar of these voices saying, "What is Emma so busily engaged in writing?" "My beautiful Troy lectures," I sullenly answered. "She will not read them," the Spirit rejoined, "we shall take away her sight."

Knowing from experience what these Invisibles could do, and might do, I had to abandon the prospect of reading, and next tried to commit my poor pages to memory. For this purpose the next day I paced for hours up and down a deserted chamber, striving to learn my lesson, until the same remorseless voice questioned, "What does Emma take such long walks for?" "You know well

enough," I savagely replied; "I am trying to learn these
abominable Troy lectures." "We shall take away your
memory," was the final answer; and thus was my last hope
shattered.

Oh, that miserable Sunday! Never can I forget the
anguish of mind I experienced as I was led into the ante-
room and for the first time that day left alone. I held
my Bible firmly in my hand, resolved, as a last resort,
to try and read two or three chapters, and then run
away—somewhere—anywhere—away from those dreadful
Spiritualists.

Conducted finally to the platform, my last clear remembrance was of listening to a lovely quartette beautifully
sung by the "Troy Harmonists," and then I had a dim
perception that I was myself standing outside of myself,
by the side of my dear father—dead—when I was only a
little child—but whose noble form I could plainly see
close by me, gesticulating to, and addressing somehow, my
second self, which was imitating him, and repeating all
the thrilling words he was uttering.

For all the words of greeting and extravagant laudations
poured into my ears when the delightful tones of "the
Troy Harmonists" woke me up from the sleep into which,
as it seemed, their sweet voices had put me, I could only
murmur, "Do not praise me; it was my own beloved
father's Spirit that spoke." I had no more any farther
doubts or fears for the evening lecture, though then, as
ever afterwards in the countless platform addresses I have
given, I have seemed, and still seem, to be two individuals—one whose lips are uttering a succession of sentences, sometimes familiar to me, still oftener new and
strange, but always unpremeditated by my second self; in
fact, I am rather an onlooker and occasional listener than
the originator of the spoken words. I often see Spirits
hovering around persons in the audience, and can often

detect the characters of those around me, especially when they are of an evil or malignant type. I can think independently of the words I utter, and not unfrequently seem to see distant places and persons.

I can give no explanation of this peculiar condition; I can only sum it up by adding, I know and can trust the good Spirits with whom I have taken service, and I am far more assured of their kind protection and power to preserve me from all evil than I could ever feel of any human employers.

It may be asked, Why cannot all human beings place the same reliance upon *their* Spirit friends? I answer, *I have taken service with these Spirits.* They were just and good men on earth, and are the same though even more powerful as Spirits. They have again and again warned me back from dangers in which they could *not* protect me; but from the many great trials and seeming dangers to which I have been subjected, UNDER THEIR DIRECTION, they have ever led me through in triumph.

On all occasions when *not* actually engaged in working for "the cause," my good Spirit friends have charged me always to use my own best judgment; never to ask of Spirits to do any work or perform any duties for me which I ought, or could execute for myself; and whilst labouring faithfully in the noble ranks of the Spiritual army, they still encourage me ever to live my own life and never to act contrary to my own sense of right to God, man, and my own soul. These Spirits allege they could not, and would not if they could, exempt me from the ordinary trials of humanity, or the griefs and personal sufferings which purify whilst they wound, but I must again repeat that in doing the work they have COMMISSIONED me to perform, had I been guarded by an army of giants I could not have been more safely led through every trial and danger. . . . Hitherto, and even up to my first great

trial lectures at Troy, on July 5th, 1857, I had clung
religiously, as I had termed it, to the orthodox faith in
which I had been brought up, nor had my experiences as
a test Medium contributed to shake that faith. Indeed
I had sometimes listened with equal horror and indignation to what I designated as the *unchristian* and infidel
talk of many of my Spiritual associates.

Thus, then, when the New York Spiritualists, stimulated
by the glowing accounts of my *début* as given by Troy
friends, invited me to occupy their platform on the succeeding Sunday, July 12th, I accepted the offer, confident
that I, through my Spirit inspirers, could so severely
rebuke the infidel spirit which I felt was existing
amongst my New York associates, that in all probability
I might convert many of them to the true Christian faith.
The Spirits had promised me that on that special occasion
I should hear every word I spoke, and so I did, but the
result of those same two New York lectures was, that
instead of converting any of my audience to orthodoxy,
I converted myself entirely away from it, nor has my
incessant study of ancient history, science, and God's
Bible of Creation ever suffered me to relapse again into
the mists of superstition invented by Priestcraft, or shaken
my assurance of my own personal reponsibility both here
and hereafter, for all the good or evil I have ever done on
earth.

For about two years from the period of my opening
lectures at Troy, I continued, without intermission, to
speak every Sunday, and many week days, in New York,
Philadelphia, Troy, Brooklyn, or such places as were easily
accessible from my temporary home with my mother and
Mrs. French's family in New York City. All this time
I continued periodically weekly sittings with friends, and
choir practices for my young singers. My choir consisted
of young, musical residents of the city, and these at last

became so numerous that one of our committee gave us a splendid practice room, where, at least once a week, we all met to study and rehearse the numerous hymns and anthems I composed for them. At these choir meetings our special friends and supporters were made free to enter, and very often the number of our visitors amounted to at least a hundred persons. On these occasions we were often, favoured with the presence of Judge Edmonds, Jackson and Mary Davis; Drs. Gray, Hallock, and Wilson; Charles Partridge, S. B. Brittan, and hosts of Mediums, through whom the Spirits gave us tokens of interest and words of encouragement. At times the piano on which my choir rehearsed to my playing was lifted bodily up in the air, obliging me to request the good invisibles to let us proceed with our practice.

My choir at last became so infatuated with the compositions I wrote specially for them that they did not care to sing other music, and when I introduced new compositions the Spirits, through some of the mediums present, would rap thunders of applause.

Every night I was either engaged in holding circles myself or attending those of other mediums, especially at the rooms of my valued friends the Fox sisters. At the time of which I write dear old Mrs. Fox, the mother of the celebrated sisters, was living with her two daughters, Kate and Margaretta.

The eldest of the sisters, Leah, was married to a wealthy and highly respected merchant of the city, Daniel Underhill, but she still continued to throw open her handsome house free to her special friends for séances, and being by far the best and most powerful of all living mediums at that time, the privilege of being admitted to these séances was, indeed, highly prized. As my dear mother and I enjoyed an intimate acquaintance with Mr. and Mrs. Underhill, we organised for some time winter evening

receptions, which were held in Mrs. Leah Fox Underhill's
splendid drawing-rooms one evening of each week.   At
these delightful reunions I may mention as amongst our
most constant attendants the poet sisters Alice and Phœbe
Carey, Horace Greeley, Raymond (editor, of the *New
York Times*), Robert Dale Owen, Fennimore Cooper (the
novelist), Professors Longfellow and Whittier, Washington
Irving, and hosts of other writers, poets, and celebrities.

By the earliest of the New York Spiritualists I was
affectionately recognised and treated as the Spiritual child
of the city—truly and spiritually born there.   I was
amongst the most frequent of the New York Spiritual
rostrum speakers, and though their fine hall was always
thronged with many of the most eminent people of the
city, my dear young singers would not consent to let me
absent myself from the leadership of their choir, and
though I might be, and often was, the speaker of the day,
nothing would satisfy them but to have me leave the
rostrum to play the harmonium for their singing, and to
return at the close of the last anthem to take my place
again on the rostrum, winding up the entire service with
one of those stirring musical appeals to God and the angels
that sent the people away almost as entranced as ourselves.

Such was the order of the early services in which I was
privileged to take, and to *play*, my part, and I look back
upon them now as amongst the happiest and most inspired
periods of my eventful life.

It was at one of these meetings that the Rev. Thomas L.
Harris, who was an occasional speaker there, tried hard to
convert his hearers to his own particular views of Christian
Spiritualism.   He often brought me small lyrical pieces to
set to music, but. his views on orthodoxy never had any
effect upon me.   I was present, leading my choir, when
this gentleman, finding he could not convert the New
York Spiritual Society by love, made use of their rostrum

to abuse and threaten them. In the midst of his denunciations of God's vengeance against their infidelity, he was interrupted by the President of the Society (Dr. Warner), and for a few minutes a tumult in these well-ordered meetings threatened to ensue between the Christian partisans of Harris and the bitterly denounced "infidels" who had engaged him.

At Judge Edmonds' stern bidding, however, Harris descended from the rostrum with the meek air of a martyr.

At night he returned, with his troop of special supporters, evidently bent upon creating a disturbance. Prompt measures were taken, however, to assure the would-be intruders that Dodworth's Hall was not a Methodist Conventicle Church, and that they could only take their places there as listeners, and not as propagandists of a vicarious atonement doctrine. Finding the infidel Emma Hardinge was installed into Christian Harris' rostrum, the crew retreated, and soon after took a special hall for Harris, where he held forth for a few weeks each Sunday to a pitifully scant set of followers. At the close of his abortive attempts to secure an apostleship Harris revenged himself by writing and publishing a poem entitled the "Song of Satan." In this *truly Christian* production he introduced all the well known New York Spiritualists under the titles of various "Devils," I being classed amongst them, no less to my amusement than gratification, as "the Devil of Harmony." Mr. T. L. Harris, I may here add, was at one time a fine medium, a splendid poet, and a man of great and varied talents. I sincerely lamented his secession from our ranks ; but of his remarkable egotism in announcing himself as a sort of Messiah, together with other eccentricities not by any means in harmony with our keenly analytical religion of PROVEN FACTS, I have already written in my voluminous works entitled "Modern American Spiritualism" and "Nineteenth Century Miracles."

Leaving the succeeding doings of the *great man* to his own report, I must now proceed to notice another phase of my experiences which, by removing me from the kind and indulgent association of my dear New York friends, sent me forth on the tossing ocean of storm and tempest, and in the far and wide fields of distant travel launched me into the midst of dangers, trials, and almost miraculous interventions of Angel guidance and protection, and enable me at this distant period of time to recall my career of strange adventure and providential assistance, and say once more, with the inspired Bard of Avon— " There's a divinity which shapes our ends, rough hew them how we will."

CHAPTER VI.

"The Song of the Stars."

"Look, look, through our glittering ranks afar,
In the infinite azure star after star."

I HAVE already spoken of the Spiritualists' Volunteer Choir, whose excellent performances contributed to render our Sunday services as attractive to the public as they were acceptable to ourselves. Finding how much our weekly gatherings for practice were enjoyed by all concerned, I resolved to institute a series of entertainments consisting of vocal and instrumental music varied with recitations and *tableaux vivants*.

This idea was eagerly seconded by my young singers, then numbering about fifty, whilst aid in the mechanical departments of the undertaking, besides a liberal guarantee fund to meet any deficit which a very small admission fee might leave, was at once forthcoming.

The New York Athenæum was engaged, and I was unanimously chosen to arrange the programmes, teach the recruits their several parts, rehearse the music, accompany the singers, invent and arrange the *tableaux*, and act as band teacher, stage manager, and not unfrequently as principal performer. The labour thus imposed upon me was certainly superhuman, if not supernatural. Still it was a labour of love, and was always crowned with success and high appreciation. We were also fortunate enough to secure the commendations of the New York Press, who, whilst affecting to rejoice in the discovery that "music in the heavenly spheres did not all consist of psalm singing," took occasion to say they did not know whether it was essential for a Garrick or a Siddons to come back from their peaceful graves to inspire and conduct the dramatic portions of the performance, seeing that they were quite well conducted under the charge of a popular actress, whose experience might save the trouble of waking up the dead.

These and similar skits upon the Spiritualists' claims for inspiration were always given in a kindly spirit, rather than in the malignant tone of the later press notices, and saved us not a little outlay in advertising our meetings. In the matter of dramatic recitations the chief difficulty I had to contend with was that whilst I could at any moment lay my hand upon at least twenty Hamlets or thirty Romeos, I could scarcely persuade my dullest scholar to appear as a Laertes or Mercutio. Then again, there was not a lady in our midst, from an elderly soprano to a twelve year old contralto, who did not volunteer for Ophelia or Juliet, but utterly disdained the part of the Queen in *Hamlet* or the Nurse in *Romeo and Juliet.*

After a considerable amount of speculation as to how I could give my entire troupe each the best part, I finally decided that the first of my entertainments should introduce all the witches' scenes of *Macbeth*, in costume (alias rags and broomsticks), whilst for the second I selected acts of Sheridan's famous "Tragedy Rehearsed," entitled "The Critic," the mock tragic parts of which were best represented by the worst possible acting.

Both these portions of the entertainments were so abundantly successful that I had much difficulty in restraining my associates from hiring a theatre, installing me as manager, stage manager, leading actress, and musical conductor. I had no slight difficulties to contend with also in the compensatory part of this onerous work; however, the real affection with which my young friends regarded me compensated me at last, without a murmur to my final decision. In other respects, too, I proved beyond a shadow of question what a mighty strength resided in union.

All our committee, and those outside friends interested in our cause, were so brave and so generous in "putting their shoulders to the wheel," that we had but to ask and to have all the mechanical assistance we needed. Materials or "properties" for *tableaux vivants*, or dramatic scenes, were also furnished promptly, to be made up under my direction. I could fill many an amusing page with details of the trials and *contretemps* the indefatigable stage manager and her assistants had to encounter, and it may not be wholly uninteresting to notice one particular phase of these petty mishaps. One of our most earnest helpers, having observed the fine effects produced in spectacular scenes at the theatres by coloured fires, had purchased a quantity of the materials to produce them, and constructed four iron pans with long handles in which to set them alight. The coloured lights, held behind the scenes, of course, by our assistants, produced such an excellent effect in some of the tableaux, that these little interludes became popular enough to embarrass me considerably; in fact, unless at least a couple of tableaux were exhibited at each entertainment, murmurs were likely to be heard. To devise dress, and arrange these same tableaux and then subject them to the action of the coloured fires, now became another part of my serious undertaking. It was in connection with this part of "the play" that there occurred some *contretemps* which preyed severely on my nerves. On one occasion, when I had designed a gipsy night scene, which I had desired to be lighted up by red fire, *à la* "Guy Mannering," the kindly assistants behind the scenes, mistaking the package of stuff they were to burn, threw on the jolly gipsy encampment a sickly glare of green fire, in which the illuminated party resembled a company of ghastly phantoms. On the same fatal night a snow scene, designed to represent a mother and three little ones, perishing amidst the snow, a tableau to be specially displayed in the commingled rays of white and blue fires, was lighted up by the dazed assistants with the gipsy red fires, giving the snow the hue of a cheerful Christmas blaze and the dying victims the appearance of a well-warmed, comfortable party. The most striking mishap, however, arose thus : A very beautiful design was shown me for a pyramidal group, the apex of which was to be a Santa Cecilia, attired in classic white drapery, wreathed, and holding a lyre in her hand. The other rounds of the pyramid were to be filled up by smaller figures variously attired, but each furnished with some instrument or symbol of the Genius of Music. The gentleman who introduced this design agreed to furnish the pyramid, dresses, instruments, etc., *provided only* that I myself occupied the apex as the Santa Cecilia.

To refuse was impossible, and having provided a performer to execute the appropriate music behind the scenes, a task which generally fell to my lot, I proceeded to arrange and finally assume my part of the tableau in question. Warned by past experience, before assuming my elevated post, I insisted upon the two gentlemen, stationed at the wings with the fire pans, examining their materials so carefully as to be entirely certain that they would throw nothing but white light on this scene. All was in due order, the curtains rose—the white fire gave us all such an angelic appearance, that after the lowering of the curtain, such were the thunders of applause and shouts of "encore" that the scene shifters were ordered to raise the curtain again.

This time the drop was lowered much more quickly than before, and the people were still not satisfied. More shouts and more cries of "encore" ensued. Amidst the persistent shouts and clappings of hands, a long wait followed. This, together with an unusual amount of hurry and bustle amongst my poor scared assistants, rendered my cry of " Raise the curtain again " inaudible. Presently, however, the curtain was raised again, but—oh horror ! from one wing appeared the lurid glow of a crimson fire, from the other shone the dismal hue of the green light, and as if to make confusion worse confounded, the two poor gentlemen who held the pans had got so choked and blinded with the fire smoke that they thrust the pans full on the stage in sight of the audience, whilst they turned their half-suffocated heads the other way. Of course, the stage became a mass of vapour, which, even after the rapid descent of the curtain, rolling in clouds into the house, sent the audience into alternate fits of laughing and coughing, in the midst of which one of my good assistants, with his face smoked into various patterns by the ill-managed fires, put his head out from the wing before the curtain, and said good-humouredly : " Ladies and Gentle-men, don't laugh, don't choke, and don't encore fire-lighted tableaux again twice. All our white fires were burnt out, and we, remembering a certain stage manager's directions, ' If they could not snow white to snow brown,' acted accordingly."

This sally restored the audience to such good humour, that when we all went on the stage to sing the spirited finale, " O for the days of Robin Hood," in tableaux costumes, it was only my own firm but necessary refusal, which prevented another double encore for our over-worn company's parting song.

These were bright days, glorious days—life and work as well as worship—life and work that contributed to bring Spiritualists so favourably to the front that public opinion began to change rapidly concerning our "ism," as well as ourselves.

Whilst Spiritualism under the irresistible influence of

its supermundane operators was spreading with a power and rapidity unprecedented in the history of any other new movement upon earth, the demand for workers in this tremendous harvest field was wide-spread and urgent.

In my own case, letters of appeal for services came pouring in upon me from all quarters, and in some instances from cities thousands of miles distant from New York.

At first I regarded these appeals as impracticable, but when the Spirits through my own and many other persons' mediumship bid me answer my letters affirmatively, and added promises of successful achievement abroad, and assurances of protection and good health for the dear mother at home, I realised that I should be unfaithful to my noble employers if I continued to resist their counsels.

It was on a certain Sunday evening at the close of my last lecture that I felt obliged to lay this matter before the committee of the New York Spiritualists, by whom I was most frequently engaged.

I pointed out to them the numbers of invitations that pressed in upon me ; how that applicants would take no denial, whilst Spirit guides enforced my compliance with their urgent persistence.

My New York friends, no doubt realising the expediency of having a resident speaker in their midst, and especially concerned, perhaps, for the maintenance of their fine choir, were at first much displeased, and endeavoured to change my decision by tempting offers of long and remunerative engagements.

All would not do, and I parted from these kind friends in the midst of a gloom of silence that weighed heavily on my spirits.

It was on the second evening from this that a letter was put into my hands, signed not only by the members of the

New York Spiritual Committee, but also by upwards of thirty of the most prominent and influential Spiritualists of the city, inviting me to take a benefit concert or entertainment, as a *temporary* farewell and *present* cessation from the "work" I had performed amongst them. Coupled with this flattering request was another equally urgent. This was that I would compose such a musical work for the occasion as would give the public a fair idea of "the talent" they (the Spiritualists) had amongst them. Mr. Carnes, the gentleman who presented this gracious missive, was himself an accomplished musician, and frequently lent the aid of his fine baritone voice to our choral performances.

To him, as a judge of the "divine art," I attempted to explain the impossibility of my composing, writing out, and teaching any work of sufficient importance to be worthy of the occasion proposed in the very few weeks I had at my disposal.

Mr. Carnes could not, or would not, recognise the force of my objections, and nothing remained but for me to write a grateful acceptance of the compliment rendered me, making, in addition, promises of achievements in the composing line which—at the time—I as much expected to fulfil as to take an immediate journey to the moon.

The invitation and acceptance being published in one or two of the local, as well as the Spiritual, papers formed the first item of the publicity which my good friends designed to give to this memorable affair.

The first problem which presented itself to my mind after Mr. Carnes' departure was—what on earth subject I could take on which to found a new composition. It should be a cantata; but where was I to find words? Several members of my choir having dropped in during the evening, I presented to them, in moving terms, the nature of the dilemma I was placed in, and asked their

advice touching a subject for a cantata. One lady
suggested "The Song of Solomon." I declined it emphatically. Another proposed the first chapter of Genesis by
way of illustrating the "Creation." I said I did not feel
quite up to placing myself before the world as the rival of
Haydn.

My principal tenor suggested a cantata on the conversion
of St. Paul, but the whole of the ladies present chorussed
out, in high indignation, that St. Paul was a crusty old
bachelor, and objected to women speaking in public. Upon
this the entire party looked sympathisingly on me, and St.
Paul was dropped.

Shakespeare's tragedies, though highly suggestive, were
deemed too long. Scott's novels, Byron's poems, Don
Quixote, the hundred and fifth Psalm, and a dozen other
absurdities were suggested and rejected, and my friends
departed with the sorrowful apprehension that they were
to look in vain for songs and solos to be ready for them by
the time appointed.

Alone with the dear mother, and preparing to retire, I
fixed my eyes despairingly on the magnificent vault of the
midnight sky above me, studded over as it was with one of
the most brilliant displays of sparkling stars that I had
ever—as it then seemed to me—gazed on before.

Whilst my eyes were involuntarily fastened, as if by
fascination, upon this glorious spectacle, some power for
which I never could account, yet never can or will deny
the operation of, seemed to me to wheel into line rows of
the largest and most dazzling of these glorious armies of
light, until they formed to my straining eyes, in letters
built up of star worlds, the clearly distinct legend of
"THE SONG OF THE STARS." The Song of the Stars!
Yes! I read once, twice, thrice; then it seemed as if a
mist came over my sight.

I still gazed upwards, but the hosts of light, though

they seemed to be moving backwards and forwards hither and thither in a strange, wild dance—all were obscured to my dim sight, as if I were gazing at the heavens through a veil. The mists rose, parted, and left my dazzled eyes free at length.

For a few moments I buried my face in my hands; then, turning my gaze once more towards the resplendent firmament, all was as still, calm, and motionless as if the myriads of stars were sleeping.

Passing to my mother's bedside, and imprinting the accustomed kiss on her dear face, I told her, simply, I had something to write.

Then, sitting down to my table, before the grey mists of dawn had melted into the crimson glory of the next morning's sunrise, I had finished the words of my cantata, under the title of the "SONG OF THE STARS."

For the following fortnight I was as busy penning down the music of this piece as I had been during the night above referred to in tracing out the words. Both were written or composed by a power that worked through my organism, such as it is and was, according to the limitations of the instrument that organism afforded. Not being a naturally gifted poetess, the words are inferior to what the power of inspiration could have produced through a more poetic temperament. As to the music, it was composed and set down in far too much haste to satisfy my own instructed taste. When, however, I called my choir together to rehearse it, the general opinion was that it was beyond the capacity of my poor amateurs, and the verdict went forth that some of the solos, at least, should be executed by professional vocalists.

Two ladies and one gentleman were engaged for this purpose, on their own terms. Each of the parties required some additional solos, all of which I composed with the same lightning speed as the rest of the work was executed

in.   The professional vocalists expressed themselves as
" more than satisfied" with what I had assigned them, and
for fear lest I should fail to please them with my own
accompaniments, we actually agreed to pay a pianist of
their own selection to practise with and accompany them.

Two nights prior to the evening announced for the
entertainment, all three of our professionals informed us
that they were warned by the organists of the several
churches at which they were engaged to sing, that they
would at once lose their situations and *be peremptorily
dismissed, if they disgraced themselves by singing at a
Spiritualistic entertainment.*

I believe some of the gentlemen interested in our undertaking did venture to remonstrate with these professionals
for leaving us in the lurch at the last moment.   All was in
vain.   They were " not going to lose their situations " for
us, nor could we blame them, except when we consider
that they might have done a more Christian act by appris-
ing us of their defection a little earlier than the time when
no possibility existed of supplying their places.   Still we
were not to be wholly defeated.

My ever kind and really capable young singers, especially my principal soprano, good Mrs. Adams, set to work
heart and soul to study the solos that would otherwise
have been omitted.   They ordinarily sang well, and gave
general satisfaction, but on the night of the entertainment
they simply sang so splendidly that no one could have
disputed their claim that they were one and all inspired.

Academy Hall, in which the entertainment was given,
was crowded, and a sort of mystic prestige, I might almost
say a halo of inspiration, seemed to pervade the entire
scene, and work all things together for good so completely
that not a single fault or failure broke the spell that was
over us.   The people cheered and encored nearly every
number rendered.   The Press, so generally insulting, or,

at least, sarcastic in their reports of Spiritual doings, were in this instance as much under the *spell*, whatever it might have been, as were the performers, and whilst some of the papers lauded both the musicians and the music, prophesying for the cantata "well-deserved popularity," the *New York Herald*, hitherto our most inveterate enemy, alleged "that whoever the Spirits that controlled Emma Hardinge might be, they could at least make good music, and the only pity was that she did not give up the shadow and take to the substance of life, when she would assuredly be one of the leading musicians and composers of the age."

Now, notwithstanding all the brilliant prophecies that were made concerning the future of my cantata, I have to acknowledge it has never been performed since its first appearance at Academy Hall, April 24th, 1857. This has arisen entirely, I may say, from my lack of time, in the midst of incessant travel and literary work, to give the necessary attention to writing out and preparing the score properly. Should time and opportunity open up the way, "The Song of the Stars" may yet make another essay of its power to convince the world we are neither destitute of harmony nor melody even in our scattered and disorganised ranks.

[And now in closing this chapter I cannot give a better idea of the earnestness and enterprise with which the early Spiritualists of New York conducted their methods of propaganda, and manifested their sense of appreciation towards their workers, than by giving a *fac simile* of the handsome programme they put out on the occasion of the complimentary concert to Miss Hardinge before referred to. I may here remark that Mrs. Britten, some months previous to her complete collapse in all active literary employment, intended to reproduce the Cantata above mentioned, with the assistance of a friend interested in Spiritualism, and also in musical compositions. For that purpose she collected all the fragmentary pages of music which she possessed of the " Song of the Stars," with the intention of re-arranging the score, and writing in the missing parts, which had been given to her New York choir for practice, and had never been returned. But failing health and inability to any longer touch her piano, prevented her from accomplishing her desire, and as the Cantata was composed hurriedly it was not very comprehensible to those unaccustomed to her style. Nevertheless, the friend to whom she entrusted the principal parts of the · composition still entertains hopes of reproducing it at no far distant period, so that the "Song of the Stars" may yet once more be heard on earth, and even though it may be unoer other auspices, and probably in an altered form from the original design, it will be heard by the arisen Spirit of her who first produced it under the control of the Angels of the higher spheres of being.—M. W.]

ACADEMY HALL,

663 Broadway, opposite Bond St.

FRIDAY EVENING, April 24th, 1857,

WILL BE GIVEN BY THE

Spiritualists of New York,

A GRAND

AMATEUR COMPLIMENTARY

CONCERT,

TO

MISS EMMA HARDINGE,

DIRECTRESS OF THE MUSIC AT DODWORTH'S HALL.

Admission 50 Cents.

Performance to commence at 8 o'clock.

TICKETS to be had at the offices of the "Spiritual Telegraph," 342 Broadway ; "Christian Spiritualist," 553 Broadway, and the principal music stores ; and at the door on the evening of the performance.

Mann, Stearns & Beale, Stationers, 141 Fulton St., N.Y.

PROGRAMME.

PART I.

GRAND CHORUS, "Vive le Roi," ....BALFE.

SONG.—BEAUTIFUL DAY...HIME.

DUET FOR TWO GUITARS. Pot-pourri.... ....

CANTATA.

THE WORDS AND MUSIC COMPOSED EXPRESSLY FOR THIS OCCASION BY

MISS EMMA HARDINGE,

ENTITLED

THE SONG OF THE STARS.

A SPIRITUAL APOLOGUE.

SYMPHONY.

———

GRAND OPENING CHORUS,

"THE WORLD WAS GEMMED."

The world was gemmed with flowerets fair—
Field and tree and shrub were there—
The breath of perfume filled the air,
    When life first dawned on earth.

The fleecy clouds in distant sky
Floated above the scene on high,
While earth and nature joined the cry,
    "Life—life at length has birth."

The day was closed, the first bright day
On which created man had sway,
And e'en the twilight's sober gray
    Had passed, and night had birth.

That first of nights, whose shadowy veil
Threw o'er the scene her mantle pale,
While darkness deep began to sail
    Around the weary earth.

And now arose that wondrous sight,
The calm majestic orb of night—
The fair and radiant moon so bright,
    That midnight hailed her queen.

At first she reigned alone, serene,
The sole enchantress of the scene,
Whose glory ne'er on earth had been,
    Except in Eden's bowers.

But one by one in sparks of light,
Came forth the jewels of the night—
The sparkling quivering stars so bright—
    The Heaven's eternal flowers.

Hark ! they are calling !—hear their voice :
Life ! life on earth ! rejoice, rejoice !
The world is made—rejoice, rejoice !
    The stars are made—rejoice !

———

RECITATIVE AND AIR—SOLO.

THE SONG OF HESPERUS.

I come—I come—from ocean's wave
    Where seas unfathomed roll,
Where unborn worlds shall find a grave,
    From North to Southern pole.

I rise from out the shining spray,
    To gild the twilight hour,
And bid farewell to parting day—
    I am the night's spring flower.

I dance before the straining eye,
Which fondly loves to trace
The parting gleam in western sky
Of sunlight's closing race.

I come—I come to sing of home,
To labour and to toil;
To warn the weary ones who roam
'Mid life and earth's turmoil.

That noontide has faded,
That twilight fast steals on ;
And e'er that path be shaded,
To turn their footsteps home.

I love to gild the bower,
Where fair and loved ones dwell ;
To float o'er dome and tower,
O'er mountain, moss, and fell.

I go—I go, still brightening
Each spot where'er I roam ;
Then fall like summer lightning,
Beneath the ocean's foam.

TRIO.
"MARK HOW THE PLANETS."

Mark how the planets swim and float,
Sparkling in ether far remote ;
Some clustering thick, like a council of light,
Or a crown formed of worlds on the brow of
night.

Some pale and pure as a virgin's sigh—
Some lone and silent in dim space lie—
Some strong and mighty as warrior's breast—
Some red and sanguine as warrior's crest.

Hark ! they are calling—their voices choir,
Loud, thro' creation—their tones like fire
Call on the nations to heed their song,
While their mighty chorus arrests the throng.

GRAND DUET.
"SATURN IS BORN."

Saturn is born—from the wrecks of a world
A lurid fire from the rim is hurled ;
Fierce and portentous the race shall be
Which claims this star for its destiny.

Saturn is born—through the midnight sky
The legion of star worlds return the cry ;
Earth hears the shout, and with pale-eyed fear
Quakes 'neath the glance of his lowering
sphere.

ARIA MARTIALE.
THE SONG OF MARS.

Proud and triumphant, in the ascendant,
See towering Mars in the zodiac resplendent ;
Earth quails with fear, while the war star
gleaming
High over victory ever is beaming.

See o'er the hosts contending in deadly
battlefield,
White victory hangs impending o'er many a
sword and shield ;
The star of Fate is beaming, in radiance wild
and fierce,
O'er every blade that, gleaming, the warrior's
heart doth pierce.

CHORUS.
THE METEOR.

But, lo ! a wild and trackless light
Shoots athwart the chorus bright;
Darting, parting through the space,
Stars and planets in the race.

Can it be some comet's sweep,
Rushing up the azure steep?
Dashing past ten thousand spheres,
Measuring ages less than years.

No ! It is the meteor's glance,
Shooting in fantastic dance,
Through the sky's immeasured arch,
Mocking, laughing at the march
Of the stately worlds of light,
Rolling through the empyrean height.

Hark ! a little distant star
Greets the wanderer from afar ;
Listen to its greeting small,
Twinkling out its whispering call.

Welcome—welcome, wandering sprite,
Homeless fairy of the night.
Wilt thou stay to deck my home?
Or must ever onward roam ?

Onward still the meteor flashes,
Wildly sparkling, onward dashes ;
But at length in chaos toss'd,
Lo ! the glittering spark is lost.

RECITATIVE.

But now a nobler song shall rise—
These starry worlds have angel eyes ;
Angel forms within their light,
Folded up like gems of night.

SONG.
"ANGEL LEGIONS."

Angel legions from repose,
'Midst those starry worlds unclose
Their eyes sublime, and o'er the woes
Of suffering kindred whisper those,
Whose earthly voices yet may reach
The human ear, and haply teach
The secrets of their wondrous sphere,
So bright, so distant, yet so near ;
And chaunted forth by that bright band,
Who breathe o'er man at God's command,
The fire divine of heavenly birth,
This song re-echoes through the earth.

GRAND CHORUS AND SOLO.

"AWAKE, ARISE!"

Awake! arise, ye souls divine!
Bid your immortal spirits shine,
Amidst the stars of heaven as fair,
As those ye mourn now dwellers there.
Awake! arise, ye sons of God,
Cast off the thoughts of earthly sod;
The stars are choiring o'er your head,
With spirits of the mighty dead.
They sing the noble themes of truth,
They dwell in ever-blooming youth;
They call you in their speechless tone
To turn your thoughts to heaven alone.

————

GRAND CAVATINA.

"WHERE THE STARS."

Where the stars of night arise,
There are watching angel eyes,
Ever proving how the loving
Hover 'round their earthly ties,
And in tones of former years,
Bid the mourners dry their tears.

Listen! listen to their tone—
Each has left his silver throne,
And around the midnight bed,
Of earth's children stand the dead.
Once again the lost are near,
Whispering soft in dreaming ear;
Father! mother! sister! brother!
Lo! thy loved and lost are near.
Wake and list, the glorious strain
Echoed o'er yon starry plain;
From shining worlds of light and love
Seraphs join the hymn to prove,
Through Creation's endless round
Love Divine in all is found.

GRAND FINALE—CONCERTED PIECE.

Love Eternal! Love Divine!
Hovers in the pale moonshine,
Reigns supreme in morning's beam.
Glitters in each starry gleam;
Love to man—rejoice, rejoice—
Echoes back Creation's voice,
Love is Life—and God is Love,
Resound the world of light above.

———————————

PART II.

GLEE.—"HAIL THOU MERRY MONTH OF MAY,"............WEBER.

DUET.—ON THEMES, from Don Pasquale, for Violin and Piano,
LEONARD AND GREGOIRE.

SONG.—"PASSED AWAY." ....Composed by MISS HARDINGE.

————•————

An ADDRESS, by Miss Hardinge, on "MUSIC," illustrated by the
following pieces:

"ARM, ARM YE BRAVE." Judas Maccabeus ....HANDEL.

KORNER's celebrated "SWORD SONG,"...Music by VON WEBER.

"MOURIR POUR LA PATRIE." Hymn of the Girondists.

"SCOTS WHA' HA' WI' WALLACE BLED."

FINALE.

"FOREST DAYS." A Prize Glee ....Composed by MISS HARDINGE.

CHAPTER VII.

RONDOUT.

"But even the very hairs of your head are all numbered. . . . Fear
ye not, therefore ; ye are of more value than many sparrows."

As this autobiography is not written with any desire for
personal distinction, but solely with the hope of adding
to the vast mass of literature already devoted to the expo-
sition of the Spiritual movement, so it becomes necessary
to mention a few places wherein some examples of those
cases were given which indicated the treatment that
many of the earlier workers in the Spiritual movement
had to receive.

In perusing the following "Notes of Travel," therefore,
let it ever be remembered that they *are* representative,
and that I, myself, as well as many scores of my early
associates, could duplicate the cases I am about to cite by
the hundred, as they have occurred in different parts of
the world.

As I gradually rose into favour with the friends of
Spiritualism, I was literally besieged with entreaties to
lecture at places to the very names of which I was a comparative stranger in America, and had never even heard
of. Amongst these appeals was one from a Mr. George
Smith, of Rondout, a place, as my correspondent informed
me, on the Hudson River, and easily accessible in my
journeyings to and from Troy, where I filled frequent
engagements. No one with whom I consulted appeared
to know anything of the Spiritual status of Rondout,
though I was informed it was a county town in a mountain district, and in the midst of vast coal regions.

Whilst pondering upon the propriety of accepting Mr.
Smith's invitation, my Spirit friends, speaking with me,

as they ever have done, by a voice which impinged as distinctly upon my spiritual ear as human voices reach my material sense of hearing, peremptorily desired me to answer Mr. Smith's letter in the affirmative, and this I did, appointing a certain Tuesday of a week when I was to fulfil a Sunday's and Monday's engagement at Troy.

At the time set, on an afternoon in the bitter month of December, 1857, I landed from the Hudson River steamboat, and was at once met by a pleasant-looking man, who accosted me by name, gave his own as George Smith, and conducted me to his buggy, which was close by the landing-stage waiting for me. After a few words of kindly welcome from my companion, he drove on, maintaining an unbroken silence until we reached his house.

As our road lay entirely up a steep mountain, more like a wall than a hill, I attributed Mr. Smith's taciturnity to the necessity he felt of concentrating his attention on the zigzag ascent of his poor horse. On reaching his home he took me into the house and introduced me to his brother's wife, and left me, promising to return as soon as he had put up his horse.

I was engaged to lecture at Rondout for two succeeding nights. After being very kindly inducted by my hostess into the room prepared for me, I returned to the parlour to find Mr. Smith awaiting me, with his naturally round jolly face lengthened into an ominously long oval. Premising that he deemed it his duty to inform me of the nature of the place I had arrived at, he went on to say that most of the inhabitants were more or less connected with the interests of that place, which was the county seat of the district, but that, whether the classes were high or low, they were all intensely orthodox, bitterly opposed to Spiritualism, and altogether a pretty rough lot. I drew a long breath. Proceeding with his narrative, he stated that a few years ago his brother—an elder Smith—then absent, had come out to be a great healer and clairvoyant. He (the speaker) became intensely interested in the cause, and in the hope of sharing the glad tidings of Spirit communion with his neighbours, he had invited Conklin, the test medium, to come there; also he had engaged the Rev. S. B. Brittan, the Rev. T. L. Harris, and quite a number of other eminent Spiritualist speakers and mediums to visit the place, all of whom had either not been permitted to land, or had been driven out of town with garments more or less damaged by the unsolicited presents of rotten eggs, mud, and even still more solid missives.

"There is a place quite handy," said Mr. Smith, confidentially, "where one of my friends resides, and to which I conveyed the Rev. R. P. Ambler and Thomas L. Harris, and where they were safely bestowed, during the preparatory time for starting by daylight next morning along routes the mob did not suspect." He added that his poor brother, the medium, had been a special mark for public execration, and although he was in an official situation himself, in the county, his windows had been systematically smashed about once a month, his garden trampled down, stable burned, and even the stone fence he had put up round the premises, had been hammered almost to pieces. Pausing in the list of calamities, but evidently only with the intention of taking breath to pour out fresh additions, I interrupted him by asking, in as steady a tone as my choking throat would permit, why in Heaven's name he had betrayed me into visiting that scene of horrors. Mr. Smith replied candidly enough, first, because I was a young lady, and he did not believe the roughest of American mobs would ever harm one such; next, because he had heard enthusiastic reports of my great successes; and finally, because the *Spirits had bidden him send for me.*

Plainly speaking, I am naturally, not only an exceedingly nervous person, but a decidedly cowardly one. The wholly unexpected favour with which my cultured audiences had hitherto received me, had contributed not a little to unfit me for ruder scenes ; but when, after the terrible pictures Mr. Smith had drawn, he gave the above-named reasons for sending for me, my mortal terror of the position he had placed me in was heightened by deep indignation, but the reproaches I was about to cast on him were interrupted by his saying, with a piteously appealing look and tone : " I have stuck up with my own hands three sets of bills announcing your coming; the two first sets have been all torn down or blackened over, I then went ten miles off to borrow the highest ladder in the county, and on this I stuck up the third set I have had printed, too high to reach or pelt at.   Oh, Mrs. Hardinge, do try to speak for me ! "

" I will," I murmured.

Rising up to go, he added : " I have hired a hall very near here.   This morning, on going to see if it was all right, I found they had taken out every seat, and except for the platform, left it empty; but, you see, I am not to be easily beaten, so have gone to a very poor fellow up yonder who keeps a day school, and agreed to give him a good sum for the loan of his school forms.   These I am now going to fetch and put in the hall."

And so, from four o'clock to half-past six, George Smith passed and repassed the window of that room, carrying on his shoulders the long heavy school forms he had hired to reseat the hall.   I sat at the window musing, like a little two-year old child, singing in low tones, all the doleful ditties, especially any dirges I knew, and watching by a street lamp outside the house, George Smith, with his heavy burdens, always turning his bright face up to nod at me as he passed.   Good Mrs. Smith brought me a cup of tea, which I was too choked to swallow, and when seven o'clock came, and I had covered up my dainty lecturing dress with a large cloak, Mrs. Smith and I sallied forth, she carrying a lantern to light my way in the midst of otherwise thick darkness, and a drizzling rain. The hall was not far off, but to reach it we had to cross the road, and before she would let me do this, the good woman picked up several large stones and made a path for me, with my thin boots, to tread on.

Arrived at the entrance, there stood George Smith, with a huge knotted stick in his hand. Slightly opening the rough overcoat he wore, he showed me a belt, on either side of which was stuck a pair of pistols.

Without a word spoken he walked by my side through the hall, stood guarding the door of the ante-room in which I took off my cloak and hood, then conducted me up to the platform, and stationed himself close beside my chair, whilst good Mrs. Smith, with a very pale face but perfectly composed manner, sat on the other side of me.

The hall was about three parts full of a rough-looking set of men, all of whom wore their hats, whilst, except Mrs. Smith and myself, there were only two women in the audience.

George Smith, stepping to the front of the platform, introduced me in a brief, manly, though highly-eulogistic speech, at the close of which, amidst dead silence, I commenced to speak.

After proceeding for about five minutes, as if at a previously concerted signal, about a dozen men rose from their seats, and with their heavy, wooden, clog-like shoes stampeded round the hall, shouting "A witch! a witch!" With a combined yell they then stampeded out of the hall.

With a calmness and composure I had never before in my life experienced, I stood still, only motioning to George Smith to be quiet until the "roughs" had gone out. I then went on again speaking for a few minutes more, when another dozen got up and repeated exactly the same programme, and this continued for upwards of one hour—I, after each brutal interruption, resuming the lecture with as much composure as if I had been addressing the most refined Athenæum audience. When I finally closed, all the time under the same amazing but resistless influence, there could not have been more than half-a-dozen people left besides ourselves, and these sat still staring at me, as if I had been an exhibition rather than a human being. On emerging from the hall we found the entire crowd waiting for us. At this sight, George Smith, giving his heavy stick to his sister-in-law, who held my arm on one side, threw open his coat, deliberately took out his two pistols, one in each hand, and planting himself on the other side of me, escorted me to his home. The mob followed, now and then shouting "A witch! a witch!" until Smith would turn round and, facing them, display his revolvers, when they at once slunk back and were still for a few moments. Finally, Mrs. Smith and I climbed the stone steps of the garden, and as we entered the house, George Smith stood at the front gate holding his pistols in each hand well displayed. A yell was set up as we disappeared, and Smith fired one of his "shooters" in the air, upon which the entire mob turned, ran away, and left us in peace and quiet within our closed doors. Then it was that, for the first time, the resolution of the strong man gave way. Sinking into a chair, and covering his face with his hands, the hitherto brave man, amidst choking sobs and fast-falling tears, refused all the efforts of his kind sister-in-law to comfort him. Speaking at length in husky, broken tones, he declared that his last hopes were shattered, his last desperate game of the one against the multitude played out. All he now regretted was, he murmured, that he had subjected the dear young lady to so shameful a persecution.

To atone for it as well he could, he said, was all that was now left him to do, and the plan that he had thought over coming along was this: About midnight, when the "roughs" had gone home, weary of their disgraceful fun, he would harness up the pony, and quietly drive me a few miles out to the house of the friends who had helped the previous Mediums and speakers to escape. I should be safe and well protected there, and in the morning I should be put in the train for home. "All I have now to do, dear lady," the poor man added sorrowfully, taking out his purse, "is to pay you, as far, at least, as dollars and cents can compensate for such usage."

Under the strong, nay, the resistless influence of the same power that had sustained me during the evening, and now held me as in a grip of iron, I said, "Put up your purse, Mr. Smith, and listen. Do you not say this is the county seat?"

"Yes, madam."

"Then you have a magistrate residing here, and a courthouse, have you not?"

"We have."

"Very well," I said (without ever having seen an American courthouse, or having the least idea of its functions); "now, what you must do is this. Go to-morrow morning to your magistrate."

"'The Squire' we call him, ma'am."

"Go to the Squire, then, the first thing; he will see and listen to you. Tell him your whole story, and how we have been treated this night. Ask him, IN MY NAME, to give us the use of the courthouse for to-morrow evening, for a second lecture from me. Ask him to come himself— listen to me, and if I say anything contrary to the law, or the peace and welfare of the people, let him arrest me; if I speak what he deems well and righteously, I call upon him to protect me. Will you do this?"

" I'll do it, and say every word of it, Mrs. Hardinge, and
may God help me through the effort," replied Smith.

"God helps those who help themselves," were the last
words my stern guides made me speak that night.

It was nearly one o'clock on the next day before I
again saw George Smith, as he entered the house on
returning home to his dinner; his kind face might have
been taken as a model for a full moon, so jolly and plump
were the proportions to which it had attained. The Squire
had received him kindly — listened with attention and
some show of indignation to the narrative of his wrongs;
at the close, the request which he had preferred had been
granted. The Squire authorised a notice of the intended
meeting to be posted outside the courthouse door, and
promised himself to attend the lecture. Even the clerk
of the weather was in sympathy with us that night, for it
was fine and dry, and the brilliant light of the full moon
made lantern and stepping stones unnecessary.

On entering the courthouse, I at once perceived that it
was crowded to excess, and that by respectable-looking
women, as well as by men of a very different stamp to
the "rowdies" of the preceding evening. George Smith
escorted me up to the judge's seat, the place that had
been assigned me, and made a quiet but effective little
speech, asking, for the honour of America, that the
audience would give a patient hearing to the English lady,
whom he proceeded to eulogise in terms wholly out of
place for the said lady to repeat.

When he retired, the Squire, who occupied some official
crib beneath me, rose up, and addressing the audience,
after looking sternly around for some time, like a school-
master facing a set of unruly children, he said: "There's
the lady; here am I; and now, behave yourselves!"

I scarcely ever recollect or can recall the text of the
lectures I deliver save when I am obliged to correct

reports of the same for publication; but that which I do
remember of that Wednesday night's lecture was that it
was the Bible story of Joseph, that it was listened to in
breathless silence till towards the end, when a number of
little choking coughs, blowing of noses, waving of hand-
kerchiefs, and faint murmurs of admiration testified to
the deep effect the lecture had upon those present.

During the questions which followed, in which the
Squire took an active part, it seemed difficult to restrain
the audience from bursting out into applause.

At the close of the service the Squire again arose, and
said : "All which the lady had taught in that lecture, and
those answers, was the kind of religion he had been
looking for and waiting to find all his life, and as long or
as often as that lady would come to Rondout and give
such teaching, she should have the courthouse to speak in
free, even if it was every week for the next fifty years."

With three cheers "for the lady" and three more for
"the Squire," propounded, as the Smiths both assured me,
by one of the very "roughs" of the previous night, the
grand meeting which celebrated the lifelong and final
triumph of good George Smith over all his foes terminated.
I never found time or occasion to visit Rondout again,
though for years after I was frequently pressed to do so.
My work there was ended, and it was enough for me to
know that the place became one of the strongholds of
Spiritualism, whilst a flourishing Children's Lyceum gave
promise that the next generation would be somewhat
wiser and more progressive than their progenitors.

CHAPTER VIII.

MONTREAL.

"God moves in a mysterious way
His wonders to perform."

IT was only a brief period after I had commenced my career as a Spiritual lecturer when I received a letter from a gentleman in Montreal, Canada, inviting me to visit that city, and give a course of three Spiritual lectures there.

The writer said he had just built a new hall (called Buona Venture) which he wished to open for the first time with me. He guaranteed to pay my railway fare to and from New York to Montreal, and as his offer to engage me was only made, he added, on the strength of the flattering reports he had received from Mr. Thomas Ranney, the good Spiritualist friend whom I had met at my first New York boarding house, my engagement must be regarded in the light of an *experiment*. If I was as successful as Mr. Ranney had led him to expect I should be, he would pay me one hundred dollars for the three nights' lectures, but, if on the contrary, *the people would not hear me*, I was to forfeit the sum in question, and be satisfied with my railway expenses only.

As I knew nothing whatever of Canada save from the representations of our friend, Mr. Ranney (a Canadian by birth), and was totally at a loss to know why it should be a question whether the people would hear me or not, I submitted this offer to several friends, all of whom pleaded with me not to accept it. The Canadian winter, they urged, would be unendurable ; the conditions implied *danger*, not *failure*, the latter of which my too partial advisers deemed "impossible."

These and many other objections were so forcibly urged, that I was on the point of declining the offer in question, when the Spirit voices pleaded with me sternly to do my duty, and go, whatever might be the result. To this charge I ventured so far to demur as to ask if the powers thus directing me could or would give me any idea of what would be the result of such an adventure? At this point, according to one of the phases of mediumship with which I was then frequently exercised—namely, by pantomimic action—the Spirits drew an imaginary line down the middle of my face, as if dividing it into two sides. Pointing to the first side they said, "Portentous and stormy," touching the second half they added, "Triumphant and glorious."

Within an hour after this my letter of acceptance was despatched to Canada, and the second day from thence I started on my long journey according to telegraphic directions received.

It was at a place called Rouse's Point, some hundreds of miles distant from home, that I had to change cars, and as it was three quarters of an hour before I could resume my journey, I took advantage of the opportunity to warm my frozen limbs by the waiting-room stove.

I had not sat there five minutes before a party of four gentlemen entered, approached me, and asked if I was not Mrs. Emma Hardinge.

I answered in the affirmative, when one of the party said he had heard me lecture in New York, and being on a business tour in Canada he had also heard that I was announced to speak at a certain date in Montreal.

Being *en route* to New York, these gentlemen had taken pains to intercept me, with a view of saving, perhaps, a friendless lady, one whom they all respected, and entreating her not to venture to go to Montreal to lecture on Spiritualism.

They then repeated in substance the Rondout story, concerning the treatment which numerous lecturers of far longer standing than myself had experienced in that city of Scotch Presbyterianism and French Catholicism.

They said they had taken counsel together, and the party ended by offering at once to purchase my ticket back to New York if I would be advised by them.

Expressing the real gratitude I felt towards my kind friends, I asked for some ten minutes of quiet deliberation on their offer.

The remonstrances and assurances of my Spirit friends decided me to proceed. So, after taking a grateful leave of these worthy men, in a short time I found myself tucked up under buffalo robes in a sleigh on what I deemed to be a broad prairie, intercepted by long rows of stunted fir trees lining each side of divers roads. I was soon given to understand by my fur-coated drivers that the prairie I thought I was riding on was the frozen River St. Lawrence, that the fir trees were branches stuck in the ice to indicate landing stages, and that the bear-skin coated drivers of the sleigh I had entered were about to land me in Canada.

Arrived, met, and welcomed by my new manager, I was taken to warm rooms in a good hotel, and comfortably lodged till the next day.

It was on Tuesday, November 16th, 1858, that I appeared for the first time at "Buona Venture Hall," Montreal. The place was full, and, to do them justice, the people listened to the lecture quietly.

But when, according to my usual custom, I invited questions, the long pent-up feeling of hostility had full sway. At least a dozen impatient and unmistakably determined opponents shouted out questions and remarks at once. One person demanded, fiercely, to know if his grandmother's spirit was there; whilst another screamed— "Tell me my mother's middle name, or I won't believe."

A hoarse voice roared out—"How could the Lord have made the earth in six days, when it takes——." The rest of the sentence was lost in the shout of "Moses says 'Thou shalt not suffer a witch to live!'—down with her!"

Just then a small voice from the gallery screamed— "Can the Heathen be saved?" and another from below snuffled forth—"Paul says 'Let your women keep silence in——.'" "Just tell me, how did God make Eve out of a single rib?" was fiercely demanded; whilst still another cried, "Why don't serpents talk now as well as in Paradise?"—"Is my old nannygoat's spirit in heaven or the other place?" etc., etc., etc.; and these are but a few of the questions, or rather the ribald remarks that were hurled at me as I stood before that hideous and insensate mob, silent and motionless.

When, as if by a spell, the hubbub subsided almost as suddenly as it commenced, I can well recall the words I— or some blessed power through me—uttered.

They were—and that amid profound silence—"God forgive them, they know not what they do."

I then quietly and calmly, to my own subsequent astonishment, said I should lecture in that place again the next night. On that occasion the audience were to select a committee of five gentlemen from amongst themselves to choose the subject of the lecture, after which I would answer such questions as belonged to that subject, and none others, and the very moment two voices spoke at once, or raised any unseemly clamour, I should quit the platform.

At this point I left amidst vociferous cheers and equally vociferous hisses and cries of "Down with the witch!"

During the next day I received numerous calls from gentlemen who were believers in my faith, several of whom had tried before, but all in vain, to introduce Spiritualism to a Montreal audience, but who had only endangered the lives of those they had engaged and injured their own standing in the city.

Amongst the visitors was my old New York acquaint-ance, Mr. Ranney, who was then acting as a book agent in Canada, and with him came the proprietor of the hall. They both assured me my inaugural meeting had made such a deep impression on the community that I positively must appear again that night, however repulsive it might be to my feelings. On that same Wednesday evening a committee of five gentlemen were chosen by the audience to select the subject of the night.

As this committee were stationed in a small room only separated from the antechamber I occupied by a slight partition, and they were over half-an-hour engaged in discussion, I had, what may be deemed either the pain or pleasure, as the case might be, of hearing their arguments *pro* and *con*. All I can now remember is, that a certain Mr. Hunt, whom I was subsequently informed was the " Queen's chemist," was appointed as chairman of that committee, and the last words I heard him utter prior to the committee's return to the audience were, " We'll break her down anyway, and that's all we have to do." The subject selected, I find by the newspaper reports I sent afterwards to my mother, was " The Geological Formation of the Earth and its Ultimate Destiny."

Again the lecture was listened to attentively, and loud applause, in which the committee, as I was afterwards informed, joined, greeted me at its close, but the end was not yet.

Sitting opposite the platform, in the front row, was one whom I subsequently learned was a Jewish Rabbi. On either side of him sat some twelve of his scholars, and it was he it seemed, who was expected by the opposition, to " break me down anyway." This gentleman, rising from his seat, asked permission of the audience to put a few consecutive questions to the speaker, and that without any interruption. A loud burst of applause being taken as acquiescence, the rabbi proceeded sternly to ask me a number of purely biblical questions.

After about seven or eight minutes' interlocution of this kind, the gentleman, turning to the audience with a profoundly sarcastic air, remarked, that " These Spirits of the lady's did not know much, as, if they did, instead of answering in orthodox biblical fashion, they would have known that such and such passages, which he repeated, were false translations. In the original Hebrew," he added, "they were so-and-so, and the translations were rendered otherwise, either to suit the opinions of the time, or on account of the translators' ignorance of the ancient Hebrew language."

I cannot now recall the passages to which my opponent referred, nor do I believe that they were indicated in the newspaper reports, but *I do* remember the nature of the answer which the Spirit power that held me—like a vice—impelled me to give, and it was to this effect: That the sentences quoted were inscribed after the ancient mode of of Hebrew writing, in which the vowels were omitted, and that the methods of *pointing* employed would render them susceptible of being translated in six different ways; consequently it was the learned scholar who was endeavouring to impose upon an unlearned audience, and not the young woman who stood before them as the mouthpiece and messenger of those who " did know Hebrew, both ancient and modern."

Before the audience could take in the full meaning of this speech, the Rabbi rose in a furious passion from his seat, and addressing the chairman of the committee, cried, "There ! I told you that girl *did* understand Hebrew."

Whether the people present did or did not understand that this scene had obviously been pre-arranged for the sole purpose of attempting " to break me down," I cannot say, it is enough that it served completely to turn the tide in

my favour. *The second half of the face of destiny was
reached.* Shouts of applause greeted me, in which the
adverse committee joined. Every succeeding question
and answer only called forth more and more applause,
until, as my delighted manager alleged, I retired from the
scene in a blaze of triumph. The success of my (Thursday)
night's lecture was now assured, and by a hastily got up
invitation, numerously signed, I was induced to lecture
again on Friday evening, also on Sunday afternoon.
Friday evening's lecture was chosen by the audience,
Sunday's was given by my own choice.

On Monday I left Montreal with a DOUBLE FEE, made up
by liberal presents from kind strangers whose very names
I did not know. Even in that bitter icy cold season,
bushels of hot-house flowers were sent me, and a perfect
crowd of warm sympathisers met me as I was about once
more to enter the sleigh to cross the vast St. Lawrence
River, bidding me God speed, and entreating me to come
again soon.

Since this time I have visited London and Toronto,
Canada, but on both these occasions I found that
Spiritualism was no longer either a strange or tabooed
subject. I was as well received in both places as I should
have been in any American city where my belief was well
established ; but ere I proceed to draw conclusions from
the scenes above narrated, I must ask my readers to
follow me to a still more remote Canadian district than any
before mentioned. This was to Picton, on what is called
Prince Edward's Island. I was giving a month's course of
Sunday lectures in Oswego, a beautiful town on the
borders of Lake Ontario, when I received a letter from a
gentlemen residing at Picton, literally entreating me to
visit "that benighted spot," to which, as he said, his evil
fortune had condemned him, after being "born and brought
up in the midst of American civilisation." He could not

exist longer without some Spiritual life, he added, and
as he had heard me lecture in the States, he thought I was
just the right one to make the people in his present scene
of exile listen to me.   It was in pursuance of this
invitation that on a certain day in June I embarked on
a Lake Ontario steamer bound for the Bay of Quinte, and
late in the afternoon I reached my place of destination.

My correspondent, whose name, if I recollect rightly,
was Mr. Ayers, met me with all kindly greeting, and we
started in his buggy for his home.   As we drove along, I
was amused at the violent ringing of a huge bell, whilst in
the intervals of the clatter, a man, with stentorian lungs,
was shouting out—" *The most beautifullest, the most
wonderfuilest, the most as—-tonishingest great prodigy
as never was*"—more furious ringing, and then commenced a fresh tirade as above.

I asked in amazement, what that creature was bawling
about, when, before my friend could reply, the answer
came in a voice of thunder, " Missis Emmy Ardin !—Come
and hear, come and hear !—*the* most beautifullest, *the* —— "
etc., etc., etc.

" Oh, Heavens " ! I exclaimed, trying to stop my ears,
" Is that the way you advertise me ?   Let me go back
again, I beseech you, or else stop that horrid monster's
noise."

" Now, don't be scared," replied my companion, half
laughing at my dismay ; " that's the only way we have just
yet of making public announcements ; why, even our
M.P.'s, when they come here to visit us, are cried about
the streets.   Weddings, christenings, fires, murders, or
Spiritual lectures—it's all one,"   Just then a good
tempered looking man rushed out of a small shop by the
wayside, and seeing the buggy slowly toiling up the hill,
called out, " Hallo, Mr. Ayers !   Got the young lady there
all safe ? "   Seeing me by my friend's side, he extended a

very black hand, shook mine most cordially, and declared
he was proud to see me—in fact, he was " pleased to death,"
for he was a great Spiritualist, he was, and only hoped we
would step in and have tea with him and his good dame.

Thanking my new acquaintance heartily, Mr. Ayres
declined the invitation on the ground of Mrs. Ayres being
in waiting for us, and the lateness of the hour. " Well,"
said my jolly friend, " you see what I is, Miss," pointing to
the sign above his door, "and any time as you can bring
yourself down to stop with such as me and my missis, be
sure you're mortal welcome, either for a week or a month,
or many of them for the matter of that." Glancing up at
the sign I read—" James McCormick, shoemaker," and
underneath, the legend—

> " I work for those that pay me best ;
> When I get time I work for the rest."

" The best fellow in the place, Mrs. Hardinge," said my
friend as we drove off. " He has paid half the rent of our
hall himself, and is ready, if need be, to pay the rest."

But our good Crispin was not the only one interested.
At least a dozen genial people met us, or came out from
their doors as we drove on still up, and up, and uphill,
offering us hospitality, shaking my hand, and extending
warm Canadian welcomes to the stranger, of whom that
awful crier was roaring out such a pack of stories. There
is little to report of the two lectures given at Picton, but I
speak of this visit simply to notice the third night of my
engagement, when I was announced to speak at Bloomfield,
a place some few miles from Picton, and where there was a
settlement of Quakers, some of whom it was that desired
my presence there. Mr. Ayers told me that I was to speak
in the Universalist Church, which had been built by a rich
Quaker of the settlement as "a Friends' meeting house,"
but as there were a large number of Universalists there,
and the residents could not afford to build another place

of worship, the two sects had mutually agreed to occupy the one church on alternate Sundays, and thus accommodate each other.

It was a very fine summer's evening, and I noticed as we drove along (Mr. and Mrs. Ayers and myself), what an immense number of different conveyances there were on the road.

"They are all going our way, you see," said my friend, "and you may assure yourself they are going to exactly the same place and with the same object."

"I may look for a good audience, then?" I queried.

"Perhaps!" was the curt reply.

Arrived at our destination, a most extraordinary scene met our eyes. A large plateau of green sward stretched on every side around a huge mound on which was erected a handsome church. Surrounding this spot, in every direction, and completely covering the green plateau, were huddled together several hundred carriages of all sorts and sizes. The owners themselves had evidently dismounted, and were waiting about in groups, listening to a dispute that was being carried on between a party of Quakers, who stood on one side of the closed church doors, and a number of what I afterwards learned were church members on the other side, disputing with the Quakers on their right to admit me and my audience into the church. We were informed that the dispute had continued for the past half-hour, and arose when the parties who really owned the building demanded the keys from the opposition. More and more fierce had grown the controversy, until it had just reached that point when the leader of the " Friends " had avowed his intention of putting his own and a few other of his partisans' shoulders to the door by way of key unless it was unlocked in exactly five minutes by a watch.

It was a curious sight enough to see the peaceful Friends standing together in a compact body, silently but sternly fixing their eyes on a watch which one of their number held on high in view of the whole crowd, whilst the opposition group were eagerly and noisily disputing among themselves.

Suddenly came a crash, followed by shouts, cries, and a rush. " There they go in, for sure," said my friend. "Think it's about time for us to go in too." I followed Mr. Ayres, until almost borne along by the surging crowd we were literally pushed up the mound, and shoved on to the very steps which led to the church door. " No more admission here," screamed a man with his arms extended from one side of the door to the other. " Full and brimming over." " All right," coolly replied Mr. Ayers, " If they won't let *you* in, Mrs. Hardinge, guess they won't have much speaking in there to-night." " Eh, what ?" replied the officious warden. " Is that the speaker ? Here, here "—to the throng inside—"stand back out of the way with ye ! Git, will ye ? " The speaker, the speaker," now echoed through the crowd outside ; and amidst cries of "What's she like ?" "Let's get a look at her." "Has she come on a broomstick ?" "Does she wear wings ?" &c., &c. I was partly pulled, partly shoved into the church, and that without tearing more than one half of my white muslin dress to pieces. Escorted up into the pulpit, with Mr. Ayres sitting below me as clerk, I looked curiously at the sea of faces beneath, around, and above me, for some daring ones had even climbed up to the windows, and were perched on the sills. Bonnet and gloves removed, I was happily inspired to open a hymn book which lay on the desk and give out a hymn, reading the first verse myself. Then, at once, and without any parley, one fine voiced man struck up a favourite old hymn tune. The words were known, the tune was popular, and the people all sang with one accord. The crowd outside joined in the sublime strain—sublime when upwards of a thousand voices were united in praise and supplication to the Father of all. In that glorious strain of harmony the spirit of discord was vanquished, and the triumph of peace and goodwill was achieved. An invocation, followed by the lecture of over one hour, ensued, during which a breathless silence prevailed amidst that jammed and seething crowd. A few questions, many attempts at cheers repressed by a hush, and the remembrance of being "in a church;" a parting hymn sung, and then amidst the fading twilight and the glimmer of a few dim lamps the masses separated and began to pass out quietly, only pausing to glance kindly at me, some murmuring "God bless you," some holding up a child for me to kiss, and not a few stretching out hands to grasp mine.

The best part of the scene to me was when a vast mass of the crowd had dispersed and Mr. Ayres led me out of the church, to see the two recently opposing parties vigorously shaking hands with one another; the leader of the one sect exclaiming, as I came out, "Why, bless my soul, dear lady, what you said to-night has been my religion all through and through my life." "I don't know about that," said the head revolutionist of the other side, "I only know it's the religion I have been waiting for all my life."

I slept well that night when I was at last permitted to do so. The next day I once more embarked on a Bay of Quinte boat, expecting to rejoin my dear mother (who was visiting kind friends at Oswego) about five in the afternoon.

On reaching Lake Ontario, however, our boat encountered one of those terrific gales which sometimes sweep over those American inland seas, making navigation more difficult and far more dangerous on what are supposed in other countries to be "peaceful lakes," than being midway on one of the wide oceans.

For many hours. and far into the night, our good boat tossed and heaved in the midst of fierce surging waves

sweeping our deck from stem to stern, whilst pealing
thunder and one incessant glare of forked lightning
contributed to render the scene as terribly impressive as
the worst storms I have ever had to encounter on the
Atlantic or Pacific Oceans. Sailor's daughter as I am, it
may be as a matter of inheritance, or perhaps from deeper
causes, that I have always rejoiced in, rather than feared,
the awful phenomena of storms at sea.

Complimenting me on what he called my bravery as he
passed my chair, which I had had lashed to the side of the
boat in a sheltered nook on deck, the captain said to me:
"They say you are one of them good Spirit folk, ma'am.
Can your Spirits tell us how soon we shall all be sleeping
in our ocean graves, for I don't see much chance of any
other bed this night of our Lord?"   "Neither do I,
captain," I replied; "that is to say, *on this night*, for it is
now nearly twelve. Those of us who live in Oswego,
however, may all be in our quiet beds by three o'clock
to-morrow morning, and you may throw me overboard as
the Jonah of the ship if we fail to land by two at the
latest."   "By the Lord, I believe you, ma'am," replied the
poor captain, staggering off on his way with a cheery
"God bless you, lady."   By five minutes to two our storm-
tossed craft was safely moored in the Oswego harbour.

Our good friend and host, Mr. Doolittle, obeying the
telegraphic signal of our approach, which he had provided
for, was at the wharf to receive me.

As I landed, the captain whispered in my ear, whilst
helping me ashore, "You don't know the good your
blessed words have done me," and by three o'clock I was
asleep by the side of my dear mother, and dreaming I was
on Prince Edward's Island, Canada, and gazing with dazed
speculation, as hundreds of others have done before me,
on the phenomenon of the celebrated "lake on the top of
the mountain."

CHAPTER IX.

THE TRUTH AGAINST THE WORLD.

To avoid repetition I have devoted the last few chapters of this work to a narration of some of those representative incidents, *hundreds* of which marked the chequered career of my thirty-five years' experiences as a Spiritual lecturer.

I have no doubt that many of my fellow workers have had to pass through similar ordeals, but because I was a wide and adventurous traveller, besides being what was called a genuine revivalist, I cannot but think I have had something more than my share of such adventures.

Whilst visiting many foreign countries, as well as during my engagements in forty-four of the North American States, I was continually solicited to open up new places, wherein, under ordinary circumstances, I should not have dared to undertake pioneer work, but I had been assured by the good Spirit employers in whose kindness and foresight I had learned implicitly to trust, that in proceeding to such scenes of effort as *they* indicated, "a park of artillery brought against me, by a legion of enemies, could not harm me."

During all the years of my far and wide pilgrimages, my custom of dividing up my time was as follows :—

I was invited to make engagements in the larger towns for one or two consecutive months, speaking every Sunday in the morning and evening, at two services.

During the Sunday afternoons I was frequently requested to give an address in the State Prisons of various cities, such as Philadelphia, New Bedford, Charlestown (Massachusetts), Providence, &c., &c.

These visits were especially interesting to me, as it afforded an opportunity of presenting to the unhappy criminals who most needed such teachings, the stern but strictly just doctrine of *personal responsibility* for all sins committed, as well as the encouraging and hopeful Spiritual assurances of eternal progress for all who, like the "Prodigal" of the scriptures, willed to arise, and return to their Father by the path of penitence trodden by their *own* unwearying efforts. Sometimes the wardens brought me special requests from the prisoners themselves to visit such a particular cell.

On these occasions I passed through some of the most tragic and impressive scenes of my life. I may note this of two particular cases, when I was privileged to deliver addresses at Moamensing, the Pennsylvania State Prison, and was called upon by one of the wardens to visit the cells of two hapless criminals, condemned to suffer the last penalty of the law on the following day. Such words of warning, and yet of hope and promise, and such unfeigned remorse and grateful resignation passed between the messenger of the Spirit world and those doomed men, as will never escape my memory, until we all meet again in the spheres of ETERNAL PROGRESS.

My noondays were mostly devoted to visiting sick or aged people, who desired interviews, but were unable to call on me. On the Tuesdays, with equally recurring certainty, I set out on fresh travels, being always engaged three and not unfrequently four nights a week in opening up new places, or effecting revivals in old "Stamping grounds." On numerous other occasions I was called upon to conduct two or more evening DEBATES with opponents to Spiritualism, such persons being most commonly clergymen of different denominations, or Secularists.

Returning towards the end of the week to the scene of my regular month's engagements, morning and afternoon calls, evening receptions, an immense correspondence, and articles to be written for the various spiritual papers constituted the chief, though not always the *only*, demands that were poured in upon me.

In my own person I give a by no means exaggerated picture of the life and work of that large class of Spiritual speakers that for the last thirty-five years have laboured with heart and soul, body and mind, time and service, to plant the standard of the Spiritual faith through the vast length and breadth of the New World. I know many of these devoted missionaries have "fallen in their tracks," and attained to the work which is joy, and the labour which is rest, in the higher life. Nearly all my own early associates, those who have so often exchanged with me words of kindly cheer and mutual sympathy, have happily scaled the blessed heights before me ; but although few of those who have succeeded them have had to encounter the fierce persecutions which were heaped upon the first pioneers of this mighty movement, or known what it was to wander so far and wide from all home ties as the writer of these pages, I repeat it, the brief summary I have drawn of a devoted and energetic Spiritual speaker's life, the work, whether in the past or the present day, so far from being exaggerated, has been purposely understated ; and it is for such labours of body and devotion of mind that modern Scribes and Pharisees so often call upon the poor medium speaker to go forth and *give* time and service "without money and without price," forgetting that every means of support or locomotion costs money, and costs price, and every other form of activity in the world is considered to be worthy to receive it.

I have not included in my list of duties the number of funerals I was called upon to officiate at, the population of babies I was required to name, or the Lyceum exercises I was expected to attend with the advice and encouragement which was sure to be forthcoming in timely addresses.

·I must add that these diverse occupations were not peculiar to the work of the movement in America, as I found myself quite as actively employed in New Zealand Australia, and during my *first* return visit to this, my native country. Neither do I claim exemption from similar toil for the American workers of the present day, whose labours and worth I see continually written of in the Spiritual papers.

In the sketch I am at present preparing, however, I speak of what I have myself experienced—what hundreds of still living witnesses will testify to—and that in promulgation of a cause which has revolutionised the realm of old theological thought, and laid foundations for the up-building of the new, the true, and the well-proven in those religious beliefs which will yet rule the entire civilised world. To return, however, to the special subject of this sketch. The only leisure time I ever found for reading was during long journeys in the railway cars, or on the steamboats. Even in the latter, on ocean transits, the captain almost always called upon me *to do* the Sunday services, and to get up musical entertainments for Sailors' Widows' and Orphans' Funds. As to holidays, I did not know the meaning of the term. My dear mother now and then accompanied me in journeys to places not more than a few hundred miles distant from where she boarded, which was generally with good friends in either New York or Boston, and when, after many long months of absence in the Far West, North, or South, I returned to share her home and gladden her dear eyes with the sight of her wanderer, it was a fixed fact that I was to lecture on the Sundays at either New York or Boston, and rush off somewhere for week night lectures on at least four evenings between the week ends, and all these far and wide wanderings were pursued for the most part under trials and difficulties unnumbered. Sometimes I spent months in the North-west, when from three to six feet of snow covered the earth. Sometimes I was half dissolved beneath the burning sun of St. Louis, Memphis, or New Orleans.

The trains on which I journeyed were often snow-bound, and I have known what it was to be nearly famished, as well as frozen and weary almost unto death. I never enjoyed vigorous health; was always subject to throat and chest affections, and often became nearly crippled with rheumatism. I do not know how it may have fared with other speakers, but in my own case I declare, and there are now scores of living witnesses who will confirm my assertion, that even the most serious indisposition, provided it did not confine me to my bed, never interfered with or marred my lectures.

On one occasion, when my mother had accompanied me to Buffalo in order to visit Niagara Falls, I heard her—ever the kindest and most tender of nurses—say to Mrs. Maynard, with whom we were staying, and when I was completely prostrated with a severe fit of influenza: " Never mind, we must dress her and put her in the carriage. She will be all right when she gets on the platform, and the lecture will cure her." And this pro-phecy was not only fully realised, but my mother spoke from what she had witnessed in unnumbered cases of a similar kind, and what I always wished to be done.

It may be right at this point to anticipate the same questioning which many good home-bred friends have applied to me before; namely, how *could* I, and why *would* I endure a life of such incessant fatigue, frequent privation, and bewildering excitement ?

I reply: I *could* endure it because good and powerful Spirits enabled me to do so, and ever supported me nobly in every emergency; I *would* endure it because the exercise of the powers with which I was endowed made.

me supremely happy because they made others happy,
reformed many a criminal, enlightened many a darkened
mind, and because I believed—nay, I knew, the truth of all
the Spirits taught through my own lips, and proved
through many other mediums' tests.   Nay, more, I should
have felt that I was guilty of disobedience to my Heavenly
Father's will had I resisted the wonderful power that had
been poured out upon me, and failed to become an instrument for the blessed Spirits in teaching and proving the
conditions of life hereafter.

I may here state that my various phases of test medium
powers, though not so strong as when they were in full
exercise by my sitting day after day for the public, never
wholly forsook me.   The good Spirits who inspired my
lectures had strictly charged me to give up test mediumship as a practice, alleging that philosophic, scientific, or
teaching Spirits could not control those organs of the
brain that were required to be used to give names, ages,
dates, and tokens of personal identity.   Such tests, they
alleged, could only be given by people's Spirit friends, or
through the medium's "Guide," or "familiar Spirit," not
through the controlling powers who inspired instructive
lectures.   "You put the magnetic wires out of order,"
these teaching Spirits would say; "and when we wish to
give our listeners the oratorio of 'The Creation,' we only
find a one-stringed instrument accustomed to drone out
the melody of 'Home, Sweet Home.'"

Neither did these Spirits ever permit me to give tests on
the platform.   They alleged that the variety of minds
assembled around a speaker produced only broken and
heterogeneous influences; also that the platform should
not be turned into an exhibition, but was designed to
expound the philosophy and religion of the movement,
whilst the small harmonious circle, or private interviews,
were organised through the science of the intercommunion

between Spirits and mortals, and should be wholly devoted to that science through which tests could be given and mortals and Spirits re-united.

I must now speak of one very important incident in my early career, and though I shrink with unspeakable reluctance from the possibility of incurring the charge of personal egotism, I feel that all I have done, or could do, is so entirely due to the control of the good and wise Spirits, whose servant I am, that I take shame to myself when I hesitate to point to one special result of their influence, and briefly note its consequences.

It was in September, 1858, that, by the command of the Spirits, who by spoken words gave me the subjects of my Sunday lectures, and who generally mapped out for me the month's course that I was to give, I commenced a series of eight lectures on the Origin of All Religious Faiths. The order of the discourses included quotations from the most ancient religious Scriptures, descriptions of monuments of India, Egypt, Persia, Chaldea, Greece, Rome, the Jews, and the Christians. To well-informed students of history there were no novelties presented in these subjects, but to communities of those who either had been, or still were, adherents to the Christian faith, the revelations of Solar, Sex, and Fire worship—in a word, the doctrines, miracles, nay, the very teachings and histories of ancient Messiahs dragged from the dust of ages, and proved to have been in existence uncounted centuries prior to the *last* of the Messiahs, the alleged founder of the Christian faith—was a revelation so new, so astounding to the mass of an uninformed populace, that this course, first commenced at Dodworth's Hall, New York, created not only astonishment, but mingled fear of consequences, and not a little indignation amongst many of the Spiritualists themselves.

Accustomed as I had been to receive the warmest tokens of appreciation from my Spiritualistic associates, I was often inexpressibly pained by the remonstrances of some of my friends against "the dangerous ground" on which I was treading, and what they called my attacks and subversions of the foundations of Christianity. These and many similar murmurs could only be silenced, when, prompted by my stern Spirit guides, I queried thus: "Is what has been taught true or false? If false, prove it. If true, how can you hope to build up a new and true religion of *personal responsibility* here and hereafter, on ground already occupied by a religion which teaches salvation only through *vicarious atonement* for sin, and belief that such salvation is wrought through one special individual, whose history has been acted out again and again ages before his time?"

That these lectures struck home to the very hearts and consciences of the supporters of orthodoxy, was sufficiently proved by the bitterness with which they were received and commented on. The editor of the *New York Herald* proposed that I should be "*shut up*" "in the *best interests of religion, and not released until I had promised never to speak in public on religious subjects again.*"

The St. Louis papers protested against my daring to revive the *theories* of Volney, Dupins, Robert Taylor, and Abner Kneeland, but the learned writers who proposed to silence me by the arm of the law, forgot to explain wherein the teachings of the great authorities cited were *false or untrue—heretical* as they might have been to believers in special sectarian faiths.

And still, though many pious ones ran away, and many savage ones stamped out of my lecture rooms, making as much noise as they could, and banging the door behind them, with what Thomas Hood has defined as "*a wooden damn,*" the Spirits whom I served insisted upon my giving this same obnoxious course of lectures in all the large centres I visited.

Very soon after this severe trial, for such was my enforced obedience to my Spirit guides, Mr. Kersey Grave's "Sixteen Crucified Saviours," Lydia Maria Child's "Progress of Religious Ideas," besides books and an endless flood of tracts and pamphlets, fairly saturated public opinion with the very ideas that had first been deemed too dangerous and even blasphemous to express publicly on a Spiritual platform.

When visiting Australia, twenty years later than the first delivery of the revolutionary addresses above referred to, and during a ten months' series of lectures in Melbourne, when I allowed a committee of the audience to choose the subjects of my lectures, the origin of *all* religious faiths as taught in various ancient lands was almost always presented as their choice. Before quitting Melbourne, I was requested by several scholarly men, some of whom were members of the Victorian University, to embody the chief points of these lectures in some printed form, together with references to such well-known authorities as would strengthen and justify the statements made. The result of this request was the publication of my work, "The Faiths, Facts, and Frauds of Religious History," ten thousand copies of which were circulated through the Colonies. The only answer that has ever been made—to my knowledge—of the teachings enunciated in that work, proceeded from a *learned Australian Bishop*, who published a pamphlet (when almost forced to do so at the request of his congregation), entitled, "The Expectation of Christ." In this *instructive* work, the only account that was rendered of all the various antique Messiahs who preceded the Christian one was, that they were the myths, and He was the real; in other words, they "were *all* only a sort of prophetic expectation of the only *original* and *the last of all the Messiahs.*"

My sole object in referring now to this *curious* episode is, first, to show the utter hopelessness of the modern theologian's case when he is called upon to demonstrate that his entire basis of doctrine is *not* a mere plagiarism of far more ancient faiths than his own. I would also point out the radical changes which have taken place during the last twenty years in public opinion on the subject of orthodox faiths, the rapid spread of what is called liberal preaching, even from Church pulpits, and the general diffusion of this liberal spirit on religious questions, not only among the masses, but also amongst the best classes of thinking people.

I ask then, from whence does this vast flood of liberality in sectarian belief spring? I give all credit to the fearless researches and bold assertions of the Secularists, and am prepared to admit that they have made a deep mark upon popular thought, but they have been at the least a hundred years in making this mark, the teachings of Volney, Dupins, Voltaire, and the French Encyclopædists dating back even beyond that period.

In the mean time, the sudden increase of ever-widening faith in true and proven religion, I fearlessly attribute to the action and influence of the Spirit world—the world that KNOWS, and therefore which alone is qualified to testify to the reality of the condition in which life is continued beyond the grave.

For the first decade of the great Spirit outpouring, the obvious aim of the controlling power was to establish, by tests and proofs, through various phenomena, its identity with the arisen spirits of humanity. The next decade, still ruled by Spirit influences, has been devoted to clearing the ground of human thought from the rank weeds of prejudice, superstition, and the domination of priestly errors and abuses.

With the iconoclastic hammer, which struck down and demolished the false, however, came along the sowers and planters, who did what no mere iconoclasm could effect, for they planted the true and the natural, and with every crumbling wall pulled down they put in its place a stone, cut "fair and square," *with the Master's mark* of TRUTH upon it. It is the laying of such stones as these that will form the foundations of the world-wide temple, in which all the earth shall yet worship that God, "who is all Spirit," led on and guided by the voice of that man who is all Spirit, and cries " I am he that liveth and was dead, and behold I am alive for evermore."

CHAPTER X.

"The mightiest souls of all time hover o'er us,
　Who laboured like Gods amongst men, and have gone
　Like great bursts of sun, on the dark way before us,
　They're with us, still with us, our battles fight on."

BEFORE proceeding further on my travels, it seems to be
in order to refer to some of the eminent personalities who
constituted the ranks of Spiritualists with whom I was
associated during my long years of public life and work.
From my first entrance into American Spiritualism, I
became well acquainted with Mrs. Fox, and her daughters
Katey and Margaretta, the so-called "Rochester Knockers,"
and one of my most esteemed friends was Mrs. Leah Fox
Underhill, the eldest of the renowned Fox Sisters.

This lady was the best test, rapping, and physical
medium I ever met, as well as one of the kindest and most
noble-hearted of women.

After her marriage with Mr. Daniel Underhill, a highly
respected citizen of New York, although she was placed
in wholly independent circumstances, she never flagged in
her devotion to the cause she had espoused, but opened
her handsome house in 37th Street, New York, for winter
evening receptions, in which, whenever I was in the city,
she kindly invited me to become her associate. At these
delightful reunions, as I have stated in a former
chapter, hosts of noteworthy Spiritualistic celebrities
were frequently present.

After the general receptions broke up, a few privileged
friends would remain to share a social supper, always laid
out in the basement dining-room, on the famous old
Rochester dinner table, at which the first Spirit circles of
the age were held, under the auspices of the Fox sisters.

At these séances of Mrs. Underhill's, the manifestations were so powerful and startling, that they would seem in cold recital too incredible to justify repetition. One occasion only I will allude to, namely, that of a séance that was subsequently reported in the New York papers by one of the parties present, and therefore there can be no impropriety in requoting the account.

"Immediately after supper we all adjourned to the suite of reception rooms, our company consisting of our host and hostess, Emma Hardinge and her mother, who were then staying at the house on a visit, Oliver and Mary Anne Johnson, Robert Dale Owen, William Lloyd Garrison, and a few others. The first Spirit that manifested by loud rappings and calls for the alphabet, was Robert Owen, who announced that he wished to give a set of Spiritual Commandments through Emma, if she would kindly submit to his control, whilst his son, Robert Dale Owen, should transcribe them as the entranced medium spoke. Upon this, Emma Hardinge, passing to the open piano, played for a few minutes a grand and solemn improvisation; then returning to the rest of the party, apparently under strong influence, she announced that she was ready to receive the good Spirit's inspiration, provided only he would give three affirmative knocks at the end of every *correct* sentence, or interrupt her by two knocks at any words that he objected to.

"The medium then commenced speaking slowly, but emphatically, and with two corrections only from the controlling Spirit, who spelled out by raps the words he wished to substitute, there were given ten Spiritual Commandments, and ten laws of right.

"After this scene terminated, Mr. Underhill asked and obtained by rappings several answers to questions concerning the fate and ultimate end of the terrible American war, between North and South, then raging. When he queried, 'What will be the next move on the great chequer board, Spirits?' the reply by raps was 'Go to the piano, Emma.'

"Emma Hardinge obeyed, and played first 'John Brown' and several of the war song tunes then so popular. Almost at the close of the first strain, a high shrill voice piped out from above our heads, 'Lower the lights.' This order was obeyed, and instantly the music was accompanied by sounds as of the marching of a heavy body of soldiers, then came repeated explosions as of the firing of musketry, all given in different tones, some like the snapping of a pistol, some like the roar of distant artillery. Anon we had clashing as of swords, then a confused hum of voices, moans and faint cries. Meantime every object in the room was in motion. It seemed as if the very carpet would be torn up, it shook so, and bulged up as if moved by a strong wind.

"At length the player broke into a march of her own composition, concluding with a magnificent performance of the Dead March in 'Saul.' So loud and in such perfect rhythm was the beating of muffled drums and slow marching of feet during this closing piece that one of our party went to the front window softly, and drew aside the blind to see if there was not a regiment marching through the street with muffled drums beating. It was then near four o'clock in the morning, and the street was all silent and deserted.

"This was the closing scene of an ever-memorable, but by no means *rare* séance with Leah Fox Underhill and Emma Hardinge. Mr. R. D. Owen and Wm. Garrison were about to return to Boston by an early morning train.

"The servants being all in bed and asleep, the ladies got some breakfast, during which (and wiping many tears from their eyes) they declared the scene they had that past night witnessed would never leave their memories whilst life lasted.—R. D. OWEN."

The séance above described was not by any means a rare one in the experience of Mrs. Underhill and her friends. We must, however, pass on to glance at other phases of New York Spiritualism, in which I was a frequent participator.

I have mentioned that my mother and I were privileged for some years to become boarders in the house of Mrs. E. J. French, the renowned clairvoyant, physician, and medium. This lady too held frequent circles and receptions, attended, however, by a different set of visitors from those who frequented the Underhills' gatherings.

Amongst Mrs. French's friends were generally a number of well known mediums, including Mr. D. D. Home, Mary and A. J. Davis, and many of the New York committees on the public meetings. Now, though I resist the temptation to write in detail of the grand Pentecostal scenes that were enacted amongst us at No. 8, Fourth Avenue (Mrs. French's residence), I must record one form of noteworthy phenomena which was projected and carried out by our attendant spirits there. This was an agreement made between Mrs. French and I, that we would spiritually telegraph to each other every Sunday, at one o'clock by New York time. This was Mrs. French's dinner hour, and besides her own family, my mother, who boarded there, several of our friends would drop in about one o'clock to test the success of the mental telegraph. The message Mrs. French would send me was written down by those present at her house, and generally one of the visitors was deputed to write to me, wherever I might chance to be, to state in full what the message sent consisted of. Meantime precisely the same formula was observed at my end of the wire. I might have been in Chicago, or New Orleans, or anywhere a thousand miles distant from New York; but always allowing for variation in time, our messages were sent and received at each end without failure or mistake for some years, that is, when I was absent on lecturing tours. Parties of friends and witnesses assembled round me, as with Mrs. French, to hear the messages received and sent, and these, with perhaps a slight change now and then in a word, NEVER FAILED. The letters sent by the attending friends around me, and from them to New York, crossed each other, but were in substance always correct. Mrs. French received her message through rappings, generally at the crowded dinner table; I mine through clairaudience, but at the same social meal.

I particularly dwell on this case, not for its rarity, for I have during many years past communicated by mental telegraph with members of the Occult Society, to which I formerly belonged, but in no instance that I am familiar with were the messages so publicly reported, or so numerously witnessed, as those mentioned above between Mrs. French and myself. I could fill a volume with accounts of the circles held, and the tests multiplied to all enquirers amongst the early Spiritualists of New York. I must now pass on, however, to notice my own special relations to "the cause" and its supporters in other great centres.

In Boston I found the reputation for high culture and learning attributed to its citizens amply proven by the characteristics of the Spiritualists with whom I was surrounded. As a general rule, they were merchants and professional men and women occupying the highest grades of society. Alvin Adams, the founder of the celebrated express company which bore his name, was a devoted Spiritualist, and he and his dear wife opened their palatial residence every week for an evening reception, which was invariably crowded by poets, authors, editors, ladies and gentlemen of the highest intelligence; and such renowned mediums as Lizzie Doten (the best, most inspired, and noblest poetess of the age), Mrs. Leeds, Mrs. Cushman (the greatest musical medium), George Redman, Colchester, Rollin Squire, D. D. Home, Mrs. Hayden, Mansfield (the great Spiritualist postmaster), Mr. and Mrs. A. E. Newton, Fanny Conant, and scores of others too numerous to mention.

At the time of my first engagement in Boston, Dr. Gardner, one of the most indefatigable Spiritual *entrepreneurs*, had organised meetings in a fine building called "The Melodeon." In that hall and several others managed by Dr. Gardner, or committees of the first merchants of Boston, I was in the habit of filling engagements for one or two months at a time during many years.

In the course of these visits, as well as when I and my family subsequently became residents of Boston, I witnessed, and partook of, more phenomenal wonders in Spirit communion than in any other part of the world. There, too, were enacted many changes in the progress of "the cause," such as the introduction of new personages and elements, and the withdrawal and sometimes the uncompromising exposure of shams, or parties unworthy to bear the honoured name of Spiritualists.

The record of all this would far transcend the limits of this autobiography. I must, therefore, in this case, as in many others, confine myself to the narration of one single illustration.

One fine Sunday in spring I entered the anteroom of Allston Hall prior to giving my afternoon lecture. According to announcement, a committee nominated by the audience were to choose the subject of my discourse. When Dr. Gardner came into the room to conduct me to the platform, he gave me a slip of paper on which was written, as the subject of the lecture, "Give a description of the Arctic regions, and the fate of Sir John Franklin." Passing on to the platform, I found the table, which was placed near my chair, literally covered with bouquets of flowers. My good friends, there as elsewhere, had noticed that I was in the habit of holding flowers in my hand during the lectures, and often drawing illustrations from them. It was for this reason that they had provided for me so liberally on the occasion referred to. Instead, however, of taking in my hand as usual any one of the finer floral tributes prepared for me, I was impressed to draw out from under a mass of bouquets, which almost concealed it, a tiny bunch of humble violets, and these I not only held throughout the lecture which followed, but I was made to mention the fact (subsequently confirmed by good authorities) that violets were the favourite flowers of the martyred Franklin, and were *àpropos* to the tragic theme of the address.

At the close of the lecture, and on retiring to the ante-room to escape the profusion of compliments that were showered upon me, I threw down my little bunch of violets on the table, when I noticed for the first time that there was a card attached to the white ribbon with which the flowers were tied. The writing on it read thus: "My dear friend, I send you these flowers in token of my love and sympathy." The card was engraved with the words "Mrs. Sisson, 18, Shawmut Avenue." At that time I was a comparative stranger to Boston, and neither knew the name of Sisson nor the place of her residence. When Dr. Gardner entered, therefore, I asked him, somewhat curtly, who was the Mrs. Sisson that addressed me as her *dear friend?* Dr. Gardner replied that she was one of the most celebrated of the Boston mediums, and so the matter ended, for that occasion at least.

On the following day I came in from East Boston, where I was staying with friends from New York, bound upon delivering a letter of introduction to Mr. Epes Sargent.

Mr. Sargent's residence, I found, was in Dover Street,

and although my friends in East Boston, who could not accompany me, had given me elaborate directions how to find Dover Street, I soon got confused with the windings and turnings of that locality. There was no number on Mr. Sargent's letter, and my friends had explained to me that he lived up a part of the street opposite to one or two corners of other openings. At length, finding myself facing, not one or two, but about half a dozen corners, I looked about to see of whom I could enquire. Whilst thus engaged, I noticed that one of the corners I had reached was marked Shawmut Avenue, and I was even then standing opposite a handsome house (No. 18), on the door of which was a large plate with the name of Mrs. Sisson.

"Why," I thought, "that is the name and the street on the card of the *dear friend* who sent me those violets, yesterday. Surely, as she resides so close to Dover Street, she would know Epes Sargent's address; I have half a mind to call and enquire there." Mounting the flight of steps, I was about to ring the bell, when the door opened and a sweet-faced little woman stood there, smiling and holding out her hand to greet me. "Welcome, Emma Hardinge," she cried; "Sir John told me to be ready, for you would be sure to come." I was speechless, and could only yield to the pressure of her kind hand as she drew me into her handsome reception rooms.

Almost before I could utter a word or explain the purpose of my call, my new friend began a series of eulogies on what she called my wonderful lecture of the previous day, thanking me warmly for holding the violets in my hand, which she said *Sir John Franklin's* spirit had desired her to send. She added that though she neither knew nor had ever spoken to one of the committee who chose the subject, the same ubiquitous Sir John, to whom she alluded so often, had, as she affirmed, assured her that the Arctic regions and his fate would be the subject chosen for me to discourse upon. "Had it not been so," continued the little lady confidently, "I believe, old Spiritualist as I am, I should have been overwhelmed with doubt."

Then, without giving me time to utter any other words than a few interjections, my hostess (who I could only presume to be Mrs. Sisson) led me to the inner reception room, and pointing to a small handsomely framed oil painting on the wall, representing a young girl of about ten years of age, with a star over her head, she said, "Do you know who that represents?" "Good heavens!" I exclaimed; "why, it is the very facsimile of one which my father painted of me when I was a child."

"Have you got that painting?" she asked. "No," I replied. "It was sold with all my poor father's effects I suppose, when he died and left his widow and four little orphans penniless." "Well, no matter," she said. "Mrs. Blantyre, one of our best Boston artists, and a fine medium too, brought that picture to me a little while ago, declaring that a spirit made her paint it and bring it to me. She said she had not the slightest idea for whom it was meant, but it would be recognised if I would but hang it up in this room."

With the same volubility as before, the dear little lady added that Sir John Franklin, who was her guide, friend, and the founder of her successes, had told her that Emma Hardinge's father had been a sea-captain, and a devoted explorer; that he had passed away from earth when I was a child; that my father and sailor brother, as spirits, were in Sir John Franklin's spirit bands of exploration. Now, in justice to one of the most remarkable mediums of the new Dispensation, I must acknowledge that all the first part of these statements was strictly true. For the second part, I must own that I had been told, through several mediums, the same story *de facto*, but I had never repeated it, having been charged by wise spirits to avoid the egotistical folly of citing great names as my "controls," and I have continued to repudiate such a course throughout my professional life. Even in the present instance I should not have referred to this my first, though by no means my last, interview with Mrs. Sisson, did I not propose to close this chapter with one of the most striking test facts of my spiritual experiences.

To sum up my present narrative, I may say that from the occasion above referred to Mrs. Sisson and I became fast friends. I was kindly and hospitably received as her guest when I subsequently lectured in Boston; and some years later my dear mother and I were received into her family as boarders for many months. I now come to the most important part of my record in connection with this lady.

Both Mr. and Mrs. Sisson were mediums, and the husband, although only holding the position of a workman in the East Boston Navy yard, was distinguished as one of the most remarkable drawing mediums of the day. All his sketches, however, were limited to one subject, namely, the Arctic regions. This man, who so far as I could judge, had never read a line concerning this awful land of ice and desolation, had drawn an immense portfolio full of chalk drawings, all being charts of different scenes, places, and passages of those regions.

Dr. Elisha Kent Kane, Mr. Morton, and several other of the Arctic explorers had examined these drawings, and declared them to be inimitably correct. Dr. Kane was a frequent visitor at Mrs. Sisson's, and Mr. Sisson's drawings and his dear wife's trance mediumship were studied again and again by the great navigator.

This singularly gifted couple held in their possession letters from Dr. Kane, as well as communications sent to different Spiritual papers, in which he and many of his associates acknowledged not only the wonderful exactness of the drawings, but also the correctness of all Mrs. Sisson's prophecies concerning Dr. Kane's various adventures.

My own share in the test facts of this strange history is as follows :—

Sir John Franklin, in his communings with me, both through my own and Mrs. Sisson's mediumship, promised that he would find some good drawing medium through whom he would give me a Spirit portrait of himself.

For some months I looked anxiously, but in vain, for the redemption of this promise. Weary at last of waiting, but impressed with an unquenchable eagerness to possess such a portrait, I determined to purchase one.

For this purpose I enquired at the various print shops in New York, Boston, and other large cities, but all in vain. The dealers assured me they knew of no portrait of Sir John Franklin in the United States. Remembering, as a young girl, having seen a print of Sir John Franklin in Colnaghi's shop in Pall Mall, London, I determined not to be baffled. I one day wrote a letter to this same Colnaghi's, assuming the business to be still carried on in that name, asking if I could obtain such a picture, and what price I was required to send. Before I could post this letter, a servant entered my room in New York, and delivered to me a long package, on opening which I found a tin case containing a life-size half-length portrait of Sir John Frankin, drawn in pencil, coarsely and inartistically enough, but an unmistakable likeness of the good Sir John, as seen in his London statue and the engravings that have fallen into my hands since I returned to England. Accompanying the case was a letter from a person signing himself "Wella Anderson," whom I afterwards learned had been a poor young man, a carpenter, who, while working at his bench, and being educated in the humblest routine of book lore, suddenly became controlled to draw portraits of Spirits. They were always likenesses of deceased persons quite unknown to him, and when not recognised and claimed by casual callers, he was instructed by a voice speaking clairaudiently to him, to send them to some stranger at a distant place, where the picture was sure to be recognised and gladly received.

This man had never left his Western home : I had never been to the West *up to that time*, and neither he nor I even knew of each other's existence. He had never seen a Spiritual paper, and he was too recently developed in his wonderful calling to have acquired such a reputation as would have reached my ears in the Eastern States. Above all, in a letter which accompanied the picture, he very modestly described how this "glorious Spirit" had come to him to have his picture taken, and without giving the slightest idea of who he was, he had simply desired Anderson to send the picture to "Emma Hardinge," at 8, Fourth Avenue, New York, a thousand miles away from the artist's own residence.

I have since met good Wella Anderson many times, had many Spirit pictures from him, some under circumstances no less strange than the one described above, but none have ever been to me a finer test of independent Spirit control than the rough portrait of Sir John Franklin spiritually promised and received as herein stated.

I have only to add that this picture, marred and cut away to some extent in consequence of injuries received in packing and travelling, still hangs over my head on the wall of the study in which I am writing.

CHAPTER XI.

Let there be Light.

AMONGST the cities in which I most frequently filled engagements in America, the leaders of the Spiritual ranks were chiefly of the best classes of society.

In Philadelphia I frequently had the pleasure of joining the circles, and sometimes acting as the Medium for the celebrated scientist Dr. Robert Hare and many of his associates.

Here, too, I met and repeatedly tested the clairvoyant powers of the celebrated Quaker blind Medium,. Samuel Paist, whose marvellous descriptions of character and physiognomy by the touch of the hand, or by clairvoyance, prevented hundreds of people who knew him but slightly from believing in his total blindness until they examined the remains of his poor eyes, sightless from childhood.

Sam Paist was a commercial traveller, drove his own horse and buggy, never made any mistake or collision either in crowded streets or roads, and when turnpike keepers, by way of experiment, would shut their gates as he approached, he would call out for them to be re-opened long before his horse could reach the gate.

Here, too, resided Henry Gordon, one of the most powerful physical Mediums of the day. He was a little over the size and stature of a child, but when I first knew him, the lightest touch of his tiny fingers would suffice to raise the most unheard-of weights.

The first knowledge the Philadelphians had of his marvellous mediumship was on one Sunday morning during the Spiritual service at Sansome Street Hall, when, in the midst of a thronged assembly, Mr. Gordon, who was

sitting quietly in the front row, was lifted up bodily by the
Spirits, carried over the heads of several rows of spectators,
and then dropped safely down in the middle aisle of the
meeting house. Mr. Gordon eventually shared the honour
with another medium of being the chosen instrument for
giving such communications as Mr. Henry Seybert's *mind*,
rather than any controlling Spirits, dictated. In this con-
nexion I may say, from a personal acquaintance with both
parties, I regard the curious idiosyncrasies of Mr. Seybert's
own character—a devoted Christian Spiritualist, and in
Mr. Gordon's no less devout predilections for the Roman
Catholic faith—as the main sources of what they both
called "Spirit influence," but which I have good reason to
believe was the result of these persons' own proclivities.

To dear Katey Robinson (one of the best trance and
clairvoyant mediums of the city), Dr. Henry Child (a fine
writing medium), and a noble band of earnest supporters
of the Spiritual cause in Philadelphia, I tender an equal
tribute of honour and regret that in their transition to the
higher life they have left so few behind to fill adequately
their vacant places.

In Baltimore I met one of the earliest, best, and most
popular trance speakers of the day—Mrs. Hyzer—who for
some years filled the position of regular speaker for the
first Spiritual society.

At this city also I became acquainted with Mr. Francis
H. Smith, author of several useful Spiritual works, one of
which especially is valuable as being a description of the
dark Spheres, in which undeveloped Spirits are being
reformed and overcoming the criminal propensities they
had too unhappily acquired on earth. The title of this
work is, "The Footsteps of a Presbyterian," and the records
it contains were gathered up at the circles established by
Colonel Danskin, the President of the first Baltimore
Society of Spiritualists, and his gifted wife, a very fine

trance medium. This excellent lady was appointed by good Spirits to hold circles expressly for the purpose of aiding in the reform of those earth-bound criminal Spirits whom human society so often creates and punishes, but so seldom reforms.

As I may not have any future opportunity of speaking of Mr. F. H. Smith's peculiar case, I may here state that he was a wealthy merchant of Baltimore, and a gentleman of unimpeachable probity.

Having heard of his friend Colonel Danskin's warm advocacy of Spiritualism, Mr. Smith—himself a devoted Presbyterian—undertook to censure his friend severely for his adherence to a cause which could only, as he alleged, result from Satanic agency or imposture.

Francis H. Smith was at the time when he made these remarks nearly blind, and suffering from a chronic inflammation of the eyes. On a certain occasion Colonel Danskin called at Mr. Smith's office for the purpose of inviting him to attend one of Mrs. Danskin's evening circles.

To Mr. Smith's solemn objections the Colonel replied that a certain negro Spirit, who was one of Mrs. Danskin's controls, *had sent for Mr. Smith*, promising that if he would attend, he—"Martin," as he called himself—would put him through some *"Gyganks"* that would restore his eyesight. Mr. Smith questioned *what Gyganks were?* The Colonel could not tell. At last, as Mr. Smith in his published work alleges, by way of proving to his friend the falsity of his *horrid faith*, the dignified merchant condescended to accept the invitation and attend the circle.

During the first part of the evening the Spirits did not take much notice of the sceptic. When at length "his turn came," Spirit Martin completely possessed the poor visitor's organism. He first nearly shook the life out of him, and then he made the elderly grey-haired gentleman leap back and forth across the circle table, clearing the lights and all the visitors' heads, but with such amazing rapidity that none could even count, much less arrest them. At the end of his wonderful capers, and when he had sunk breathless and exhausted into a chair, Mrs. Danskin, the medium, cried, under the influence of the irrepressible Martin, "Well, Frank, how do you like my gyganks?" Then, before the panting victim could answer, the medium added, "Read that!" She then handed Mr. Smith a hymn book with very small print, which the astonished and hitherto nearly blind merchant read off without the slightest difficulty.

Amazed alike at the superhuman power exerted over him, and the marvellous restoration to even temporary recovery of sight which these "gyganks" effected, Mr. Smith submitted to a periodical process of similar performances extending through several months. At the end of this period he not only permanently recovered his eyesight, but he saw and heard enough to convert him into an ardent Spiritualist.

During one of my visits to Mrs. Danskin's séances, Mr. Smith being present, "Martin," the darkie Spirit, announced that he wished "Frank" to go through a performance of "gyganks" for the enlightenment of the Great Preacher, as the Spirit politely called me. It was all in vain for Mr. Smith to remonstrate. Before half of his intended speech was uttered he was across the large wide table, and back and forth he leaped with a power and rapidity that I would defy the most skilful gymnast in the world to equal, much less excel. More detailed descriptions of these remarkable séances will be found in "Footsteps of a Presbyterian," by Francis H. Smith, of Baltimore.

During one of my last visits to Baltimore, I met my dear old Rhode Island friend, Dr. J. R. Newton, the renowned Healer. Dr. Newton had just returned from Philadelphia, where he had been subjected to a trial for "malpractice" on the following grounds. A young woman had come to his rooms, amongst hundreds of other sufferers, to consult him for a chronic lameness of the hip. In her case, as in hundreds of others, he had laid hands upon her, instantly cured her, and bid her leave her crutches behind. In the young woman's excitement of joy, on leaving the Doctor's presence she ran downstairs, "skipping," as she afterwards described, "like a fawn." In this way she missed her footing, slipped, and fell. On her return home she found she had slightly hurt her back, and in her anxiety to boast of her miraculous cure to her own doctor, she consulted him about the injury she had sustained in her fall.

This, the jealous medical practitioner attributed to "mal: practice" on Dr. Newton's part. On this baseless charge he was arrested. His trial lasted for six weeks, owing to the immense number of witnesses, who journeyed to Philadelphia on purpose to testify their gratitude to Dr. Newton for the marvellous cures he had effected in their several cases. The indictment was eventually dismissed as a groundless charge, but the Spiritualists all rejoiced in its proceeding, malicious as was the complaint brought against the beneficent healer, seeing that in that way only could have been popularised the multitudes of miraculous cures effected through his ministrations.

At the United States capital, the beautiful city of Washington, I met a constant influx of my Spiritual fellow workers, to say nothing of the number of others of the same faith, who through the favour of the noble President, Abraham Lincoln, held prominent official positions in the city.

I may here remark that though I have the warmest regard for the lady who wrote the recently published work

" Was Abraham Lincoln a Spiritualist ?" I consider such a question to the important matter contained in that book quite unnecessary, as Mr. Lincoln's interest in the cause of Spiritualism and frequent interviews with spirit mediums were items of knowledge too well known to need any other confirmation than common report.

Amongst the most notable mediums in Washington, I must especially mention the Laurie family, each member of which was distinguished for some gift of mediumship. Both Mr. and Mrs. Lanrie were excellent drawing and trance mediums ; Mrs. Miller, their daughter, was a powerful physical force medium. At the house of General McEwen, whose guest I was, I saw the General (himself a heavy man), General Banks, and four other gentlemen at an evening séance, all seated on a grand piano, which was driven round and round the room with the six gentlemen seated upon it, by *invisible power*, and that through the touch only of Mrs. Miller's finger, in a brilliantly lighted room. And this remarkable exhibition was by no means rare in this lady's mediumship.

There were also many other startling phases of power exhibited at Washington by variously gifted persons, that great city seeming to form a rallying point of no less interest in the Spiritual than in the political ranks of American society.

Passing over innumerable scenes, persons, and places forming milestones in my ceaseless wanderings, I pause for a few pages of description at Columbus, the capital city of Ohio, where my first visit was marked by some passages of peculiar interest.

I was engaged by Mr. Savage, a jeweller and prominent citizen of Columbus, residing in Main Street, nearly opposite the Capitol Buildings. The first evening of my reaching Mr. Savage's house was on the Saturday prior to my next day's lectures. Mr. and Mrs. Savage had invited a number of Spiritualist friends to meet me, distinguished amongst whom were Dr. Fowler, a physician of the city, widely celebrated for his skill, as well as regarded with awe for his wonderful clairvoyant powers, and Mr. George Walcutt, a Spirit artist of the most astonishing endowments. Up to this evening I had never spoken to any of my Spiritualist associates of my experiences in Occultism, nor my belief in Elementary Spirits—beings of whose existence the general phenomena of Modern Spiritualism afforded no proofs. During the evening Dr. Fowler, whose singular experiences formed a leading topic of conversation, not only avowed his belief in, and intercourse with, Elementary Spirits, but, he added, pointing to me, " that young lady is also aware of the existence of the Spirits of the elements, and will this night be controlled by one."

The Doctor at this point broke off into a long address in an unknown tongue, a phase to which it would seem he was frequently addicted. At the close of his singular outpouring, addressing me in our own tongue, he ordered me to translate what he had been saying to the company. Under a new but most powerful influence, I was made to give the translation of Dr. Fowler's speech, which was to the effect that if the party then present would visit the mysterious ruins at Newark, a place a few miles distant, and hold a circle by moonlight, amongst the works attributed to the lost races, or "Mound builders of America," they should find an evidence that the unknown people who had founded those strange works were "*freemasons*."

It was then pleasant summer weather, and several of those present agreed that they would form a party to take me to the ruins in question during the following week.

Before the entrancing power that tendered this interpretation had left me, the Doctor asked who the controlling Spirit was. The answer came that the control was " a fire

Spirit also, that the truth of this statement should be proved that night, as he, the Spirit, was about to attend the biggest fire that had ever happened in Columbus, and to give a solid proof that the *prayers of the wicked never prevail.*"

It was in vain that those present pressed the Spirit for clearer information. With the rapid words, " Be of good cheer, I'm off to prepare for the fire," I was at once released from the trance, and no further manifestations could be obtained that evening.

Whilst at supper, Mr. Savage explained to me that all through the past week, previous to my arrival, and directly after the friends had posted bills about the city announcing my lectures in Armoury Hall for the following Sunday, the bigots of the place, of whom there was a large preponderance, had organised a series of Union prayer meetings, at which the principal theme was a prayer *that the Lord would take the Devil out of Armoury Hall who was to appear there next Sunday, or choke her impious utterances.*

Now, although this atrocious act of bigotry was by no means rare in those early·days of Spiritual propagandism, I should not have named it now, or the incidents that were to follow, if I could not give, by reference to my diary, the exact time, as well as name the scene of what I relate. The date of my first lecture in Columbus, Ohio, was Sunday, September 4th, 1859.

The prayer meetings by which the Almighty was instructed how to treat the young girl that was to appear amongst them took place *every day* during the preceding week, the cursing praying party no doubt deeming that the Lord needed to be reminded of his duty sufficiently often. What follows, therefore, transpired in the memory of many still living residents of Columbus, Ohio, at the date above mentioned.

It must have been between one and two in the morning
of Sunday, September 4th, that I was suddenly awakened
by a great clamour in the street and a light in my room
as bright as if the sun was pouring in at the window.
At the same time my bedroom door was opened, and
Mrs. Savage entered with a countenance pale as death,
crying "Get up! get up, my dear! the whole city is on
fire, and we may all be burnt in our beds. Oh that fire
Spirit!" she added, "Surely it is he who is doing this
fatal work!" "Don't be afraid of him," I answered,
jumping up and dressing hastily, "he's all right and will
take care of us, never fear."

Whilst I was dressing, Mrs. Savage informed me that
the fire was in the next block of buildings to our own, and
that as it was raging all through the block, Armoury Hall,
which was the last end of the row next to our block, must
be destroyed with the rest. As my friend spoke I shivered
violently, and under a sudden and powerful inspiration
was made to exclaim: *The good Spirits will protect you,
and Emma will lecture in Armoury Hall this Sabbath,
morning and evening.*

By six o'clock that same morning, the splendid and
effective American fire brigade of the City—all too well
accustomed, unfortunately, to such work—had completely
extinguished the fire, but left the entire block destroyed,
with the exception of the great end building, consisting of
two fine shops on either side of a double door and handsome staircase which led to the hall used by the soldiers
as a drill room, called ARMOURY HALL. For the information of those who have not visited the New World, it may
be proper to state, that in nearly all the great cities of
North America, the principal streets are divided into
blocks, ten of which constitute a mile, each block being
separated by streets running at right angles—or east
and west, when the main blocks point north and south.

Thus, then, the extent of the terrible fire referred to above may be estimated, by remembering that it occurred in Main Street, the principal business centre of Columbus, facing the Capitol Square and grounds, and raged through all the shops and houses for one-tenth of a mile, *with the exception of the grand hall* in which I was announced to lecture. As the crowd gathered around this scene of desolation, it seemed to think the building, thus miraculously saved, might still have been rendered unsafe by the destruction of all the adjoining houses, and therefore that the anticipated meetings would not take place.

Mr. Savage and a party of his friends obtained my consent to put up large written notices that the meetings would be held as announced, and at ten minutes to eleven they escorted me in a perfect procession of kind followers to Armoury Hall.

Here the immense throngs of people standing around, but all *outside* the building, watched us with curious interest as we entered and ascended the stairway. For a few minutes the whispered words circulated amongst the crowd : "There is the Spirit medium ; if she goes in there's nothing to fear."

Whether it was these words or the singular impression produced by the fact that the Union Hall, in which the praying bigots had invoked destruction on my head, *had been destroyed*, whilst our place of gathering had been so wonderfully preserved, I am unable to say, nor will I even venture to pronounce an opinion on the subject. Suffice it to say, before we could even commence our services, the hall was full to repletion ; so full, indeed, during the morning lecture, that Mr. Savage, fearing the effect of the still greater overflow taking place in the evening, engaged a number of assistants to put up great props against the side of the building abutting on the burnt district.

This rendered assurance doubly sure, and enabled the largest crowd ever before gathered together in that city to sing with a power and unity that swelled up in one mighty chorus through roof and dome to the homes of the watching angels. The parting hymn, which I well remember, ran thus—

> Father of all, in every age,
>   In every clime adored,
> By saint, by savage, and by sage,
>   The universal Lord.
>
> Thou first great cause, least understood,
>   Who all my sense confined,
> To know but this, that Thou art good,
>   And that myself am blind.
>
> If I am right, Thy grace impart,
>   Still in the right to stay ;
> If I am wrong, oh, teach my heart
>   To find the better way.
>
> To Thee, whose temple is all space,
>   Whose altar earth, sea, skies,
> One chorus let all beings raise,
>   All nature's incense rise.

CHAPTER XII.

"There is no death, what seems so is transition."

AGAIN passing over an immense array of far and wide travels and wonderful experiences, but reserving my narrative for representative cases of Spiritual interposition, I pause, only for a brief space, at Delphi, Indiana, to give a condensed account of the singular Spiritual phenomena I there heard of, and, in part, witnessed myself.

The gentleman that had engaged me, Dr. Beck, an eminent and highly respected physician, had for many years bravely and openly proclaimed his adherence to the cause of Spiritualism, and by his skill in his profession, no less than by his singleness of heart and nobility of character, fully lived down every prejudice that his unpopular faith had raised against him. Up to the time of my visit I had only known of Dr. Beck and his esteemed wife by report, and my first evening's residence beneath their hospitable roof fully confirmed me in all the favourable accounts I had received of this estimable family.

It was on the morning after my arrival at their house that Dr. Beck suggested that a drive in the bright summer morning's air might dispel the fatigue of the last evening's lecture and prepare me for another effort that night. The Doctor himself set off to visit his patients in a one-horse buggy, assigning the phaeton and a pair of fine horses to Mrs. Beck and myself for the proposed drive.

The fine summer morning, and the romantic scenery of the country in the Wabash River district were equally charming. At length we came upon a long white road with a gentle ascent, and thick forests on either side.

Mrs. Beck informed me that the termination of this road was a high plateau of rocks, from which we could have a splendid view of the Wabash River, with its celebrated valley scenery. Whilst she was speaking I was looking anxiously forward along the road, upon which a tall man dressed like a carter was standing right in the middle of the path we were traversing, and directly in a line with our carriage. "See that man!" I cried. "Surely he must be deaf, and does not hear the carriage approaching him!" "Call to him," I cried again and again to the driver, who, however, took no notice of what I said. Meantime the horses rushed on at full gallop as if they had been lashed to madness, though no whip had touched them. I screamed and stood up in the carriage, waving my arms and shouting frantically, but the man in the road never stirred, and the horses, as if possessed by fiends, dragged the carriage on at a mad pace, passed over the immovable figure and then stopped, panting and covered with foam. In an agony of horror I jumped from the carriage into the road, and began to search for the crushed remains of the victim. All was in vain; there was no sign of any such victim, no trace that any one had been there. Breathless as I was, I still managed to explain to Mrs. Beck and the driver what I had seen. Neither of them had beheld the sight so clearly apparent to me; but when, after their inquiries, I described, as I could do accurately, the dress and great stature of the figure I had beheld, both agreed it must have been the ghost of one Bill Nye, who was run over and killed just at that spot, in a terrible scene, the particulars of which I was to hear on my return home.

"Why not now?" I asked. "No, no," replied Mrs. Beck, "we will just drive up to the edge of the rocks, and then hurry home." As we rode on, I still noticed the agitation of the horses, and finding that we were advancing up a ledge of rocks which seemed to terminate in a sheer overhanging precipice, I persuaded Mrs. Beck to dismount with me, and we walked on together to the edge of the rocks commanding a most enchanting view of the river valley and forest land beyond; but it was not the landscape on which my gaze was fastened, but on a narrow path far beneath us, little more than a bank of earth that ran by the river's brink.

There I saw emerging from a projection of rocks at one end of the path a tall Indian dressed in war paint and feathers, carrying his war hatchet upright in his hand, bow and arrows at his back, and trotting rather than walking or running by the river's side.

I cried to Mrs. Beck—"Look! look! at that tall Indian warrior! See! there's another—another—a fourth—a fifth!" and so I went on counting aloud, as if I must do so, until I had numbered up to twenty-five. "How many did you say?" murmured Mrs. Beck in a low subdued tone.

"Twenty-five, all in single file," I answered.

"Where are they gone?"

"Round that other mass of projecting rock—there, there! There go the two last of them. Don't you see them?"

"I see nothing," she replied.

"Good Heavens! Why did you not look? They were such a grand line, and looked so noble, yet so terrible, in their war paint and feathers."

"Describe them to me."

I did so, but again questioned why she did not see them when she was standing so close to me. Mrs. Beck replied, solemnly: "Alas! my friend; my eyes are not opened into the realm of the invisible world as yours are. Those whom you beheld were not beings of this earth, nor is there any path there now. That fatal bank has been broken away, and the waters flow over it now. Look again!"

I obeyed, and to my amazement found *there was no path*, only the waters of the river flowing as if against the foot of the rocks, on the top of which we were standing. In fewer words than I can write, Mrs. Beck then informed me that many years before, when the white men first discovered and came to settle in the Wabash Valley district, there was a tribe of Indians inhabiting a camp on the banks of the river beyond the first projection of rocks from which I had seen the Spirit warriors emerge.

They were a fierce and warlike tribe, and gave the white invaders much trouble, disputing, as they well might, the right of the stranger to come and possess the lands hitherto occupied by their own people.   At length one of the most influential of the white settlers proposed that they should hold a conference in a grove on the banks of the river, reached by the path which was once the line of communication between the two rocky points which marked the fishing ground of the belligerents.

To attend this conference, a chosen band of twenty-five of the grandest of the Indian " braves " were selected, and these, decked out in their full insignia of war, trotted, as was their custom, one after another in single file along the path to the scene of the conference ; but, alas ! for the ever-lasting story of the white man's treachery towards what he insolently denominated as "*inferior* races," a band of perfidious monsters, far more worthy of being called "savages" than the hapless aborigines, met one after the other as they turned the angle of the second group of rocks and killed them in cold blood, not staying their murderous hands until the last of the doomed twenty-five was destroyed.

The legend affirms that a white man in league with the murderers *(one Bill Nye)* was stationed·in the road above to prevent any approach to the scene of the massacre, and that this man, who refused to allow a cart and horse to pass to the spot where we were then standing, was run over and killed.

"And now, my friend," added the narrator, "*What is it, and who are those that you have seen?* I have often heard of others who claim to have seen the unfortunate man Bill Nye in this very road, said to have been run over and killed by a cart and horse, and equally often heard of people who claimed to have seen the Spirits of the poor Indians trotting along by the river's bank to their scene of massacre; but never before did I take a medium to this spot, and one, too, a total stranger alike to the scene and the terrible story connected with it. Truly then I must believe it was the victims of the very tragedy enacted in this region which have appeared to you this morning."

This opinion I heartily concurred in, unless, indeed, the "Psychical Research Society" are prepared to render some other account of an incident bruited about all through the neighbourhood, and called in those comparatively early and matter of fact days a SPIRITUAL manifestation.

I must now notice some other manifestations occurring in that same section of country, and though I was not an actual witness of the scenes, I received the account I am about to relate from Dr. and Mrs. Beck, and at least forty eye and ear witnesses, and for some time after leaving that part of the country held direct and instructive communication with the Spiritual hero of my narrative.

In my "Nineteenth Century Miracles" I have given an extended account of the case I am about to cite. In these crowded pages I can only quote a few extracts from the above-named publication:—

"The following narrative is well known, and has been thoroughly investigated. It is on the life, times, and doings of 'Bill Dole,' both as a mortal and a Spirit, and I am furnished with numerous affidavits from the parties who have conversed with his invisible ghostship by the hour together. I have visited the scene of the hauntings too, and though the parties in whose house the marvels occurred have moved away, numerous residents of Logansport still bear their testimony to the facts, as follows :—

" It was soon after the first commencement of the disturbances at Hydesville that a family named Lewis, German by birth, residing at Logansport, were annoyed by singular and unaccountable noises and erratic movement of their furniture. A sound too was often heard in their midst like the whining of a small animal, and this would taper off (to use their own expression) into low whisperings. The family were religiously disposed persons, and at no time were favourable to the idea of Spirit communion.

" Disliking publicity, and repelled from every attempt to communicate with their invisible tormentor, they endured these hauntings for some time without mentioning their occurrence, until, as the newspaper accounts relate, they were startled with a distinctly audible voice.

" At first their names only were called, then connected sentences were spoken, and finally an invisible personage established himself in the family, conversing with them as freely as any mortal inmate could do, and though annoying them greatly in respect to his supermundane character and presence, yet manifesting all the predilections and characteristics of a regular member of the family. His own account of himself was, that he had been in earth life a tailor by trade, his name, ' Bill Dole.'

" Some accounts represent him as having been a man addicted to drink, and dying under the influence of delirium tremens ; but the most authentic history of his exit from the mortal sphere, represents it as occurring through an act of suicide.

" He affirmed that he had dwelt some time in the Spirit world, but found his position there far from satisfactory ; in fact, so contrary to his inclination, that he had resolved not to stay there, and finding from some power in and about that family that he was unable to define, that he could make himself at home amongst them, he had resolved to take up his residence there ; and ' there he meant to stay,' and *did stay*, for a period extending over upwards of two years.

"Bill Dole's adventures in his self-elected home would occupy volumes, but we need not dwell on details which present a great similarity of character, save to notice that the invisible performer was, as in each case of the preceding instances, a person of entirely different habits and temper from his earthly associates. Bill Dole interlarded his conversation with rude oaths and profane remarks, besides manifesting extreme self-will, and when thwarted, propensities to violence, and even mischief. He would knock, stamp his feet, run about the house with a great clatter, and 'knock things around generally.' He manifested a great contempt for orthodox religion, and on one occasion, when a clergyman, who frequently conversed and remonstrated with the Spirit, offered up a fervent prayer in his behalf, Bill Dole called out, in hearing of the minister and all assembled, ' Well ! I don't feel a d——d bit better for that.'

" On two or three occasions he accompanied the family to church, where his remarks were clearly heard by the whole congregation, who affirm that he pronounced the sermon preached at him, 'all d——d stuff.'

" On other occasions he was heard to vociferate 'Amen !' and ' Good for you, old fellow !' (meaning the clergyman) with great unction.

" Generally however, during religious service, at church, or 'to hum,' as he called the house he favoured with his presence, he contented himself with making tremendous poundings, always giving the Christian names of the lady or her daughters who were supposed to be the Mediums.

" At times the cloth and every article necessary for a meal was laid suddenly, whilst the family were absent from the dining-room for the space of a minute or two. Bill would sometimes carry heavy loads about for them, and when in a good humour, perform many little kindly offices. He was especially fond of the children ; would guard and watch over them with wonderful power, and obvious affection ; indeed, their mother complained that Bill spoiled them, as he would get for them whatever they asked of him.

" On one occasion, when the mother was preparing their lunch to take to school, Bill, in his usual authoritative way, desired that they should have some jam spread over their bread.

"This they had asked him to procure for them, but the mother refused, alleging that it was not good for them. Bill swore they should have it, and during the recess in school time kept his word, by dropping down a pot of jam before them.

"On several occasions when one of the daughters, to whom Bill seemed especially to attach himself, was indisposed, he would demand, with no gentle oaths, that she should not be sent out in the rain, or made to exercise herself in household work. On one occasion, when her throat was tied up with a severe cold, Bill lifted her into the house from the garden, carried out a basket, and gathered all the fruit and vegetables he could lay hands on; then bringing it swiftly into the house, he set it on the hearth, lifted up the cover of a large saucepan, and tumbled the things he had gathered indiscriminately into the boiling water. At times he would attend when visitors were present, horrifying them by moving things around without any visible agency, and scare them almost into fits by taking part in their conversation, and reminding them that he was the Bill Dole they had formerly known when he lived among them. On one occasion a lady, making a visit to the distressed family, incautiously expressed her disgust that a wretch of the well-known bad character of Bill Dole should, as report alleged, come back to make Spiritual manifestations.

"She openly expressed her disbelief of the popular rumours, alleging that it must be some trick of the neighbours, which would ultimately be discovered. Whilst speaking, the family became extremely uneasy, judging from the kicks and poundings on a bureau in the apartment that the subject of the visitor's unfavourable criticisms was himself listening to them. Nor were they mistaken. In a few minutes the voice of the spirit was heard in clear and distinct tones, saluting the visitor as 'my dear,' and asking affectionately after the little boy Arthur, 'whom you know, my precious one,' the mischievous imp added, 'I am the real father of, though you do try to hide it by abusing me.'

"The tricks, and sometimes the mischief enacted by this invisible persecutor were beyond all description weird and powerful.

"By night and day his pranks were continued, and though he always yielded to the remonstrances of kindness or gently entreaty, opposition only seemed to convert him into a being little short of a fiend. The little ones of the family dearly loved Bill Dole, and some witnesses of the scene informed the writer that they had seen the children visibly carried, lifted, danced, and jumped about by their invisible attendant.

"It seemed that the attachment he conceived for his entertainers might have become mutual, and reconciled them to the strange and mysterious guest who had forced himself upon them, but the weird reputation which 'Bill Dole's ghost' brought on the household, the influx of marvel seekers that intruded on their privacy, and the scandal that the circumstances entailed upon them, at last so wearied the family that they positively refused to communicate for or with the Spirit any longer.

"They broke up, and changed their household and all their plans of life, until they finally succeeded in driving their unwelcome visitor from them.

"The voice ceased, and even the loud knockings and movements of furniture were discontinued. Bill Dole was driven away, and his weird voice and mystic presence at last passed from human observance, but not from memory. There are still hundreds of persons in Logansport who remember to have heard him converse, and can contribute items of hearsay evidence to this brief notice, which would, if published, swell the narrative to the extent of the volume. Something of a sequel, however, we will add to the history which may not prove uninteresting.

"After conversing with a gentleman from Logansport who was well acquainted with the whole transaction, and had frequently held conversations with 'Bill Dole,' a Spirit purporting to be that individual presented himself one night to the author, and desired to make a communication to her concerning his present situation.

"He affirmed that when driven away, as he called it, from his earthly refuge, he wandered around for a long time, in the vain hope of finding another home in the same sphere. Not succeeding, he fell into a state of bitter anguish of mind, during which he received consolation from kind and wise Spirits, who counselled him to lift his thoughts above the earth, and strive to elevate his aspirations to the better land, to which, as a Spirit, he now belonged.   At first the task seemed hopeless, as his earth-bound nature rendered aspiration almost impossible.

"At length, by the divine aid of angels from the land of light, he attained to a happy and peaceful home, and one moreover where he was a welcome guest, and assimilated with the Spiritual existence of which he was a part.

"In short, he had passed on to a higher life, and when idly solicited by some who had witnessed his marvellous performances to repeat them for their amusement, he gently but kindly replied, that though his life was now devoted to the task of obliging others, yet he had lost the physical aura which had once bound him to earth, and enabled him in its atmosphere to perform the material feats which had distinguished him as an earth-bound Spirit.   Bill Dole, such as he was, exists no more.   The sunlit butterfly has arisen from the chrysalitic shell of the earthly worm, and he now 'sings with the angels,' instead of astounding the marvel seekers of earth with the dread sound of his ghostly merriment and terrible Spirit voice."

It was some time after I had visited the scenes referred to above that I became a guest at the residence of Governor Talmadge, formerly Governor of Wisconsin, and one amongst the earliest, bravest, and most intellectual of the converts of Spiritualism.   Being invited to give lectures in several parts of the State of Wisconsin, Governor Talmadge kindly insisted on my making my home at his charming residence, Fond-du-lac.   There, in the society of the Governor's accomplished daughter Emily, herself a fine writing and clairvoyant medium, I found a happy genial home on my return from incessant travel and lecturing during several weeks.   My object in referring to this visit is to call attention to some remarkable phases of the Spiritual phenomena occurring in the Governor's presence, amongst a tribe of Red Indians who were encamped near his residence.   On one occasion they were invited to assemble on his lawn, and give an exhibition of their strange powers to a party of guests.

After performing one of their characteristic war dances, three of the young men proceeded to dig holes in the ground, in which they placed their poles, stretched their canvas, and formed a tent of about twelve feet in height. The top of the tent was not fully closed, leaving an opening of about a foot in diameter. From this opening depended several strings to which were attached a drum, two tambourines, a pair of cymbals, and two or three other musical instruments.

The tent set up, they invited the Governor and several of his guests to enter and examine it. Having keenly watched its construction, they found nothing within the canvas but what I have described.

After this they called upon an Indian to come forward, whom they named Johan, their "medicine man."

At the request of some of the chiefs, Governor Talmadge and two other gentlemen "bound" the medicine man hand and foot with ropes until he was completely immovable. The two principal chiefs then took him up between them, and threw rather than laid him down on the grass beneath the tent, pulling the canvas together carefully as they emerged from beneath it.

From the time when this arrangement was completed, nearly all the rest of the Indians began trotting round the tent uttering low monotonous sounds, evidently after the fashion of an invocation.

Two or three of the red men meantime seated themselves on the ground, beating their wooden drums like Chinese tom-toms.

In less than five minutes after the disappearance of the bound medicine man, several large white birds flew out from the opening at the top of the tent, and soared away out of sight. These birds were the size of wild geese, purely white, and flew away with immense rapidity. " Where did they come from ? " was the cry immediately circulated amongst the whites, whilst the Indians bowed their heads, and covered their faces with their hands as if in worship.

Directly after came a loud harsh blast as if from one of the wind instruments. This was followed by the beating of the drum, the blowing of horns and pipes, the thud of the tambourines, and a combined clamour of horrible discordant sounds. Happily for the brains and ears of the listeners, the awful concert soon terminated ; all the instruments, one after the other, being thrown out at the top opening of the tent, the whole of the distracting noise ending by the tent curtains being violently dragged open and thrown back, whilst the medicine man himself, fast bound with every cord, knot, and fastening in its place, and apparently sunk into a deep sleep, was thrown out upon the grass, some distance from the tent, and apparently by invisible hands. The tent now being open, and fully exposed, was searched by a party of the amazed spectators, but not a sign or vestige of any presence save that of the bound and sleeping Indian could be discovered.

Fully and firmly as I trust the truth of every item of this weird spectacle, as related to me by Governor Talmadge himself, I should have scarcely ventured to repeat it had I not in my own person beheld a similar performance at Rock Island, Iowa, given by a party of Indians assembled there.

Some of the manifestations were even more weird than those above described, but the Indians with whom I conversed, gravely assured me *they knew* the operators to be the Spirits of great chiefs, gone to the happy hunting grounds, and only returned on *that* occasion to do honour to the white prophetess (*me*, they meant).

These and similar manifestations, I must add, have been again and again described to me as of frequent occurrence amongst some of the Indian tribes, the witnesses giving me the accounts themselves, but when I described in turn the performances given by Spirits through the Davenport Brothers, said witnesses assured me *that* was all imposture.

CHAPTER XIII.

"And He shall break every chain, and rend the bonds of slavery in twain. . . . . For the Lord hath said it."

PASSING over the endless panorama of scenes, places, and events which were marked by my missionary labours—always organised and sustained by my faithful Spiritual guides—I now proceed to notice a flying visit I made to the Southern States of America, during the years 1859 and 1860, the eventful period immediately antecedent to the breaking out of the terrible civil war of 1861. My first visit was at Memphis, Tennessee, and although no intimation of the war spirit was manifested throughout the South in any direction, it was plain to note the prevalence of the bitterness that was rankling in the hearts of the slave-holders towards the advocates of freedom, especially to the openly avowed Anti-Slavery party of the Northern States.

Presuming, I suppose, that I, as an Englishwoman, and hailing, as it was termed, from New York, must have "come South" for the purpose of speaking what the planters chose to designate as *incendiary doctrines*, my first appearance at Memphis did not afford a very favourable augury of what was to follow.

The scene of my opening Sunday lecture course was a fine hall up one flight of stairs, with a platform placed opposite a row of windows looking out upon a plateau of leads. When my morning's lecture had proceeded about half way through, a violent crash at the window was heard, and a huge stone was launched against me with such a skilful aim that it fell directly at my feet, and only missed crushing them to pieces by its weight, and the force with which it was launched, because it fell on the flounce of my extra long silk dress. I am under the impression that the entire audience rose at this outrage, some to stare at the windows or rush out to try and find the cowardly assailant, others to advance towards me to ascertain if I was hurt. All that I can remember of my own share of the proceedings was that I went straight on without stopping even for a moment. I was informed afterwards by Mr. and Mrs. Chadwick, the kind friends who had engaged and entertained me, that not the slightest change was observable in my face, voice, or manner, and when, after a few minutes, the alarm of the audience had subsided, no one present would have known that such an act had been perpetrated had it not been so universally witnessed. In closing the morning's address, I was for the first time influenced to notice the outrage by saying, in allusion to the antagonism with which Spiritualism had been received by the press and the pulpit, that such arguments were *like stones*—very striking, but not convincing. As I was further impressed to take up and hold in full sight the stone that had been hurled at me, by way of illustration, the entire audience burst into shouts of applause and cheering.

Whilst the near prospect of death or mutilation which this abominable act threatened did not suffice to interrupt the control which Spirits exerted over me, not so the unmistakable evidence of human sympathy, manifested by my warm-hearted audience. No control could keep back the starting tears that filled my eyes, or steady the broken tones in which I said in one of the pauses of the cheers, "Thank you all, and bid the God who has preserved me, bless you."

I believe Mr. Chadwick—an estate agent of the city—was himself a New York man, and though living in the centre and focus of slavery, he had no sympathy with the institution.

The reputation he had thus acquired, and the fact of his having engaged the advocate of an unpopular cause to lecture in Memphis, might have seriously prejudiced the citizens against me, had not the tide of public sentiment been completely turned in my favour by the cowardly outrage above described. Under an impulse that my amiable stone-throwing friend could never have anticipated my meeting on the evening of that memorable day was crowded to suffocation. And so did the entire of my engagement continue throughout the period of my visit.

As it was my custom to amuse, as well as to cheer my dear old mother's heart, by sending to her far off distant home (a thousand miles away) clippings from the newspapers of my various lecturing stations, so I find, now that she has entered into her rest, in the land of Spiritual sunlight, numbers of journalistic records of what I did, and *did not*, say and do in my far and wide wanderings.

Amongst these scraps I am reminded that I sustained one entire month's correspondence, through the "Memphis Appeal" with the opponents of Spiritualism, and the enemies of progress generally. Above all I again read that I was impressed to do, what every true Spiritualist CAN DO IF THEY CHOOSE, namely, to DARE my opponents TO DISPROVE MY CASE.

All this kept my Sunday as well as week meetings so alive, that I could not enter a concert room, public meeting, or even a *nigger* minstrel gathering, in which I was not recognised, and shouted for to make a speech or recite a poem.

It was only when I entered the States of Louisiana, Mississippi, Georgia, and the Carolinas, that I realised the full horrors of the "*divine Institution*," as the barbarian ministers of the churches in the South called slavery, or that I understood its full wickedness both to God and man.

I characterise it now from what I personally witnessed as LUST, AVARICE, and CRUELTY. The details are too shocking and incredible, and I dare not now repeat them. It is enough to say that after passing once through the Southern States to fulfil my engagements, I never visited them again. I must do justice, however, by adding, that I met with many noble men and women, who loathed "the slave institution" as much as I did, and who would gladly have shaken themselves free of it, even though all their property consisted of their slaves, had they known how to do so without placing their lives in jeopardy from the State authorities.

Amongst those who most warmly sympathised with me in my loathing of slavery was good Colonel MacCrae, of North Carolina, a planter and a noble gentleman, who, just before the commencement of the war nobly, gallantly manumitted a large plantation full of his slaves; but after giving them their liberty he was compelled to fly for his life to the North, where he and his once rich daughters had to support themselves as best they could, by needlework or teaching.

I had the honour of visiting at Colonel MacCrae's house during one fortnight, and in company with my esteemed host, called at several of the negroes' houses on his plantation, where I found many excellent mediums.

Amongst them was a man whose truthfulness had converted his noble master. Colonel MacCrae had a son in the army, who died of yellow fever at the time when his regiment was stationed at New Orleans.

The distance was far too great for the mourning father to attend the funeral which, according to custom, was obliged to take place in that burning climate, within a few hours of the decease.

A year after this, Colonel MacCrae was preparing to visit New Orleans on a matter of business, and had arranged with his daughters to have a fine marble monument placed on his son's grave and inscribed to his memory.

The evening before his departure, when passing round his plantation, the wife of one of his best negroes called him into her hut, wherein her husband, in a deep trance, was giving Spirit communications. The moment the colonel entered, his own Spirit son addressed him in characteristic phraseology, and begged him not to have any monument placed in the New Orleans Cemetery to him, because, added the Spirit, "my body has been taken out of its first burying place and burned, and that of a female has been put in its stead."

Now the negro medium had been born and reared in North Carolina. He had never visited New Orleans and was totally unaware that the city, being below the level of the Mississippi River, from which it was only protected by a high levee, or artificial earth bank, the authorities never allowed graves to be made in its watery ground.

The dead were—at the time I write of—placed in little cells, built into sets of walls, about and around the cemeteries, and as in all probability the number of the dead far exceeded the means provided for disposing of their remains, it was an open secret throughout Louisiana that cremations of the mortal remains were constantly carried on; therefore, that the cells in the walls, or "ovens" as they were called, were periodically cleared of their contents, and sold over and over again.

Of all this the North Carolina medium was totally ignorant; not so the master.

When, therefore, on visiting his son's reputed grave in New Orleans, and under the excuse of transferring the remains to his own estate, Colonel MacCrae had the cell opened, the coffin deposited there, proved on examination to contain only the decaying form of a recently interred *female.*

It is needless to say that this, combined with many succeeding tests, sufficed to convince the good Colonel that the Spirit, and not the poor mortal body, is the real man, and can and does survive the shock of earthly dissolntion.

Taking it as a whole, I was most kindly received by a portion of the population of the South, found many warm friends there, whilst Spiritualism was far more rife, and mediumship more highly developed, than in the more materialistic communities of the North.

Beyond very successful meetings, fine circles and a general Pentecostal outpouring of the Spirit in my own person, and that of many others, I met with nothing of peculiar mark that I can relate beyond a curious experience in the State of Alabama.

I had for months previous to my visit to the South been engaged to lecture at Mobile, by Mr. John Bowen, an excellent gentleman known to me by report, and whom I anticipated meeting with much pleasure.

On landing from the steam boat at the bay of Mobile, Mr. Bowen and a large party of friends met me, and whilst driving to Mr. Bowen's residence, where I was to stay, they pointed to two large flaming placards on the walls; one was the announcement of a certain Madame Somebody—whose name I forget—to the effect that she would tell fortunes by palmistry, cards, or other arts. The other was the copy of an order from the State Legislature, forbidding Emma Hardinge, or any other *infidel lecturer* calling themselves Spiritualists, from speaking, teaching, or lecturing in halls, rooms, or any other public places within the State of Alabama.

Grieved as I was at this official prohibition, and joining with my friends in the wish that my lectures, instead of being announced as teachings from the Spheres of Heaven, had been dated from *the other place,* and promised to tell lies in the name of palmistry, &c., &c., I still expressed my regret that the good friends should have exposed themselves to public odium, by allowing me to land at all. This they would not hear of. On the contrary, they not only endeavoured to persuade me to prolong my visit even beyond the time I had myself appointed, but they held circles with me morning, noon, and night, at which some startling test phenomena were exhibited.

One afternoon during my stay in Mobile, Mr. Bowen, and quite a party of friends, urged me to visit the State House, and tread on the ground where that liberal and enlightened legislature had sat, who passed the law forbidding my giving any public lectures in Alabama.

At that time, namely, the winter of 1860, let it be remembered, as I have before stated, that not the faintest whisper of the coming rebellion had been breathed abroad.

The sluggish spirit of self-indulgence and luxurious enjoyment which distinguished some of the planters seemed to forebode as long a continuance of idle ease and comfort earned for the white masters by the hapless black slaves as life itself should endure.

Without warning or premonition therefore on my part, almost the moment I stood in the midst of the legislative hall of Alabama, a Spirit power overshadowed me, compelling me to speak in tones which echoed and re-echoed through that vast hall, words which a young press reporter of our party took down, and which ran as follows :—

"Alabama! Land of present peace and surface tranquillity! Woe to thee! Woe to thee! Thy sons shall be driven from the fields, and thy daughters from the homes of luxury. Thy streets shall be filled with mourning and lamentation for the slain. Thy land shall become desolate ; the grass shall grow green between the stones of thy streets ; the moth and rust shall eat away thy splendour. Thy fields shall be beaten down by the tramp of the war horse, and thy young men shall lay here, even here, beneath the very roof which has resounded to the decree which banished the Spirit world from thy fair land ; here, even here, side by side, shall lay the rows of the slain; on this very floor shall be heaped up piles of the silent dead.

"Ere two more years of tribulation have dimmed thy glory this very place shall be full of thine unburied dead, and the oppressor and the tyrant shall lay down their arms and become homeless and wandering spirits, like those whom they have driven hence. Fair and hapless Alabama ! in less than two short years shall there be more Spirits than mortal forms within thy borders, and where now the chains of slavery clank and the words of denun- ciation against the messengers of Spirit life are published along thy walls, the sound of dropping tears and the sob of broken hearts even in this very place shall proclaim the requiem of Alabama's sons and Alabama's glory."

I have only to add that this terrible prophecy, forced from my lips by a power that no effort of my own will could stay, listened to in awe-struck silence by my sur- rounding friends, and published again and again by them in different places, was only too fatally realised in all its minutest details.

During the ensuing war between North and South, commencing in 1861, a year after the utterance of this prophecy, not one of the Southern States was more active in the defence of its slave' institutions, or suffered more fearfully in the loss of its bravest sons, than Alabama. On several occasions, when hosts of the slain were brought back through the grass-grown streets and deserted cities of Alabama, the fallen warriors' remains were carried unshrouded and placed in rude coffins side by side on the floor of the State house, where the mourners assembled to hear a few hasty funeral words said over them ; in short,

in the desolation and ravages of war, and the destruction
and ruin during which it raged, every word of that sad
and wholly unpremeditated prophecy was fulfilled to the
very letter in the fate of Alabama.

In my wide travels through wild and remote districts of
America, I have been wonderfully guided and protected
by my kind Spirit guardians, and there are numerous
instances, difficult to verify, in which I could discern how
the most momentous events of my life have been shaped
by Spirit friends.

Out of countless instances of this kind I shall only
attempt in this place to cite the following cases, representative, however, of innumerable others of similar guidance.

In one of my extended pilgrimages amongst the cities
of the Far West, my first journey to Springfield, Illinois,
was undertaken in the depth of the severe winter of 1860.

The prairies intervening between Ohio and Illinois were
literally under water, and the train which was announced
to arrive at Springfield at six p.m., after labouring through
innumerable difficulties in consequence of the heavy rains
and melting snows, only reached Springfield at half-past
one in the morning which succeeded my expected arrival.
As the telegraph wires were all down, no tidings could be
be sent or given of our situation.   I was engaged at
Springfield by the State printer, Mr. Richards, but on
reaching the station eight hours later than the appoined
time, all was dark and deserted.   The waiting-rooms were
shut, and not a living creature was in sight. Our stove fires
in the cars were out, the coal exhausted, and provisions
ditto.   The guard of the train came to me, kindly asking
if I would prefer to stay in the train to landing at the cold
dark station.   "Land!" sounded the Spirit voice, in my
ears, that had never betrayed me.   I obeyed, and soon stood
on the platform hungry, desolate, half frozen, and in thick
darkness.   I saw my heavy trunk put out, and watched the

lights of the train disappear, leaving me, not alone, for as
I stood there in utter bewilderment, the same dear voice
spoke, saying, "All's well, keep still. I will bring you
help." Almost as the voice ended, I saw a distant light
gleaming over the prairie and evidently approaching the
station. In a few minutes more I heard the swish and
splash of wheels toiling through the watery ground, and
then came a man's voice shouting, "Any one from the
train landed?" Joyfully indeed did I respond, asking as
loudly as I could, "Can you take me off?" More swishing
and splashing, and then a little buggy was shoved up to
the side of the platform, and its only occupant, a muffled-up
man, held out the lantern he carried to take a view of the
unfortunate who solicited his aid.

"Where d'ye want to go?" he asked. I mentioned the
name of the street I was due at, but not the person.
"All's shut up to-night," said the man. "The train has
long since been given up, and no one's awake in the city.
You'd best get into the buggy and take shelter in my
shanty for the night; it's close by, and that's how we
happened to see the train come in and hear the whistle."
"You may trust him, go with him," said the Spirit voice
in the usual noiseless way to my spirit ear alone. I
advanced to the edge of the platform, when the man said,
"Got any baggage?" "Oh, yes," I responded, "my trunk
is here." "I can't carry that," he rejoined, "I've only a
small trap, just big enough for two, but I'll come and
fetch it the first thing in the morning." "Leave it,"
whispered the voice, "it shall be all safe, we'll guard it."

It was *on that assurance* that I left my little possessions,
including all the money I had earned for the past six
months, utterly unguarded, in that trunk on the open
platform.

I entered the buggy, was driven or rather *sailed,*
through the dripping prairie for about a quarter of a mile,
then landed at a small wooden house.

To the call of my escort, " Wife, there's a lady from the train," a woman appeared, half dressed, with an oil lamp in her hand.

I began to pour out explanations and apologies which the woman cut short by saying, " We hav'n't got no one in our Polly's room now, so you can just go in and stay till morning."

Gladly turning into *Polly's room*, I retired, needing only a good fire, a cup of tea, or the driest possible crust of bread to complete my happiness. As none of the last three requisites to a·half-frozen and completely starving traveller were forthcoming, I just drew the clean-looking truckle bed across the door, as the only fastening the room afforded, and curled myself up till morning, when the same dear voice as before awoke me with the words, " Look, Emma, look."

Starting up, I ran to the uncurtained window, and there to my delight I saw a man, whom I took to be my host, drawing along on a railway truck, the precious trunk I had left at the station.

As I ran out in my cloak and hat to meet him, he accosted me far more respectfully than before, asking if I was the Mrs. Hardinge to whom that trunk belonged.

Upon my assuring him that I was, he explained that he was a workman in the employ of Mr. Richards, the very party who had engaged me, and whom I expected to meet at the station.

The man had heard that a Mrs. Hardinge was coming to his employer's house, to lecture at Springfield, but without having the slightest idea that the forlorn traveller of the night before was the expected guest, he yet declared that when he heard the train come in, though it was at half-past one, something seemed to say to him, that he must take out his horse and buggy, and go over to fetch a passenger from the station.

In after years, when I had become a frequent visitor at good Mr. Richards' house, I heard of this same man as an excellent impressional medium, and of his constantly referring to the incident narrated above, as an act of irresistible spirit impression; one, too, which in all probability saved me from being frozen to death on that dreary railway station.

The second representative case in which I consider my own life and that of others was saved by the same blessed influence that rescued me as above detailed, was this :—

I was visiting in the family of Mrs. Neal, a lady residing in a lonely spot reached only by carriage roads graded on the side of a range of hills, about three miles from the city of Cincinnati, where I was engaged to lecture for several successive weeks. We generally drove into the city from Mrs. Neal's place in a "carry-all," drawn by a very old, very stout, but favourite black horse.

At an engagement prior to this at Cincinnati I had been accustomed to ride about in a carriage drawn by an immensely fast bay horse ; so fast, indeed, that I had given him the nickname of "Lightning," by way of con-trast to Mrs. Neal's old black steed. I called the latter "Thunder," a name which was afterwards adopted in merry humour by the whole family. Mr. Lovell, Mrs. Neal's father, had informed me that there was a tradition that Thunder had once, in his extreme youth, run away, but the old gentleman added: "We have had him now some twenty years, and he has never been known to be guilty of any such indiscretion." On the evening of my lecture, my host and hostess, and Mr. Lovell, accompanied me to the hall to fulfil my engagement. After the lecture, as we were returning home in the "carry-all" drawn by "Thunder," on arriving at a lonely part of the road where no other persons were travelling suddenly, and without any warning, several armed robbers sprang into our path, and surrounded the carriage. They threatened us with death unless we gave up to them all our money, and anything of value we had about us. My friends were terribly alarmed, but again I was conscious of the presence of my beloved Spirit brother, and I heard the well-known voice saying, "Have no fear, sit still." At that instant I saw him by the side of the driver, from whom he seemed to snatch the reins; and to the amazement of my friends, "Thunder" reared, and dashed through our assailants, scattering them. The Spirit held the reins, and urged him on, and he simply flew with the speed of lightning, not stopping in his mad career till he had landed us safely at the door of Mrs. Neal's house.

Dear old Thunder, under the control of our Spirit driver, had saved our lives.

The robbers were never afterwards heard of, but dear old Thunder was; in fact, he became celebrated as the horse that had saved four people's lives under the direction of a Spirit driver.

The third case I have to report speaks even more clearly than those described above of the guidance of the loved and loving Spirit brother, whose tender watch and ward over his wandering sister, in countless cases rather than the few briefly detailed in this chapter, illustrate the divine promise that "He shall give his angels charge over thee to keep thee and guard thee in all thy ways," and truly that prophecy has been realised by me in a thousand ways in my far and wide wanderings for missionary work in the cause of Spiritualism.

The next place I visited was Dixon, Illinois, where a gentleman of some standing, Mr. Henry Bacon, begged me to give a lecture. Mr. Henry Bacon, who was himself anxious to become a good test Medium, asked my Spirit brother if he would not occasionally come to him and give similar tests to those which occurred during my visit.

This promise being made, I returned to Rockford, Illinois, where I was engaged to give a month's course of Sunday lectures. At that time the winter season had set in most severely. The snow lay several feet deep on the ground, and a large number of poor Scotch emigrants that had come to Rockford in the pleasant season of the autumn were now unfortunately in great distress from cold and privation. My good kind hostess, Mrs. Blim, devoted all her time and means for the relief of the sick and suffering people in her neighbourhood.

I therefore joined my good hostess in her noble work of visiting the sick and afflicted, and for several days we drove about so effectually in our little sleigh that we had nearly set every one to rights in our own immediate neighbourhood.

Returning home late one bitter afternoon, a child ran after our sleigh, begging Mrs. Blim, whom she seemed to know, to come in and speak to her mother. Driving up to the door we found a family of poor emigrants in the sorest distress for the want of a cooking stove. The father was ill in bed, the children half frozen, the poor mother with a baby in her arms was vainly trying to build up a fire on a bare stone hearth. Some kind Samaritans had sent them a load of coal, and others had furnished them with meat and flour. All they now needed was a good cooking stove, but this they could not procure, as their last dollar was gone and the father was too ill to work.

Mrs. Blim and I well knew where we could get a good stove for five dollars, but we had exhausted all our own resources to the last cent, and begged and borrowed and taxed every taxable source so thoroughly that we did not know where to turn or what to do for help. "Let us go home," I cried, "something will turn up, and we will come in again bye-and-bye." Upon this we got into our sleigh in silence and sadness.

Arrived at home, the usual pile of letters was put into my hands. The first I opened was from Mr. Henry Bacon, of Dixon, the gist of which was that "Tom," my Spirit brother, had come to him through a good medium who had called suddenly at his house, to say that I (Tom's sister) was in immediate want of five dollars. Upon the strength of this communication Mr. Bacon said he had taken the liberty of enclosing a five dollar bill to me, and only hoped I would excuse him and let him know if it was all right.

I did let him and many others know that it was all right, but not before a five dollar cooking stove had been bought and sent down to the poor emigrants, whilst one of Mrs. Blim's domestics went over to help the family light the said stove, bake the bread, and dress up such a delightful stew that the flavour thereof reached our distant home and set Mrs. Blim and I off that night into the sweetest sleep we had ever known.

For some years after this I kept Mr. Henry Bacon's letter by me, and by showing it to numerous enquirers into the *uses* as well as the facts of Spiritualism, I made "the Spirit sailor boy" quite a popular character amongst the Spiritualists of the Far West.

My fourth and last personal illustration of direct Spirit interposition in human affairs I give as an extract from a pamphlet published at the *Banner of Light* office, Boston, entitled THE SPIRIRITUAL INVENTION.—"Autobiographic Scenes and Sketches.—By Frank Chase. 'Its name is Inside Self-adjusting Blind and Shutter Fastener. It is simple in construction, but perfect in principle. They can be made of brass or iron, burnished ; are equally well adapted to palace or cottage. He can get a patent for it, and it will be a very great success. All we ask is, that he will publish to the world how he came by it, that they may know whence they receive great inventions.'—*Spirit*."

To explain this matter in the briefest as well as plainest possible way, I make the following quotations from my own article published in the *Banner of Light*, April 5th, 1862, and subsequently reprinted as a preface to the pamphlet named above:—

"We all acknowledge with Thomas Paine that there are some thoughts that bolt into our heads, coming we know not how or whence. Inventors, composers, and writers will be especially familiar with this experience, and to those who may be willing to accept of a Spiritual solution for this apparent spontaneity of thought, the following incidents of travel may not be uninteresting:—

"Last November I went to Sutton, New Hampshire, to fulfil a long standing lecture engagement. I found my correspondent, a Mr. Frank Chase, almost the sole representative of Spiritualism in three villages, and, if time and space would permit, I could give a history of modern martyrdom, endured during a five years' warfare, single handed, by this brave young man against bigotry, cowardice, and village politics, that should stimulate the despairing to hope under the most adverse circumstances, and put to shame the murmurs of the 'well to do' Spiritualist, who, after enduring a few cold looks, and paying out a few dollars, to sustain 'the cause,' with the self-satisfied assurance 'that he has made sacrifices enough for Spiritualism, and means to do no more.'

"Not so my brave ally, Mr. Frank Chase, who, with scarcely any means, and the entire battery of Sutton influence levelled against him, by aid of a few Quixotes, whose chief inducement to lecture is the need of the people, rather than self, has managed to keep Spiritualism so unmistakeably before Sutton eyes, that they know with the heart what they reject with the lips. Although none of Mr. Frank Chase's family were Spiritualists, I was hospitably entertained in his house.

"One day, whilst receiving visits from the neighbours, in company with Mr. Chase's mother, I noticed to some of my visitors the presence of different spirit-friends they had brought with them.   As those I was so fortunate as to perceive were recognised with many expressions of gladness and surprise by their friends, Mrs. Chase remarked—'she supposed she was not good enough to be visited by spirits, as I had never recognised any for her.'   In apparent answer to her remark, a tall man appeared at her side, who called her *'a kind of sister of his.'*   This, in connection with other tokens of identity, assured her it was *a half-brother of hers*, and excited much curiosity and interest in her mind.

"Some time since, my host, Mr. Frank Chase, had invented a new window blind, for which he had obtained a patent.   Mr. Chase always claimed that the thought of this invention had come into his head in a manner so singular, that he was perfectly sure it was a 'spiritual impression.'   The spirit of the uncle now before me, informed me that he (himself an ingenious workman) had been the author of this thought, but as the assertion contained in it no special proof, it was not received by the company with much favour.   Ere he disappeared, the spirit added : 'I will give Frank another proof of my care and love for him, and do something greatly to his benefit.'

"That night, the moment I extinguished my lamp on going to bed, the tall man stood by my side, kindly quieted the fear which the miserable prejudice of early education has still left on my nerves of spirits, and after exacting from me a promise that what he was about to communicate I would freely give to his nephew, he proceeded to show me an invention for closing window blinds, opening, shutting and most securely fastening them, and all from the inside, and without the cold and troublesome process of opening and shutting the window.

"The machine was, and is, exceedingly simple, can be applied to any window, is the most secure of fastening when closed, against burglars, and equally so when pushed back, against the action of the wind.

"My shadowy mechanical friend took the pains to show me the instrument made in two kinds of metal, the one plain and inexpensive, the other more showy and expensive.   With another charge to *'give* it to Frank,' together with the assurance that he should obtain a patent for it, and, more apocryphal yet, be actually loaned the money which was to procure said patent without any difficulty, my good instructor went over again the screws, hinges, joints, material, &c., and bade me kindly good-night.

"The next morning, almost at dawn of day, saw me fitting on to a frozen window, and in the midst of a blinding snow storm, a paper model of the spirit's machine. Mr. Frank Chase, a ready and ingenious mechanic himself, at once understood the idea, and with the promise of the spirit (which he did believe) that where my description failed he would inspire him, and a further promise (which seemed so wild in Sutton finance that he did not believe it), namely, that the means for obtaining his patent should be found, I quitted Sutton.

"About one week after my departure, I received a letter from Mr. Chase, announcing that the machine was made, tried, and pronounced by several mechanics of the vicinity perfectly satis-factory and complete in all its details. A few weeks later, my correspondent informed me that the money was readily obtained, and the patent followed; that the spiritual machine is now in successful operation, and great demand, and can be had of Mr. Frank Chase, Sutton, N. H., &c., &c.

"As I have the permission of the parties concerned to publish this statement, and as the various witnesses can and will testify to the above, I think I am justified in saying that in me (in whom I presume none of my acquaintances would look to find germs even of mechanical genius) there is one evidence, at least, that we need but to see the wheels that move the machine, and obtain glimpses of the invisible workmen who are engaged in the machinery, to find where those thoughts fraught with gleams of untried possibilities, and rife with gems of useful discovery, come from. "EMMA HARDINGE."

CHAPTER XIV.

ONE OF THE MOST REMARKABLE INSTANCES ON RECORD OF MODERN VAUDOOISM.

"There are more things in heaven and earth . . . than are dreamt of in your philosophy."

IN every phase of life, as well as in the characteristics of living actors, there may be seen (to the keen observer) two sides to every picture, and this duality in Nature applies no less to the two sides of every story than it does to the diverse views which diverse minds entertain concerning all that affects human opinions, Spiritualism not excepted.

Hitherto it has been my pride and pleasure to point to the DIVINE side of the great Spiritual movement, and record how often good Spirits come and do help us, both consciously and unknown to ourselves, to outwork the destiny that lies before us.

In the following narrative I am about to call the reader's attention to the dangers and abuses that may grow out of the practice of occult powers, when undertaken by ill-regulated minds, or persons who yield up the reins of judgment or conscience, to the *alleged* control of any Spirit, whether in or out of the mortal form.

In a small pamphlet published by the late Mr. Stainton Moses, entitled "The Transcorporeal Action of Spirit," there is a reprint from the *New York Sun*, bearing the inapt title of "Mrs. Hardinge's Shadow." Few persons glancing cursorily at this heading, would understand that the article treats of one of the most tremendous problems of Spiritual power, and relates to the action of the embodied rather than the disembodied soul's possibilities.

Ignoring the many garbled reports that somehow have crept into many of the American journals concerning the following two cases, I shall narrate them only from the facts of my own well-attested experiences.

It was during the time when I was filling a lecturing engagement in New York that I received a letter signed " John Gallagher." This letter, although addressed to me on the envelope, and commencing with my Christian name, was evidently, *as it then seemed*, sent by mistake to me, it being an enthusiastic love letter expressed in good enough language, but carrying in its context the idea of being addressed to a very dear and intimate friend of the writer's. Coming, however, from a person whose name I had never even heard, and containing language which no human being then in America had the right to address to me, I could arrive at no other conclusion than that the writer, whoever he might be, had penned two letters at once, and put this effusion into the wrong envelope. Rational as this idea seemed, I was soon disabused of it by receiving another, and yet another letter of the same kind within about a week from the receipt of the first.

Horrified at the possibility of such documents falling into any other hands than my own, and convinced that if they did, no sane person would doubt but that I was engaged in some secret intrigue, I resolved to show the letters to, and consult the friends with whom I was boarding, namely, Mrs. French and her assistant, a dear soul, popularly called in our household Uncle Culbertson.

On reading over these letters, my confidants both came to the conclusion that some unfortunate woman of the town had assumed my name (a case that had happened before in the experience of a public lecturer), and that her correspondent had mistaken the party he meant to address for me. Even this vague idea we felt obliged to abandon when a letter followed of the same character, but commenting in the most extravagant terms on my precious Sunday's lecture and the beauty of my costume, the description of which actually corresponded with that I had worn.

"The wretch who writes is a madman," I remarked. "That is impossible," replied Mr. Culbertson, "the language is too good to be the work of insanity; yet insanity, if not something worse—it seems to be."

From this time, other letters of a similar character, letters too which referred so clearly to my lectures, dresses, and appearance, that it was impossible to doubt that they were meant for me, kept pouring in with such frequency that I resolved at last to consult the police in the matter. Hitherto I had begged my friends not to mention the matter to my mother, lest she should share with me the terrible distress that these missives occasioned.

As, however, my permanent address was at my mother's boarding place in New York, and during my lecturing tours I always commissioned her to open my letters, and only forward on such as required my personal attention, Mrs. French pointed out to me the astonishment and horror she would feel should such missives continue to be sent, and come into her hands without any previous preparation. Influenced by these suggestions, we took my mother into counsel, and she at once, with her clear strong sense, suggested that the whole thing might be the work of some enemy who would first *assume* the position that I was in correspondence with him, and then manage to have his letters fall into the hands of those whose interest it was to disgrace me. Plausible as this idea seemed, it was too repulsive to our sense of honour to permit such a proceeding to pass unnoticed, and so in sheer despair we consulted Mr. Matson, an old and experienced police magistrate, also a friend who was a shrewd lawyer. Neither could throw any light on the subject, but they pointed out that though the post mark was Boston, or some of the various towns in Massachusetts, the writer showed too intimate a knowledge of my doings in New York to be at any great distance off. As to the signature of John Gallagher, that might be, and most likely was, assumed; hence an enquiry into the whereabouts of all the John Gallaghers in the United States would reveal nothing. In a word, my official counsellors, like my friends, could offer no other solution to the affair than vague surmise, and thus the matter was left in profound mystery. I am not quite certain of the year in which this frightful persecution commenced. I believe it was in 1858.

Certain it is, however, that from that time forth for a period of at least two years, these dreadful epistles followed me everywhere.

In the Far West, through the Eastern States, and finally in the South, this abominable persecution continued. As time wore on, I commenced to realise a still more terrible infliction. I began to sense the near approach of these hateful letters, first by a feeling of cold chills, and not unfrequently by the realisation of some evil presence around me. Sometimes these perceptions were so powerful that I felt involuntarily impressed to place my chair close up against the wall, *lest the dreadful thing which I knew had entered the room should get behind me.*

The only relief I experienced from these torturing sensations was to speak of them to the friends with whom I was visiting, and though I never found one single individual who could afford me any clue to the mystery, it was something to realise that friends sympathised with me.

As to the Spirits, though I repeatedly questioned them on the subject, their only answer was, that *the evil power around me was a human one, and for the time being was too far removed from their sphere to enable them to control it. All they could do was to assure me of their present protection and final release.*

As an evidence of the *direct* action of the invisible power by which I was beset, I may mention that during one of my month's engagements at Providence, Rhode Island, I had agreed to give a week evening lecture at Pawtucket, a place only a few miles distant from where I was staying. My friends at Providence had arranged to drive me over to my lecture, and bring me back in a " carry-all," a double-seated covered conveyance.

The night was intensely dark and cold, and during the ride home, our driver determined to stop at a roadside house he knew of to borrow a lantern.

Arrived at the halfway house, my three friends, a lady and two gentlemen, got out to warm themselves as well as to procure the lantern. I was too tired to move, when suddenly, sitting in the " carry-all" by myself, the horses began to rear as if frightened, and I felt a cold hand *doing something to my head,* on which I wore a cloud, or knitted scarf.

I called out loudly to my friends, " Come here, some one's in the carriage ! " Instantly all was quiet : but again the horses reared, and my friends ran out with the lantern. No one was to be seen ; but when we arrived at home and went into the sitting-room, to my friends' astonishment and my own we found a spray of lilies of the valley stuck in my hair, which to my dying day I insist was not there when I left for the ride home. I told my friends then, and persist now, that we had no such flowers with us, and that some one or *something* got into the carriage and placed those lilies there. The next morning's post brought me one of the terrible letters, complimenting me on wearing those lilies during my ride home, lamenting the presence of the strangers with me, and speaking of *words I had said after* my return.

Passing over many terrible months fraught with similar mysteries, I now reach a period memorable in my changeful life as being the only occasion when I visited the Southern States of America, in which I had several engagements. It was in the winter of 1860 that I proceeded to Macon, Georgia, to lecture for two months, during which time I was the guest of Dr. and Mrs. Andrews. The doctor was a well-known and respected physician of the place, and though after the lapse of some thirty-three years I do not know whether this excellent couple are still on the earth side of life, I think there must be in Macon some friends who will remember my visit, and to many persons there I spoke of my abhorrent and mysterious persecution.

One day, whilst sitting in my own room writing, the feeling of intense cold came over me, which heralded-in one of the well-known dreadful letters. I had hardly pushed back my chair against the wall, to *prevent an unknown presence from stepping behind me,* when Dr. Andrews himself knocked at my door, and, on being invited to enter, presented me with several letters, one from my tormentor amongst them. I had already apprised my good host of my terrible following, and, by way of proving my confidence in him, and the nature of the mystery by which I was surrounded, when I recognised the all too well-known handwriting, and the postmark of Boston, I handed the letter unopened to Dr. Andrews and bid him read it. He did so, and, giving it back to me, we found that *some one* in Boston had described the very scene that took place the evening before in my lecture hall in Macon, Georgia, over a thousand miles away! All talk on such a mystery, all conjecture was in vain.

Dr. Andrews left me to attend his patients, whilst I sat down to write a letter to a Major Rhynders, then chief of police in Boston. In this official letter I enclosed several missives from this same "John Gallagher," received at different places during the past few weeks, and, having a slight acquaintance with Major Rhynders, I told him I wanted him to trace this John Gallagher, or find as best he could the writer of those letters. I told him that in six weeks from that time I should be in Boston to fulfil a two months' engagement, and that the entire of my fees— 200 dols.—and all that I could raise in addition if required I would pay to arrest and help prosecute the villanous author of these letters. I had just sealed and directed my packet to the Boston chief of police, when the voice of one of my best beloved Spirit friends, my sailor brother Tom, spoke to me, and the following colloquy ensued :—

Spirit : "Who is Emma sending such a huge package of letters to, and why?" I answered, "You know; you will not or cannot help me, so I will help myself."

Spirit : "We will and do help you when we can; Spirits are not God, and cannot do all we wish or mortals demand."

Emma : "Perhaps so. Then I repeat I will help myself."

Spirit : "Emma's fire is low, and the weather is chilly; pray make up your fire with those letters?"

Emma : "I WILL NOT! and unless you give me some explanation of this horrible mystery those letters shall go to the Boston chief of police."

Spirit : "Poor Emma; how she will repent her work!"

Emma : "What do I care? I have no one to help me. The letters SHALL go!"

Spirit : "Will our Emma wait, for her own soul's sake, and to please her Spirit friends, for six weeks?"

Emma : "On this day six weeks I shall be in Boston. What then?"

Spirit : "Wait till after the first Sunday to-morrow six weeks, when you speak at Boston. If you are not GLAD THEN that you did not send your letters to the police *at that time,* we will not remonstrate against your sending them or publishing them abroad in any way."

Emma: "I agree; six weeks ONLY, remember. . . ."

In six weeks from the date of this conversation I arrived in Boston, Mass. I had been travelling for eighteen hours, and arrived on a Saturday, about two o'clock in the day.

The friend who met me took me to the house of Mr. Farrar, in Hancock Street, president of the society by whom I was engaged.

Mr. Farrar was one of the most prominent and highly respected merchants of Boston, and his good wife, my esteemed friend, had arranged for me to stay at their house during my engagement in Boston.

Retiring to my room, after a three o'clock lunch, I begged Mrs. Farrar to let me be entirely quiet, in the hope of gaining some rest prior to the six-thirty dinner hour. I had just prepared for my much needed repose, when Mrs. Farrar herself knocked at my door, and, on entering, besought me to give audience to two ladies who had implored her interest to obtain an interview with me on what they declared to be a matter of *life and death.*

Overpowered as I was with fatigue, I could not resist my kind hostess's pleading, so I descended to the drawing-room, only making the condition that, as I myself had no secrets, Mrs. Farrar should be present at the coming interview.

We found awaiting me two ladies, the youngest of whom, speaking in a refined and graceful manner, said, "Allow me to say, Mrs. Hardinge, we are mother and daughter, both widows, and have come to you on a most singular and embarrassing errand. This is my mother, Mrs. Gallagher."

I need hardly say that I started as I heard this hated name.

"Do you not know my brother, Mr. John Gallagher?" the lady added, anxiously. "Not personally," I replied, "but," I added, bitterly, "I have had some dreadful letters from an individual signing himself thus."

Then it was that, with many tears, in which the poor mother joined, the daughter explained that they had both been warm Spiritualists for many years. Her brother John, who was a custom house officer, in an excellent situation, and the sole support of both his mother and sister, had no belief in the cause until they persuaded him some two or three years before to go and hear me lecture.

He became so deeply interested on that occasion, that he continued his enquiries, and most unhappily fell in with one of those self-styled *mediums*, who was always preaching as well as practising the doctrine of " Affinities." Having soon discovered that her unfortunate visitor had conceived a sudden and violent infatuation for the first female lecturer he had ever heard or seen, the cunning impostor flattered her trusting dupe by *pretending* that "the Spirits" influenced her to say that I, Emma Hardinge, was this man's "affinity," but, that, in order to win me, he must direct all his actions under certain laws and rules.

In league with this impostor was another of the same kind, a man (all too well known in Boston), who claimed to be an adept in East Indian Magic. This precious pair so wrought upon their victim, that after putting him on a régime of fruit and vegetables, and reducing him by fasting, etc., they commenced to teach him abominable Vaudoo arts, by which he could go out of his body and visit as well as follow me about as a Spirit.

The ladies added, that he neither kept his infatuation or his practices secret from them. On the contrary, he showed them continually the book in which the records of his visits to me were inscribed. Therein was described the dresses I wore and what I did and said, and the houses I stayed at during my travels. The sister added, that when he found I was announced to come to Boston, he had besought his mother and sister to visit me, carry his book of records with them, show it to me, and if, as he believed it would be, found correct, they were to tell me how long and faithfully he had spiritually followed me, and entreat me to grant him an interview.

When these ladies proceeded to show me the book of records, and I found how evidently I had been traced, my dresses described, the very pieces I had played on the piano named, and my walks followed, etc., etc., etc., I became almost frantic with rage and horror. "See him!" I exclaimed, "Never!" I added, what was true, that nothing but pity and compassion for his mother and sister prevented me from publishing his conduct to the world and holding him up to universal execration.

The poor mother went on her knees to me, pleading that I would see and remonstrate with him, but grieved as I was for her, I sternly refused. Then came the terrible problem of what they should say to him on their return. Mrs. Farrar urged that they should tell him the truth, and represent the abhorrence in which I regarded his conduct, but, I, alas! in my blind rage counselled another course of action, and one which I shall ever repent of. I said what I then thought most truly, that the best, perhaps only way, to cure him of these dreadful fetish practices was, to allege that all he had recorded was *wrong*, *fanciful*, and *false*, and that no such powers as he claimed to possess appertained to humanity.

I was sincere in my wish to serve these afflicted women, without considering that falsehood can never be right. Enough to say that the poor mother and sister left me deeply sorrowing, but most reluctantly promising to *attempt a cure* of the unhappy man's infatuation by following my counsel.

According to promise, they wrote to me in a few days, informing me that they had followed my directions, but the result was still more terrible to them than even his former unhappy practices.

Whether under the belief that he had throughout deluded himself, or that the nature of his practices had destroyed his mental balance, none could say. It is enough to add, as the conclusion of this deplorable narrative, that John Gallagher's widowed sister called on Mrs. Farrar one day during my absence, to inform her that she had just returned from the Worcester Lunatic Asylum, where she had left her hapless brother a raving maniac.

Let me add, that in pity for the poor mother and sister, the only part of this sad narrative which I can recall with any satisfaction was the burning of all the maniac's letters, especially of those I had intended to put in the hands of the police.

As a duty that I owe to the noble cause of TRUE SPIRITUALISM, no less than as a warning to those who either dare to abuse its potencies or to insult its divine realities by misuse, I feel bound to say that the narrative I have written out in the preceding pages was not the only case in which I was made the victim of base attempts to put the horrors of Vaudooism upon me.

In several other instances, additional to the one narrated in this chapter, my general successes, I presume, stimulated base attempts on the part of Vaudooists to drag me into the snares of their magnetic influences.

Some of the most wicked of these, my persecutors, are already too notoriously known to the communities of the past thirty or forty years to need farther publicity. But whilst I look back with horror upon my would-be captors, I am no less indignant with those traders who, under the pretence of mediumship, talk to their sitters of "Affinities," and teach them the same arts and base attempts at the projection of mental influences as are common amongst the Fakirs of India and the Magi of most Eastern lands.

When Spiritualism is regarded in the light I have always claimed for it, namely, as a RELIGION, neither Spirits or mortals will dare to pollute it by the introduction of magical arts, whilst the powers of SOUL, whether in public or private use, will form the highest and yet the most sacred of all studies now undistinguished in the general and little understood term of SPIRITUALISM.

CHAPTER XV.

A Modern Son of Man and Affinity Hunter.

"Watchman! What of the night? The morning cometh."

As I was engaged between thirty-five and forty years in travelling and lecturing in various countries in the promulgation of the newly revealed faith of Modern Spiritualism, and was generally greeted by large audiences and surrounded by many warm friends, and often by important public personages, I presume I was a favourable mark for the attention and experiment of that class of reformers who follow in the track of success, some of whom would fain prey upon those more fortunate than themselves, or, still oftener, of that class of persons who deem the new and widespread revelation of Modern Spiritualism sanctions all the wild and fanatical ideas which can be cloaked under the cover of a mystical new religion.

Presuming that all public persons, especially those connected with the new and wonderful revelations of Spiritualism, are especial marks alike for fanatics and impostors to test their powers upon, I ought not to have felt either surprise or indignation to find myself a special attraction for the attempted operation of these nuisances; but though I might fill a volume with the names and operations of the two classes referred to above, I am happy to say I have rarely had to deal with the horrible conditions of Vaudooism, as described in the preceding chapter. Still I feel as if I should be unfaithful to the facts and lessons of history did I fail to describe one amongst numerous other instances of wild fanaticism which came immediately under my own special notice. I

give this history as a sample of unnumbered other cases of
a similar kind, and record the characteristics of this mania
in the present chapter in full, selecting as my subject
one well known case and person as an evidence of the
insanity that may possess a commonplace mind under
the influence of powers higher than those of humanity,
especially in the direction of personal vanity, and the
attempt to make itself the centre of a new religion.

In Buck's "Theological Dictionary," also in a reprint
from the above in a little tract called "Notes and Queries,"
are to be found accounts of some twenty-five or more
impostors who at various times and in various countries
have claimed to be "Messiahs," "Christs," and either
reincarnations or divine successors of the Jewish Messiah.
Modern history is not wanting in supplemental examples
of this same Messianic fever operating in many pretenders,
some of whom under the influence of sectarian fanaticism,
or stimulated by the T. L. Harris aim of personal ambition
and love of rule, have announced themselves as new
" Messiahs," and for a time succeeded in obtaining a small
and inconsequential following.

Of all the crazes that our nineteenth century has
presented, however, none perhaps can exceed in fanatical
folly and audacious impudence the one which I am now
about to describe; indeed, it is something to say that it
even transcends in folly and pretension the horrible
haunting detailed in the previous chapter.

As I have kept no diary except of the places and times
of my lectures, I am not quite certain of the date at which
I first received a long letter, written in *pale blue ink*—a
colour, as I was afterwards informed, adopted in compliment to the colour of the silk dresses I always wore at that
time on the platform. The writer of this letter informed
me that he was the second Christ or "Son of Man," *that I
was his " Affinity,"* and the sooner I consented to see him

and become what I suppose he meant as *the Daughter of Man*, the sooner the decrees of Heaven would be realised, and the world redeemed by our joint Messiahship.

Whatever the date of this first choice epistle might have been, I know it was some little time only after the terrible finale to the persecution recorded in the last chapter. At first my second would-be "Affinity" contented himself like the former one by writing me the most extravagantly fanatical and complimentary letters, but the next move was a still more abominable one. Wherever I went or lectured, a cadaverous-looking, long-haired, pale-faced man stalked into the hall and stationed himself—standing in the passage or aisle—nearly opposite the rostrum on which I spoke.

Warned by my former bitter experience, I complained at every station where I lectured of this hateful nuisance. The matter soon became publicly known and talked of, and at Quincy, Massachusetts, Mr. Richards, one of the *Banner of Light's* most popular and admired correspondents, the chairman also at my Quincy Sunday lectures, not only turned the man out of the hall, where he planted himself staring at me, but when he subsequently stood close by the carriage when I was getting into it to drive home, Mr. Richards drew his large horsewhip heavily across the man's shoulder's. Even at this insult the meek "Son of Man" never stirred; and then, as in several other places, the friends whom I consulted assured me upon judicial authority that so long as he did not venture *to speak to me none could disturb him, seeing that he had not broken the peace.* On two or three occasions the conductors of the cars, when they were persons acquainted with me, became so well informed of this man's insane acts in following me from place to place, that they refused to allow him to ride in the same car as I did.

Still the persecution continued, and still my friends were

unable to take any proceedings against a *quiet* individual who never attempted to accost me, and never even replied to any of the harsh and insulting language with which those informed of his proceedings often drove him from his post opposite the platforms on which I spoke. Most commonly, when he was thus literally chased out of the halls, he would return again and seat himself near the door with a meek aspect of suffering humility which left no pretext for disturbing him.

It need hardly be said that in a case so publicly obtruded upon notice as this, the man's name, origin, and history were and are familiarly enough known.

I was rather gratified than surprised therefore one day to receive a letter from a woman residing in a certain Western State, informing me that she was the wife of the obnoxious "Son of Man" and the mother of his children; that the said Messiah's head had first been crazed by a Christian Revivalist, and next by the doctrine of *Affinities* put forth by some of the *Affinity*-preaching Spiritists. That in this (as in the former miserable narrative), the hateful teachers of this doctrine had fixed the unfortunate man's unholy predilection for me by assuring him that I *was* "*his Affinity*," and that it was in association and partnership with me that the new "Kingdom of Heaven" alone could be founded ōn earth.

It is in pity to the poor wife and children of the fanatic that I now withhold a name which many who are yet living and have heard of the fellow's pretensions can still be familiar with. It is enough that I wrote at once to his wife, not only assuring her of my abhorrence of the man's proceedings, but offering all the means I could raise, together with assistance from my friends, to procure her husband's incarceration in a lunatic asylum.

I never received any answer to this letter, and as the intolerable nuisance continued, this is the mode by which

I ultimately quenched it : As I was about to proceed to California, I agreed with some of my most valued friends in and near Philadelphia to occupy a small estate on the Delaware River, where my dear mother in my long absence, with an efficient housekeeper and surrounded by good friends, would enjoy a pleasant country home. Shortly before leaving "Rose. Cross," the name of our chosen retreat, our housekeeper informed us one morning that a "tramp," as she named the intruder, had entered the garden on the previous night, taken his night's repose amidst our flower beds and bushes, and on being ordered off the next morning by a man employed to dress our garden, had left a letter in a sealed envelope addressed to me. I at once recognised the blue-inked missive, and having perused the rhapsody it contained, I found "the Messsiah" was still hovering about in the neighbourhood for the answer he implored me to write and leave in a certain indicated spot. Without a moment's delay I hastened off to a neighbouring estate close by, occupied by a worthy magistrate, and an excellent friend of my own and my mother's. I had already acquainted Mr. Fletcher (our magisterial friend) of my persecution, and he was therefore not surprised when I laid my morning's complaint before him.

Acting under the authority of the New Jersey law, in which our home. at Delanco was situated, Mr. Fletcher bid me hold up my hand, and swear that I considered my life in danger from this fanatic. This I attested with equal truth and candour, whereupon the "Son of Man" was at once sought out, arrested, and brought before the magistrate (Mr. Fletcher), charged with having trespassed on my grounds for illegal purposes.

To the first part of this charge he pleaded guilty; the second part he denied, meekly urging that he had brought his own provisions with him, whereupon he produced some dry bread and *a pot of honey*, which he affirmed was the only sustenance he allowed himself, in order to follow the example of his great prototype "John the Baptist," all except in the matter of the *locusts*.

Being fined, warned severely, and forbidden to reappear in that district again for a specified time, he was discharged, and before the expiration of his time of taboo I had embarked in the "North Star," bound for California, and my dear mother was safe under the protection of good friends at Concord, Massachusetts.

The last public account I ever had of the "Son of Man," was that for a few weeks he had invested the cash which should have been devoted to the support of his wife and children, in a small miserably ill-written paper printed *in blue ink*. The title of this precious document, well known enough to many of the early Spiritualists of America, I now suppress in pity to the man's family, and like many others of kindred character, I presume, it ultimately went to the rest which it deserved, and was never heard of on earth more.

As to its publisher, I confess to having occasionally seen his name attached to certain inconsequential articles in some of the Spiritual papers, but, happily for me, the course of my subsequent far and wide travels has deprived me alike of the attentions of a modern "Son of Man," or the opportunity of becoming one of the co-founders of the new "Kingdom of Heaven."

As the subject of Spiritualism and man's relation to the Spirit world is not only very dear, but absolutely sacred to me, so it hurts, and shocks me beyond expression to find the cause abused or made a shibboleth for the aims of the visionary, the fanatic, or the self-interested in any direction.

As I have already turned to the shadow side of the picture, and shall be loth to leave the noble field of divine

revealment in future chapters to follow out any other
tortuous aims of humanity under the name of Spiritualism,
I will e'en bridge over and anticipate many years of time
and notice now, in connection with the two preceding
narratives, one of the darkest eras that has ever overshadowed the Spiritual movement in America.

Returning on one occasion to the United States after
many travels in other countries, I learned, first by report,
and subsequently by personal observation, that a strange
new sect had arisen in the United States, originating, it
would seem, with persons of some mark and talent, and
commencing with popular appeals for reform in the
marriage laws. From this starting point arose a still more
dangerous but wide-spread epidemic of popular thought,
which has obtained the sobriquet of "The free love movement." I have already touched on this subject in my
"Nineteenth Century Miracles," and, *at the time*, written
extensively and bitterly enough against the prevalence of
this well-known "craze."

In this place it must suffice to say that as the origin of
the doctrines promulgated was attributed—and not without good cause—to certain members of the Spiritual ranks,
I, in my determined opposition to the possibility of
identifying the already tabooed cause of Spiritualism with
any teachings that might label it with a still more
obnoxious reputation, publicly announced my determination not to speak on any platform, or take part in any
organisation in which the advocates of the "Free-love'
movement were engaged.

As I might as well have attempted to stem the tides
of ocean as to stay the contagion of thought which had
grown up so suddenly and powerfully on the above-named
subject, nothing remained for me at the time being but to
announce my farewell lecture amongst the Spiritualists,
just so long as the leaders of the Spiritual cause allowed

the *known* advocates of the free-love doctrine any place on their rostrums.

As I had good reason to believe that these same doctrines were held in more *general* abhorrence in Boston than in any other city of the Eastern States, and that the committee of gentlemen who had engaged me in that city were as bitterly opposed to it as I was myself, so on the Sunday announced for my farewell I repaired with my husband to the Music Hall to fulfil my last engagement there. I must here state that besides the ordinary means of propagandism there was a paper published especially devoted to the ideas of the free-love party.

On arriving at the hall, the doorkeeper who admitted us informed my husband that one thousand copies of this paper had been sold at the door, and that the purchasers had all, as if by preconcerted arrangement, pressed up to the front rows of the magnificent building called the Music Hall, and planted themselves directly opposite the platform on which I was to speak.

To an audience of over three thousand people, surrounded as I was on the platform by a mixed assembly, I took leave of our noble and inspiring Spiritual cause. During the tremendous indictment that my Spirit Controls brought against any party who would allow the pure and elevating teachings of Spiritualism to be soiled by association with "Free-love" doctrines, hundreds of papers from the front rows of seats were flirted in defiance in my face. I heeded them not at that time, though I shrink and tremble now whilst I write at the memory of the terrible scene I then passed through.

The secular papers of Boston were all with me. Many warm friends came forward to support me, and the good Spirits cheered me with assurance of better days and unclouded skies, when the storm should pass away. It is enough to add that in the study of the curative powers of electricity, and in their practice with my husband, I spent the next few months still pleading for and defending my noble cause every Sunday evening in a hall hired by my husband, and well sustained by a large and sympathising attendance of Boston Spiritualists.

As for the epidemic of which I have been writing, like storms in general, whether physical, mental, or moral, it passed away, leaving not a few of those who had once been prominent in the "free-love" craze ashamed now to acknowledge that they had ever been identified with it. As to the original promulgators themselves, as I understand, they have sought and found fairer pastures for their operations and warmer sympathisers with doctrines which make animalism a philosophy and give licentiousness a place in ethics. In America, at least, amongst the most prominent and respectable portions of the Spiritual ranks, the sunshine of pure true Spiritualism has dispersed the midnight darkness which once enshrouded the noble cause (whose temporary obscurity is only remembered as the visions of an unquiet dream), which now marches on in due time and order until it is proved that startling reforms in one direction of human thought can for the time *pervert* but never ultimately divert the order of God's law as revealed in the impulse to " do right though the Heavens fall."

CHAPTER XVI.

FIRST VISIT TO THE PACIFIC COAST.

" I have wrestled stoutly with the wrong,
    And borne the right ;
From beneath the footfall of the throng,
    To life and light." —WHITTIER.

IT was in October, 1863, and during the height of the
great American Civil War which had then been raging for
two years, that I embarked on the " North Star " with two
friends as my room mates, and about twice as many
passengers as a fine ship of the Vanderbilt Line could
fairly accommodate, bound for California.

The aunt and niece who shared my state room were,
like myself, full of youthful spirit ; hence, we did not care
for the many inconveniences which beset our crowded
unaccommodations.

We talked of, and thought out history, when in the
course of our voyage we stopped and landed for a couple
of hours at San Domingo, trod on the ground discovered
by Christopher Columbus, and sat for a pic-nic lunch
beneath the shade of the ancient palm trees which formed
the great navigator's first audience chamber with the
hapless natives. It was fourteen days from the time when
we left New York before we landed at Aspinwall, where
we were greeted by crowds of monkeys wandering about
the place in every direction, and freely mingling with the
little brown semi-nude aboriginals, male and female, the
latter being dressed up in honour of the ship's arrival in
their full court costume—*i.e.,* gauze dresses, given them
by some of the white population of the town, and the
only garment worn over their brown bodies.

Amidst the crowds of parti-coloured inhabitants of this strange mélange of nations, I almost danced for joy to recognise "Charley Simonton," once the principal baritone of my early New York Choir, now come in his official capacity of American Consul at Panama, to superintend the transshipment of our steamboat's goods and passengers from Aspinwall to Panama.

As we were not to sail from Panama till the evening, and our official friend gladly accompanied us in our forty-five miles railroad journey across the Isthmus, by his favour we stopped when and wherever we pleased at any part of the road, and provided we were careful when we landed not to step on the huge alligators that lay by the roadside in mistake for logs of wood, we enjoyed our ride all the more for the privilege of calling now and then at the garden gates of some of the beautiful residences on the isthmus, and admiring the splendid blossoms, huge handfuls of which were freely given us. In this way we had a most delightful ride, enjoyed the scenery, the fruit, and the flowers, and arrived at Panama at midday.

Here I trod on another memorable spot, for Mr. Simonton took me in a boat to one of the islands in the beautiful Bay of Panama, memorable as the home of the band of daring pirates, headed by the once celebrated "Henry Morgan," whom King Charles II. of England, either in sport or mockery, knighted. It was this so-called "Sir Henry Morgan," that two hundred years later assumed the control of the renowned Davenport Brothers ; he, as a Spirit, alleging that his former career of crime and power gave him that peculiar physical strength which enabled him to perform those astonishing feats in returning to earth again which would have been impossible to more highly sublimated Spirits.

Now it is a fact that this very Spirit, "Morgan," is one and the same so often cited by the physical mediums of

England as the ubiquitous "John King." Without much interest in, or respect for, the Pirate Spirit, whose chief haunt I visited in his island home in the Bay of Panama, I still felt it a privilege to linger in a scene as famous in history as in my own career as a wandering Spiritualist. Meanwhile Mr. Simonton kept us highly entertained by recounting the many curious legends connected with the scenes around us.

Evening coming at length, we took a kind farewell of our friend, set off in a new steamboat on our long Pacific Ocean voyage, and landed at San Francisco, November the first, 1863. Here I was met by Mr. J. V. Mansfield, the celebrated medium for answering sealed letters, and a friend with whom and his family my mother and I had been intimately acquainted during our residence in Boston. Mr. Mansfield had been some months following his mediumistic profession in California, and, indeed, it was chiefly at his earnest solicitation, and by his advice, that I had then visited the country. My room mates were also met by their friends residing in a distant part of the State, and accompanied by them we all went to an hotel, where we hoped to find rest after our long voyage.

Mr. Mansfield, according to appointment, called on me in the evening, and evidently came freighted with intelligence of no very encouraging kind.

In the first place he spread out before me three huge twenty dollar gold pieces, which a Mr. John Birdsall, a good kind San Francisco Spiritualist, had sent me as a loan, seeing that "greenbacks," the only currency in use during the war in other American States, were sternly refused in California.

This was my first startling piece of news, compelling me to accept the loan in the same kind spirit in which it was tendered.

The next piece of information I received was no less

discouraging. Besides a perfect flock of worthless adventurers who had rushed off to the "land of gold," thrusting themselves as all such scum of society ever do on every new reform, and disgusting the citizens of the Pacific State with the very name of Spiritualism, Mr. Mansfield also informed me that a certain well-known party had come out to California to lecture, and left such a bad reputation behind him that the people were set bitterly against the entire cause, a prejudice which had been strengthened into deep antagonism by two idiots of the "John Gallagher" description—fools and fanatics ; such as cling to the skirts of every new movement and hope to harness their own petty hobbies to every advancing car of progress.

I knew nothing about the difference between gold and "greenback" currency; nothing of the crazy adventurers who had been disgracing a noble cause with their tricks and vices in California, and I had been led to expect that instead of going to an expensive hotel, a home, such as every place in the distant States had afforded me, would be open to receive me. I did not reproach poor Mr. Mansfield in words for suffering—nay, urging—me to come out under such fatal delusions ; but I thought it all, and began rapidly running over in my mind the possibility of my going down to the wharf the next day and humbly begging to be carried back to the States on the promise of future payment.

It was during these woeful mental speculations that four gentlemen called upon me, announcing themselves as Spiritualists, and professing their willingness and desire to serve me if they could. These gentlemen informed me that they had been cognisant of several meetings lately held in San Francisco, in which my advent as a Spiritual lecturer had been announced, and in which the parties in council, most of them members of the celebrated Californian "Vigilance Committee," had come to the conclusion to "steamboat" me. Upon enquiring what this phrase meant, I was told it was to put me out of California anyhow. What did my friends advise, then, in such an emergency? They replied. that they had heard I was in the habit of lecturing on astronomy, geology, social, and other sciences. Would I not introduce myself to the San Francisco people on these lines, and trust to future popularity to commence on the much-abused doctrines of Spiritualism?

I asked: "What can or must I do to secure a hearing?"

Answer: "Advertise in the daily papers lectures on some of the scientific subjects you are familiar with."

"How many papers are there in San Francisco?"

"Four."

"Then," I rejoined, "If you will call on me to-morrow I will have four advertisements ready of what I *will* and *can* do." -

This being agreed upon, the next morning two of the visitors called on me for the announcements in question.

I have, at present, no copy of those announcements, but I well remember their context. I said, I had understood that Spiritualism had been talked of and *misrepresented* in that State shamefully; that I, as a firm and determined Spiritualist, had come there on a long twenty-five days' voyage, to teach those who would listen, what Spiritualism really was.

I added, that I meant to lecture—meant to lecture on Spiritualism, and intended that all who were willing to listen to me should have an opportunity of doing so. If my audience did not approve of what I had to say, I would agree to be silent evermore in that city, and, if desired, would be prepared to quit the country; but go I would not, until I had been privileged to show that Spiritualism was divine—even if many so-called Spiritualists were simply human.

As may well be supposed, the good friends who had arranged to call for my advertisements, were considerably startled, if not shocked, at their tone; but finding me immovably opposed to modify them, they reluctantly departed with a considerable instalment of good John Birdsall's gold dollars to insert my advertisements in the daily papers, and hire Platt's Hall—the largest and finest in the city—for my lecture.

On the night appointed for my first appearance, a very large audience filled the splendid building, and received and listened to me with such genuine kindness and obvious interest, that I fearlessly announced a second lecture for the following SUNDAY.

This was indeed a bold and daring move, but it was one in the right direction and secured for me a triumph which never waned or faded.

I took a quiet lodging for myself—lived in restaurants— amongst multitudes of the kindest friends I have ever known, and surrounded by loose unfriended dogs, who also lived in dog communities in those early mining days in that city.

I stayed there lecturing three times every week for ten months, every lecture being crowded, and the warm-hearted, dear, good friends helping me, caring for me, and the people of the city loving me so dearly, that I look back upon those ten months as amongst the happiest of my wandering life.

Numbers of Mediums arose during the occasion of my first visit. I might have been there, by the urgent invitation of many of San Francisco's best citizens, to this day, but the word came then, as ever, from the higher Spheres, to "move on," and I did. I visited numerous important centres in the State, invited thither by some of the earnest Spiritualistic residents. I went through all sorts of strange scenes, encountering fact and fanaticism, fraud and faith each playing their alternate parts.

At length I came to Virginia City, the great centre of Nevada Territory—not then, even, a State. There was at that time a perfect *furore* in Nevada from the discovery of many rich silver mines; terrible corruption, wild enterprise, and stranger scenes than ever, before or since, were witnessed, prevailed in that place.

The Pacific railroad was not then built, and in response to an old Baltimore friend's pressing invitation to come to Virginia City to lecture, I had to make the journey thither through the wild Sierra Nevada mountains by the stage coaches, since celebrated by "Buffalo Bill" as the "Dead-wood Coaches."

Cheered in my long and fatiguing journeys with the remembrance of my parting promise to my dear San Francisco friends, that I would soon be amongst them again, my two chief objects in travelling so far and so constantly were, first, to spread abroad the tidings of the glorious faith to which I had devoted myself, and next to procure financial aid for the "Sanitary Fund," the aim of which was to provide hospitals for the wounded soldiers of the Union army ; clothe the ragged, help the widows and orphans of the martyred dead, and in a thousand ways to meet the exigencies of a war in which several millions of men had been suddenly called upon to leave home, family, and all they held dear on earth, to fight for the cause of freedom, and the safety of the great New World's Republicanism. I had vowed all through the war to devote my week-night earnings to the Sanitary Fund, reserving only my Sunday fees for the dear mother at home.

Arrived at Virginia City, and kindly cared for by my friend Colonel Meacham, I commenced my lectures at Macguire's Opera House, to thousands of kind supporters, and soon became popular enough to contribute piles of money to the Union cause. All this, of course, was taken charge of most thankfully by the Sanitary Committees which were established everywhere and in every district.

On one occasion an enthusiastic devotee of the Union cause had carried on his shoulders a sack of flour from place to place, exchanging flour for gold pieces to give to the Sanitary Fund. I had that sack of flour brought on the platform at one of my lectures, and placed in the midst of a Committee of the Sanitary Fund. The admission was free, but after my lecture I demanded help for the Soldiers and their Committee sitting around me, Almarin B. Paul, a great banker of the place, being my Chairman. That audience fairly pelted us with gold pieces. The stage was covered with them; and when those present thought they had not money enough, they threw Californian gold brooches, pins, and nuggets on the stage, which the Committee gathered up and stuck upon the sack. It is worth while to add that Mr. Almarin B. Paul, polished gentleman and eminent banker as he was, went out the next day in a large cart filled with a band of amateur musicians and the immortal sack of flour in their midst. Mr. Paul was the driver, the speaker, and the revivalist, and after an eight hours' pilgrimage in and about Virginia City, he returned at night with a contribution of twelve thousand dollars to the Sanitary Fund. I am in truth and in duty bound to add that Mr. A. B. Paul generously and even publicly attributed his success in procuring the enormous sum he returned with for the Soldiers' Sanitary Fund to the absorbing interest created by me on and at my previous Sunday's lecture at Macguire's Opera House.

CHAPTER XVII.

" Press on, press on, be bold, be brave,
Press on, press on, and thou shalt have
A sure reward at last."

DURING my first fifteen months' visit to the Pacific coast
my life was one constant scene of new and strange
adventure, the recital of which might prove equally
exciting and amusing did time and the limitations of space
permit of my so doing. As the watchwords of my present
undertakings are : " Press on ! " I shall merely say, as I
have before observed, that as the demand for aid to the
poor soldiers of the Union army was constant and
imperative, so every true man and woman in sympathy
with this side of the dreadful conflict, was taxed to the
utmost in purse and person to contribute to the working
departments of the Union army.

Amongst other resorts we used to hold "Sanitary
Fairs," in which, with merry mock auctions, we sold all we
could lay our hands on, good, bad, and indifferent.

Seeing that I was so constantly engaged in addressing
the public, my more *diffident* associates frequently called
upon me to be the auctioneer on the occasions of our
heterogeneous sales.

At the time of which I am writing, namely, in 1863 and
1864, Nevada (then only a northern Pacific Coast Territory),
was renowned for two products, and these were "sage
brush" and silver. The former was a species of wild
lavender, which covered the ground for hundreds of miles ;
the latter tunnelled the ground in almost the same pro-
portion. Trees, flowers, or even humble grasses were
unknown in Nevada, and nothing but the dismal grey sage
brush was to be seen betwixt earth and skies.

It was by way of introducing the mirthful element into
our otherwise pathetic occupation of aiding the necessitous
victims of the war, that I made one of my friends dig up
a root of the poor sage brush, plant it in a painted box of
earth, label it "Sanitary Sage Brush," and then, when the
auction was growing dull and flat, I brought out *my
treasure*, carefully covered up in white paper, and after
descanting glibly for some time upon the splendid object I
was about to display, and stimulating the curiosity of the
listeners to the highest pitch, I would gently withdraw the
cover, and exhibit the TREASURE in the form of a piece of
grey old sage brush !

Shouts of laughter inevitably followed the unveiling,
and amidst these favourable symptoms, I carried on my
auction, selling *the prize* again and again, but always
begging it back at the end of the play, until our committees
have realised as much as a hundred dollars at a single
mock auction.

At the close of the war in 1864, the editor of the *New
York Herald* (once one of my bitterest foes) affirmed, that
I had collected and donated to the Sanitary funds of the
Union cause "no less than twenty thousand dollars."

I am unable to pronounce upon the truth of this statement, as I never kept any record of the sums that I gained
for the Union committees, but this I do know, that my
poor sage brush alone earned some fifteen hundred dollars
in the way I have described above. I am now about to
refer, however, to what the said sage brush did FOR ME,
and that on a very memorable occasion, when my own
life was in danger. During my stay in Nevada I received
an invitation to lecture at a town in the Pacific Coast wilds,
some two hundred miles distant from Nevada, namely,
"Susanville," a place in Plumas Co. My correspondent
was a Dr. Chamberlain, surgeon to a garrison stationed
near Susanville, and as there was neither railroad or stage

road by which I could reach his station, only a rough way, beaten down by the ox waggons of the teamsters that in great numbers traversed those districts, so, he informed me he would send a good carry-all, two fine horses and a trusty youth to drive me, if I would consent to come.

The doctor added, that the young man he would send knew the road well, would arrange at all the places where I could stop each night, and his own good wife would be delighted to see and entertain me even if I would stay a twelvemonth.

The friends at Virginia City grumbled at my determination to accept the invitation, and prophesied all manner of disasters during my long journey. The Spirits urged me to go, and promised all manner of successes, and good to the cause.

I need hardly say the latter prevailed, and in due time, after my acceptance of Dr. Chamberlain's offer, the carry-all, drawn by two fine mustang horses, and driven by a bright intelligent youth of about eighteen, arrived to fetch me. As the last and only piece of advice I would follow from my Nevada friends, I let them take charge of my trunk containing all my earthly possessions.

This they were to send on to Sacramento, where I was engaged for a lecture course two months from that time. For the interim, I only took with me a valise, some light band-boxes, and my now famous " sanitary sage brush."

The reason why my friends urged this precaution was because quantities of " treasure " were sent through the districts in which I was to travel, although it was carefully guarded and all sorts of precautions, and even disguises, were resorted to, as the intervening country was so infested with brigands, that my poor trunk might have fallen a prey to the " gentlemen of the road."

At first, these suggestions made me feel nervous, but when after two days of peaceful travel no sight of a

Jack Sheppard or "Paul Clifford" appeared, the excitement of such a possibility faded away in delight at the varied scenery and amusement at my intercourse with the lonely people at whose places I was quartered.

I was beginning to be fearfully tired, however, as the evening of the third day's long pilgrimage began to close around me.

"Shall we never reach that Robinson's Ranch?" I asked of my driver.

"Seven long miles yet, ma'am," was the answer; "but I might make it a deal shorter by going through the sugar pine woods."

I was just about to ask, why in the name of wonder he didn't drive up there or anywhere, to keep us from dropping by the way with fatigue and hunger, when an authoritative voice shouted to us to "Stop!" and a band of some five men surrounded our carriage and began asking questions as to who we were, whither going, and where was *the expected treasure* hid away.

The poor driver's teeth chattered too fearfully to speak, and though I was very little more composed, I answered that I was only a visitor going to stop with Mr. Chamberlain. To this, one of the party replied, "Gammon," another "Bosh," and still another, "Why it's only a young woman and a lad; they ain't got nothing."

"Jist the same cusses that has said so; anyway, we're going to see what they have got, that's a fact. Now then! Get out."

Pistols in hand, and two of the party around with muskets, did not command our doings in vain. The driver descended. One of the band quite politely helped me out, whilst two more began inspecting the contents of the carriage.

Whilst tumbling over the articles in my valise, one of the party espied under the seat my carefully covered up sage brush. "Hallo, what's this?" he cried. Then snatching at the paper cover he discovered my poor sage brush, and read out in a loud voice the letters painted on the box—"SANITARY SAGE BRUSH. EMMA HARDINGE."

"Good God!" cried the man. "Are you, then, Emma Hardinge, and is this really *the* sage brush of which we have heard so much?"

"Even so," I murmured.

"Then, God bless you, Emma Hardinge, you have helped to save my life, and my poor brother's—since dead. God bless you, dear and good lady." Thunderstruck and amazed, I could only listen as the young fellow described how he and his brother had been soldiers, wounded in battle, being brought in carts to Philadelphia on a certain night a few months ago, when all the hospitals were "*chock full*" of victims. There was no place for them to stop at, but to lie in the street all night, saturated with blood from stumps of arms and legs shot off. It was then that kind nurses came along, and took them all into the "coopers' shop," which had been turned into a "soldiers' refreshment room," supplied with mattrasses, provisions, boots and shoes, nurses and doctors.

Since my name has often been connected with that building, and I have *now in my house* a handsome certificate recording the gratitude of the founders of this noble charity to me for services rendered, I may as well say that during a long engagement I fulfilled for the Philadelphia Spiritualists I gave all my week night earnings to this same Soldiers' Refreshment Room. It was at first designed to be only a temporary place of rest, but in the increasing exigencies of the war it became a regular hospital, and many a valuable life was preserved by the ready means it afforded of aid to the wounded soldiers. Of course the voluntary contributions of money and goods, which were the sole means of supporting this institution, were highly prized, and humble as was the assistance that I could give, it was sufficient to render my name amongst others deeply cherished by the sufferers who benefited from this excellent charity.

It so happened also that the kind people who had charge of this building thought it would be a relief to the poor souls who could sit up and listen, as well as an advertisement for the place and its purpose, if I gave some lectures in the large refreshment room adjoining the hospital. This I used to do once a week, always calling for and obtaining a handsome collection for the hospital at the close of my addresses. Thus both my name and personality became known to the poor men sheltered in this place; and thus it was that the one-legged discoverer of the little sage brush and another battered ex-soldier, one of the band, came forward with the warmest greetings and apologies for *annoying* me, mixed up with pathetic reminiscences of their stay in the Philadelphia temporary Hospital, of which they affirmed, with equal vehemence and *falsity*, that I was the founder. The sage brush next came in for its share of admiration, especially when a young fellow, who seemed to act as the leader of the band, came forward and placed in my hand a slip of paper, on which was written in pencil, but in a good clear hand— "Pass Emma Hardinge and the Sanitary Sage Brush, for John Melville, Honey Lake Valley." "This," the donor explained, with a significant wink, "might be useful in case you should happen to meet any more of *our* people; you know, ma'am." I did know; and though I had not the honour of any future encounters of that sort, I was not sorry to have such a *pass* through the wild and lonely regions in which I now found myself. I must add that when my new friends had replaced my little belongings, and respectfully handed me back into the carriage, one of their number humbly asked if I would honour them by stepping into a neighbouring shanty close by and partaking of a little refreshment. This I declined on the plea of the lateness of the hour; but having begged and obtained a pail of water for the poor horses, we shook hands all round, and with uncovered heads and waving hats, those poor lost creatures set up such a cheer as I drove off as re-echoes in my memory even to this day. If it be asked how it came about that men who had helped to serve their country as soldiers should have been unable to find any better occupation when disabled than brigandage, I must answer that in a sudden and improvised war, wherein millions of men were engaged, the worst as well as the best of characters were pressed into service, besides which, to provide even medical aid and temporary shelter for the wounded was often a difficult problem, much less to organise pension lists or maintenance for the disabled.

I must pass over my final arrival at my destination, the warm welcome I received from Dr. Chamberlain, his dear wife and son, and the many scenes of adventure, Spiritual aid, and delightful intercourse which illumined my five weeks' stay in that remote yet busy and enchanting valley. Although my kind entertainers combined in begging me to prolong my stay for months instead of weeks, the imperative word had come to "move on," and on I had to go.

My next engagement was at a station above a hundred miles from Susanville, and in a wild mountain district called Indian Valley. This place I had been entreated to visit for the purpose of delivering a Fourth of July oration, that being the Independence Day of America, and the occasion on which all parts of the great New World unite in celebrating the birth of their grand Republic.

I found that Dr. and Mrs. Chamberlain had friends whom they occasionally visited in Indian Valley, and when I agreed to accept the invitation of my correspondent, a Mr.

Blood, to deliver the oration, a feat of oratory which I had frequently performed before, my good host and hostess kindly promised to drive me themselves and accompany me on my two days' journey to Indian Valley.

Our ride was delightful, our night encampment no less charming, and that despite the visit of the poor harmless beast they call there the California lion; our wanderings in sugar-pine forests, gathering pine burrs, not less than two feet in length—all was enchantment and happiness until the third of July, when my kind companions took leave of me at the door of Mr. Blood's house, and passed on to visit their own friends.

I soon found that Mr. Blood's history was in Indian Valley precisely the same as that of George Smith's at Rondout.

Besides the fact that poor Mr. Blood had, like my Rondout friend, to encounter all sorts of opposition on the question of Spiritualism, there being but few of that persuasion in the vicinity, Mr. Blood was crippled from the effects of a severe accident, and was only enabled to walk with two crutches, whilst, worse than all, he was determinately opposed in politics to most of his near neighbours, he being an ardent Republican, whilst they were what was then called ultra Democrats or "copperheads."

When he related to me all the bitter struggles he had gone through, especially in the act of his having engaged a Spiritualist, a *lady*, and "an Englishwoman," to deliver a Fourth of July Oration, I certainly did wonder at my host's temerity, and still more at what my fate would be about that time next day.

When the eventful morning arrived, I put on my best summer attire, with something of the sentiments which I imagined might have possessed the martyrs of old, when preparing for death by fire, or the beasts of the amphitheatre.

My poor crippled friend walked on one side of me, my good hostess, with her veil down to conceal her pale face and tearful eyes, clinging close to me on the other side.

Arrived at the speaker's stand we found a large party of Indians, with war hatchets and tomahawks, surrounding the stand, just as Mr. Blood had placed them the night before to prevent its being pulled down by the opposition, *for the third time.* The scene in which I was to speak was literally what the place was styled, namely, "the washbowl of the mountains," shut in on every side by vast ranges of the Sierras, the winds howled dismally through the canŏns and gave forth a wailing sound which some of the anxious women present likened to a "prophetic dirge" for what was to happen.

There was an immense concourse of people around the stand, some seated on the ground, others in traps, carts, or on horseback.

After I had mounted the platform, the old gentleman who presided made a few remarks which nobody seemed to hear, and then proceeded to read the famous Declaration of Independence from a book, the leaves of which were continually blown over and over by the wind.

"I am afraid you won't be able to read a word of your speech for the wind," the old gentleman said to me in a hoarse whisper.

"I don't think I shall," I replied, laughing at the bare idea of my *reading* a speech.

What I had to say being upon the History of Nations, America in especial—The principles of true freedom— National life, and the history, power, and possibilities of the grand New World; taking for my text also the famous passage, "GOVERNMENTS WERE INSTITUTED FOR THE BENEFIT OF THE GOVERNED," all shades of politicians and religions in that immense assembly were satisfied, none hurt, none dissenting.

The cheers grew into shouts; the clapping of hands into perfect leaps and yells of applause; and at the end of about an hour's address (without experiencing a shade of hoarseness), I was literally pelted with flowers.

The women kissed my dress, and held up their dear little children for me to kiss also, whilst the men almost wrung my arm out, and my hand off, with grips and shaking.

The climax was reached when Mr. Blood cried out, "Now, friends, you'll all be at the Sanitary Fair to-night."

Then arose a perfect scream of—"And the lady, too—the lady, too!"

"Yes," I said, "I'll be there, and be one of the auctioneers, too." I then descended to join Mr. and Mrs. Blood.

Fortunately, we had scarcely more than a quarter of a mile to go, or I think I should have got home minus my hat and feathers, which I kept nodding and nodding in "good byes till the evening." Arrived at home, after each of us had enjoyed a hearty good cry for very gladness, and just as we were about to sit down to dinner, Mrs. Blood cried, pointing to the front garden gate, "Look there!" Round that gate was a party of at least a dozen men on horseback, who to Mr. Blood's anxious enquiry of what they wanted, replied, they wished to see the lady, *to decide a wager*.

In a minute I was out with them, when one of their party, doffing his hat, said, "We are told, madam, that you claim to make all your public speeches through Spirit influence. May we ask, is that so?"

"Undoubtedly," I replied.

"Why we ask, madam," said the spokesman, "is this. We have a heavy wager on the matter. I say I know for a certainty who the Spirit is that spoke to-day. Others say it isn't so. Now, dear lady, won't you please decide the wager, and tell us who the Spirit was?"

"I will do so," I said, "on one condition. You shall write down the name of who you think it was. I will write the name of who I know it was. We will then compare notes."

In a few seconds, Mr. Blood procured us pens, ink, and paper. I wrote: "*The Spirit that controlled me this morning was General Edward Baker.*"

Our horseman wrote: "*If that was a Spirit that spoke this morning, it was my former General, Ned Baker, killed at the battle of Bull Run.*"

When another of the party read out the two papers, consecutively, more shouts and more cheers followed.

Then still another of the party tried to explain to me that which I knew already, namely, that Edward Baker was an Englishman, and a lawyer by profession.

When the war broke out, this gallant gentleman, a warm partizan of the Northern side, entered the army, rose step by step, renowned for his bravery, until he was killed at the battle of Bull Run. "He was my commander, Mrs. Hardinge," said the first speaker, "but before the war I have heard him speak many and many a time. I knew his style, his manner, his very words, and if ever I heard Ned Baker in my life, I heard him this very morning on your platform."

The night's auction followed, the next morning's fare-wells were exchanged, and then, the *adieus*, spoken to beautiful Indian Valley and its warm-hearted friends—for ever—on earth. . . . Back again to my home at ocean-girt San Francisco.

What tales I had to tell! What adventures to narrate! Scenes and places, and incidents crowding upon each other, such as would fill volumes!

I shall give but one more phase of my California life, and though the narrative is all too full of myself to satisfy me, besides its being an oft-told tale, it relates to scenes of

too much importance in the history of a memorable cause
to be omitted in this place.

The record from which I am about to quote is a small
pamphlet got up by the late Benjamin Coleman, a wealthy
and influential gentleman, and a well-remembered and
esteemed Spiritualist, of London, one of the first friends to
welcome me on my return with my mother to England,
in 1866.

Arrangements having been made for me to give three
lectures on "America," in St. James's Hall, London, Mr.
Coleman, at his own expense, got up and distributed by
thousands the pamphlet which I am about to quote as
illustrative of my closing work two years previously in
California. I may add that as the pamphlet in question
was compiled entirely from the American papers, the
record may be accepted as a more truthful one than if it
had been written by a too partial friend for a special
occasion.

The title page of the pamphlet is thus inscribed :—

MRS. EMMA HARDINGE'S POLITICAL CAMPAIGN.

*For the Union Party of America on the occasion of the Presidential
Election of 1864.*

Mrs. Emma Hardinge is widely known throughout the United
States of America as one of the most eloquent advocates of the
Spiritual Philosophy. Her name has for years been identified
with a widely-spread and philanthropic effort to ameliorate the
condition of poor fallen women, amongst whom her missionary
labours have obtained for her the designation of "The Outcast's
Friend."

Mrs. Hardinge's eloquent discourses have frequently been
delivered in the jails and penitentiaries of the United States, and
many touching incidents are related of her visits to the cell of the
prisoner.

Since the commencement of the late American War she has devoted a large part of her time and services to the aid of the soldiers' families, hospitals, and funds ; and has held a prominent place as a political speaker in the Union cause.

As Mrs. Hardinge is comparatively unknown in this her native country, a few friends, interested in procuring for her an impartial hearing before an English audience, have thought it advisable to circulate the following sketch of one passage in her public career, which cannot fail to interest all who sympathised with the Union cause in America during the eventful period referred to.

From a work entitled "Sketches of California," we learn that after having lectured through California and Nevada, making what the American journals admitted to be an unprecedented success, and establishing her reputation as a "wonderful and eloquent speaker," she determined to return to the Eastern States to recruit her exhausted strength after her fifteen months of indefatigable labour.

At a farewell reception tendered by her numerous friends, an urgent requisition, with an immense number of signatures, was presented to her, begging that she would hold a final public meeting, and in view of the agitating political contest prevailing in anticipation of the next Presidential Election, which was to decide the fate of the nation, Mrs. Hardinge was requested to take for her subject, "The Coming Man ; or The Next President of the United States."

Mrs. Hardinge consented, but as her time in the States was limited to ten days, the promised lecture was arranged to take place three days after the request was made.

The high reputation of the lecturer, and the deep interest which the announcement of such a subject awakened in San Francisco, sufficed to crowd the great hall at so early a period that an hour before the set time for commencement already two thousand persons were seated, and nearly as many more were standing within and without the hall anxiously awaiting the appearance of the lecturer.

From this point we follow the narrative of the writer herself, which was printed in the New York and California journals shortly after the occurrences they describe.　Mrs. Hardinge writes thus :—

"For years I had been lecturing to masses of people, many of whom I knew were opposed to the opinions I advocated.　On occasions of great social and religious interest I had often been called upon to address assembled thousands, but never had I stood face to face with a mass of persons so moved by a sense of deep feeling as that which had gathered this assembly together.

"It would scarcely have mattered who was the orator; the subject announced was the chord that had vibrated through that thronged city, and drawn that eager multitude together : they had come to listen to an address on 'The Coming Man; or The Next President of America.'　No doubt every voter present had already predetermined which side he would espouse, nor did he expect to hear aught that could induce him to change his opinion; but the feverish anxiety which throbbed in the national pulse in those days, urged the multitude to hear the prevailing thought of the hour discussed, and the passionate flow of their own fervid street oratory echoed.

"I knew that the entire disruption of the Union of American States, the enfranchisement of six millions of human beings from slavery, besides countless other problems of national interest, were all to be solved by the simple act of individuals recording a preference between Abraham Lincoln or George McClellan as next President of America.　I knew the political history of the country. I also knew much of the life of one of the candidates, and quite enough of that of the other to determine that if in my own person the division of every atom of my mortal form could ensure for each atom a corresponding vote for Abraham Lincoln, I would cheerfully have devoted myself as a willing sacrifice upon the altar of American liberty to secure his election.　.　.　.　.

"Let any one who has traced the history of America's uncrowned king, from the backwoods of old Kentucky to the White House at Washington, and followed his career as the woodsman's boy, farm servant, boatman, petty clerk, lawyer's drudge, then partner; captain of a militia company, then advocate, legislator, Congressman, and, lastly, President of the New World, and Commander-in-

Chief of an army of eight hundred thousand men, and those who have followed this wonderful career may judge what a case I had to plead, and one showing that the power that had made the title of 'the rail splitter' one of the earth's noblest patents of nobility, had been the power of honesty, the might of integrity, the strength of goodness, and the light of genius.

"In truth it was no merit to plead for Abraham Lincoln, and only required a fearless hand to strip away the mask of political prejudice from his honest face, and a glib tongue to rehearse in its true proportions the details of his noble life, to enshrine him where he belonged, in the affections of every true American, and the honour and respect of every true man or woman of all countries.

"I, in especial, may look back with glad memory to that night when, in my first public plea uttered in his honour, I declared that the day was not far distant when every true American would say, that 'If George Washington was the father of his country, Abraham Lincoln was its preserver.'

"If cheers and tears, warm pressures of hands, and showers of blessings, but above all a noble roll of unexpected votes which the next day's record showed in favour of my client, could have been reward to any one, I was repaid indeed for that one night's work.

"The next morning brought to my apartments two or three acquaintances deeply interested in the Union cause, and who were urgent upon me to go out and 'stump the State for Lincoln.' Of course these suggestions were *unofficial*.

"The Union State Central Committee, whose campaign orators were clergymen, Congressmen, men of the highest place, wealth and talent, but always *men*, could not for a moment condescend to the indignity of employing a professsional speaker, and that speaker *a woman*. Yet whilst this was understood to be the sentiment of the committee, *as a committee*, divers were the persons that day, in uncommittee-like fashion, who urged me to perform the work which they needed.

"It may be questioned why I hesitated to undertake what my avowed interests in the cause may appear to have rendered a duty incumbent upon me; I answer that I had already had to *conquer* my way to public favour, amidst every imaginable obstacle that prejudice against a female speaker and bigotry against my faith could array to crush me. I had been *permitted* to lecture for the benefit of soldiers' funds, because money was imperatively needed; I had been *allowed* to speak for charitable institutions, for the mere advantages to be obtained; but to invade the sphere of politics was a step too daring to contemplate.

" And in addition to the terrible repulsiveness which a political election of such a gigantic character was to open up to the action of a female campaign speaker, the country had been suffering from a whole year's drought, and the ordinary furnace heat of California, and incessant travel over roads made of boulders like those of California at that time, made the prospect of the proposed campaign an act, which, to unaided reason, seemed little short of actual insanity. I resolved it would be better to endure the pain of refusing such a service than to fail in the attempt, to say nothing of being exposed to the taunts of a ribald opposing press, the execrations of a political mob, or perhaps the tar and feathers of an insensate multitude. At last, fairly worn out by incessant solicitations, I purchased my ticket for a passage to the Eastern States, announced my immediate departure, and prepared for an early flight. It was just six days after the delivery of my lecture on 'The Coming Man,' that I received a visit from the treasurer of the Union Central Committee of California, by whose earnest appeals in behalf of the cause as dear to my heart as to that of my eloquent and esteemed visitor, all my scruples were overcome, and I parted from this gentleman at last, pledged to speak for the Union party every night up to the day of the election as far as human strength and power would allow.

" The chief difficulty that arose between me and my kind visitor was as to the terms of the compact between us.

" The Committee agreed to pay all my expenses, arrange all my meetings, send me from place to place, transact all preliminary business, and pay me any sum I chose to demand.

" The special fee I required, however, was more than my friend chose to promise me, for it was nothing more nor less than the ELECTION OF ABRAHAM LINCOLN. If I took more, I argued, the people would not trust me; less than that I would not risk my life for. Mr. S. mildly replied that as he did not believe in my sybilline powers of prophecy, he could not promise me the price I asked ; but if, as he justly argued, I had sufficient faith in my own powers of prevision to accept such terms, he could do no less than accede to them. Both parties being thus satisfied, we parted on the condition that I should deliver lectures constantly up to the time of the election according to my utmost capacity, taking as my pay the election of Mr. Lincoln.

"From that time up to the day of the polling, I delivered in thirty-eight days thirty-two lectures, each address usually occupying some two hours or more in delivery, and the time spent in congratulations and greetings.

" These lectures were given in different places, obliging me to travel, in oppressive heat and dust, from twenty to forty miles each day. I was, besides, often stopped on the road by vast multitudes and compelled to deliver a speech from my carriage, or a mountain rostrum by the wayside. I was often obliged to pause on my way to and from the large cities in which my meetings had been arranged, to address a mining camp or an extemporised mass meeting, gathered together in the midst of Nature's halls, such as California's wild mountains and giant forests afforded.

"Sometimes the largest buildings were found insufficient for the multitudes that thronged to hear the female speaker—the now renowned 'Campaign Orator '—and my friends were obliged to remove the windows and even the frame walls of their halls.

"Scaffolds were erected in every available place ; bonfires were lighted to stretch away into field and forest to make room for the vast multitudes that came to listen. Sometimes I spoke from the balconies of the hotels where I was planned to stop, whilst to summon the multitudes to the meetings rockets, fireballs, and salutes of cannon were employed.

"Sometimes my audiences assembled in long processions of two or three thousands, carrying lighted torches and paper lanterns, preceded by flags, and marshalled by bands of music, and thus they would form around my platform, and with the flare of torches below and the silver light of heaven's eternal lamps above my head, I spoke to eager multitudes of the stupendous issues of a contest that was to determine the destiny of the great New World. Who would not have been inspired in such scenes as these ? And let it be remembered, that never, on one single occasion, did I receive a word of insult, or even interruption, except from the prolonged and enthusiastic cheers of my auditory ; neither must it be supposed that these tokens of approbation were due to the presence of partisans alone. It was generally acknowledged that the opposite party, who would not honour the meetings of the male campaign speakers for fear of swelling their numbers, resorted to mine in multitudes, moved to do so, no doubt, by curiosity and the novelty of the occasion.

" The result, however, was a large accession to their roll of voters, and an aid in enabling them to flash across their wires the splendid majority of those thousands which have enwreathed the name of the Golden State with the ' Loyal California !'

" Many were the touching, many the ludicrous passages of this campaign of mine.

" My matter-of-fact committees had heard, and ' pooh-poohed' my claim of speaking ' only as the spirit gave me utterance.' Some amongst them, however, questioned me in private seriously on the subject, confessing their astonishment at the continuation of my unflagging strength and never-failing *memory*. Sometimes they followed me from place to place, commenting with astonishment on the variety of the addresses, which I believe were generally adapted to the hour and varying circumstances of each meeting. Many a time I have been folded to the hearts of weeping women, who loved ' Father Abraham,' and thanked God that one of their own sex, at last, could echo the fervent prayers and blessings they had put up for him to heaven, in the ears of the world. Many a time my hand has been clasped in the rough grasp of the miner, or half crushed in the warm pressure of the mechanic, as he cried, ' Thank God for thee, brave lady, and thank Old England for sending thee to our help.'

" On the eighth of November, 1864, the thirty-ninth day from the time I set forth, I took my pay in full for all my labour in the triumphant election of Abraham Lincoln as President of the still United States of America. . . . ."

When next Mrs. Hardinge spoke of Abraham Lincoln it was exactly thirty-six hours after his fearful martyrdom, when, by the request of some of the citizens of New York, she delivered the first oration in that city on his death—an oration which has been pronounced by the best critics a masterpiece of composition and eloquence.

When next she beheld his honoured face it was in the old Independence Chamber of the State House, Philadelphia. In that place, where the sires of the American nation had signed the famous instrument which made America a nation ; and there with the painted faces of all that nation's heroes, veiled in the drapery of death, face to face with the only uncovered canvas on the walls, which bore the effigy of Washington, "the Father of his country," lay Abraham Lincoln—*its preserver*—dead !

In closing this rough but most truthful sketch of my first visit to Calfornia, I cannot do better than by reproducing the improvised poem with which I took leave of my good San Francisco friends on the last occasion of my farewell social gathering with them. The poem, taken down and subsequently printed by some of the numerous press reporters, reads thus :—

FAREWELL TO CALIFORNIA.

By Emma Hardinge.

Farewell to the land of the sunset and gold,
    The wild and the wonderful West,
Where the curtains of evening the dying day fold,
    As it sinks in the ocean to rest.

Farewell to the mountains, whose giant peaks rise,
    Like the hands of huge Titans upreared,
To write with their fingers of snow in the skies
    Their history so ancient and weird.

Coast range of brown hills, which the Sea Kings have tossed
　From the waste of the storm-beaten shore,
Stretching far, far away, till in mist they are lost—
　I shall gaze on their bleak face no more.

Oh, mammoth green forests o'er whose solemn brows
　The ages eternal have rolled,
Writing records of centuries on your green boughs,
　Which the history of man leaves untold.

Oh, valley and gorges, whose dark depths profound
　The foot of the hunter ne'er trod—
Whose stillness was never yet broken by sound,
　Save the voice of great Nature and God.

Hoarse roar of the cataract, wild clash of the flood,
　Tinkling stream like the lone mountain's bell;
Pattering rain drops as precious as Nature's heart-blood;
　Endless wealth of spring-blossoms, farewell!

Farewell to the myriads of faces up-turning
　In wonder to gaze in my own—
They, around me like stars of the night, fixed and burning,
　I, a wild-flying meteor, alone.

Farewell to the love, which, with many a blessing,
　Has strewed my rough road with sweet flowers;
To the hate which the bigot lip, scarcely suppressing,
　Has clouded my day with dark hours;

To the wild shout of triumph, the greeting, the cheer,
　The applause of the multitude's breath,
The hiss of the serpent which falls on the ear
　With the purpose of poison and death.

To the dear, very few, who may greet me no more
　Till the sun, never setting, shall shine
On them and the wanderer on Heaven's cloudless shore,
　And their loved hands again clasp in mine.

Farewell to them all—wondrous people and land,
  All my blessings I give thee again!
Thy curses, alas! must return to the hand
  That has launched them against me in vain.

As I pass through the Golden Gate closing for aye
  On the footprints I've made in the land,
Though my memory in sunset that evening may die,
  This promise eternal shall stand:

For the welcome the wanderer has met on thy shore,
  Thou hast angels received in thy home,
Who shall bear for the land of the West evermore
  Her record in God's Kingdom come.

CHAPTER XVIII.

" All things that are on earth shall wholly pass away,
Except the love of God, which shall live and last for aye."
                                                    —BRYANT.

FOR about two years after my return from California, I pursued the same unresting course of missionary labour to which I had been previously devoted.

At length I felt impelled to yield to my dear mother's urgent entreaties that we should return to her much loved native land, and " retire into private life."

Although without much expectation of realising any such views of our future destiny, I was quite willing to give my good mother the opportunity of revisiting her own country, were it only for the sake of temporary rest, and renewal of old associations.

Having received from my kind American friends the warmest tokens of their high appreciation, we embarked on our homeward bound voyage with many loving fare-wells and prophetic assurances of our speedy return.

It was on the night previous to our expected landing at Liverpool that one of those " visions " which has always formed a marked phase of my mediumship, was presented to me.   I thought I saw an immense ship, bound, like our own, for England.   On board this ship were tens of thousands of Spirit people of all ranks and classes, amongst whom were scattered numerous North American Indians.   The entire throng was marshalled by the only Red Indian Spirit that has ever controlled me, " Arrowhead," a glorious being of gigantic proportions, and whom I have good reason to believe has exercised his beneficent protecting power over me on many occasions of imminent peril.

Presently I saw, our ship sail into port, its visionary hosts landing and stretching out under the direction of their Indian leader, until they filled every town, city, village, and street of England. As they passed on their way, I saw that, though so plain and life like to me, they were assuredly Spirits, and invisible to the people whom they encountered.

None saw them, but all felt their passage. The rush of the mighty hosts stirred all things around them as in a resistless wind. Added to this, they struck right and left at all the people they passed, and these, not beholding their invisible assailants, turned angrily upon each other, until the entire land was a scene of discord and contention. The invisible hosts struck at the grandest palaces and the tallest buildings, until some fell, and the foundations of others were shaken. They struck at the churches wherein the wondering people sought refuge, but the tottering walls and crumbling columns, the broken images, and ruined ornaments, compelled the refugees to fly into the woods and fields, where all was peaceful and quiet.

At length the mighty iconoclasts ranged themselves before St. Paul's Cathedral, which I at once perceived to be representative of the National State Church. Here the work of demolition proceeded with such force and speed that I soon expected to see the great edifice become a shapeless ruin. When, however, the huge dome fell, and the cross that surmounted it was sinking amidst the ruins, "Arrowhead" snatched it up, and for the first time I heard him speak and say: "This emblem has been held dear to the human heart, and is the visible symbol of such religion as the people alone can understand. It is too sacred to be lost amidst the ruins. Take it then," he cried, as he lifted it up towards the heavens, "and keep it until the people of earth know better how to use it, than to fall down and worship it." As he spoke, a luminous

cloud in the sky opened, and countless little white hands
stretching down to receive it, he tossed it up towards
them. They caught and carried it away, and disappeared
behind the clouds.

Then for the first time, turning to me, " Arrowhead "
said: "Behold! the soldiers of the new Reformation!
Amidst the unrest, discord, and contention caused by these
invisible warriors, all things are coming into judgment.
Mourn not that ·we strike down or uproot the old, the
effete, and the idolatrous. Before the soul of man can
enter the new heaven, it must grow into manhood on the
new earth, and the Lord and Master of life Himself cannot
lay the foundations of the new, the true, and the beautiful,
as long as the ground is occupied with the worn out ashes
of the dead past. When the clamour of war and the
voice of strife is in thine ear, child, look aloft, and the
dawning light of the new Reformation shall assure thee
' The morning cometh.' "

Arrived at my native land, and installed in a pleasant
lodging in old Chelsea, London, the quiet retirement my
mother had anticipated was not of long continuance.
Hosts of Spiritual friends found us out, and soon
persuaded me, alike from a sense of duty and responsibility, to enter upon a course of winter evening lectures,
first to large and aristocratic assemblies in a handsome
semi-private hall, and finally to well-announced gatherings
of the public in regularly organised Sunday meetings.

Amongst the many noble and esteemed friends whom I
met in my first missionary work in 1866, in London, were
Mr. and Mrs. Howitt, Mr. and Mrs. S. C. Hall, Mr.
Benjamin Coleman and his family, Mr. Robert Cooper, the
proprietor and founder of the *Spiritual Times*, Mrs.
Macdougal Gregory, Drs. Ashburner and Elliotson, Mrs.
de Morgan, and a perfect host of titled, aristocratic, and in
many instances *illustrious personages*, all devoted to, or
interested in, the cause of Spiritualism.

It must suffice to say that retirement from the public work of the movement was simply impossible on my part. My old friend, Dan Home, was then in England, and active as usual in manifesting his wonderful phenomenal powers; but that, chiefly, amongst his aristocratic friends and illustrious patrons. Mrs. Everitt also, one of the best and most wonderful mediums of this or any other age, was in high request, especially amongst the aristocratic classes, who would not condescend to consult professional mediums.

As Mr. Everitt was at this time in business in London, and he and his noble and gifted wife gave abundant hospitality to their visitors, as well as *free* circles, it is needless to say they were thronged alike with visitors and solicitations to attend private circles in the most aristocratic and influential quarters.

I may here state that it was my good fortune to include dear Mr. and Mrs. Everitt amongst my earliest and warmest FRIENDS, as well as amongst my mediumistic assistants, the *former* relations of which I hope to retain until we all meet again in the higher and better world.

It would be almost impossible for me to number up the eminent and even illustrious believers in the great cause of Spiritualism, who met and greeted me on my first arrival in London, and who professed open allegiance to Spiritualism and its wonderful revelations. Professors Alfred Russell Wallace and Crookes, and hosts of other scientists, to say nothing of those distinguished aristocrats who, in a country of *caste* and *class* exercised the most profound influence upon Society, were amongst the most earnest enquirers and the warmest supporters of the Spiritual movement at the period of my return to England in 1866.

Should the question be asked me, Where are these influential powers and potencies now? I should be obliged to refer the querists to the annals of the life hereafter to

which many of the earliest and warmest of the English
Spiritualists have passed on, or to the effects which antagonistic public opinion has produced upon the least worthy
of its early supporters.

As I have made some twenty-six ocean voyages during
my missionary efforts to promote the cause of Spiritualism
in different parts of the world, I shall only recur now and
then to these changes. In reference to my first return
to America, after about one twelvemonths' residence in
England, I may say that during my first period of absence
from the United States I was besieged with earnest
entreaties and not a few temptations to return,

It was towards the close of my first year in England,
then, that my brave mother united her entreaties to those
of my American friends that I would go back to the life
and enterprise of the bright progressive New World.

As an illustration of the eminent favour in which
Spiritualism and its advocates were held by the upper
classes of English society during my first year of residence
amongst them, I may mention that when it was known
that my mother and I were about to return to the United
States, a splendid farewell reception was tendered me at
St. George's Hall, Langham Place, on which occasion a
vast concourse of friends, including authors, writers,
scientists, and titled personages of the highest position in
the land formed the assemblage, Gerald Massey, the
renowned poet and writer, being the chairman of this
memorable gathering. Towards the close of the meeting
a finely illuminated testimonial was presented to me (now
hanging up in the study wherein I am writing), the
chief value of which consists in the signatures of the
good friends who were instrumental in making the
presentation.

After some months of work and residence in America,
ever most dear to me as the land of my Spiritual birth, we

were induced to return to England again at the entreaty
of our now only living relative, my sister Margaret, whose
husband having been appointed manager of St. George's
Hall, London, they besought us, the two last of the once
large family circle, to combine with them in making a home
together. This change, being equally acceptable to each of
our little family quartette, was readily effected, especially
as I proposed to reserve some quiet hours for writing and
compiling a great work assigned me by the good Spirits,
whose servant I was and am, namely, the origin, history,
and progress of the first twenty years of Spirit Communion in America, under the title of "Modern American
Spiritualism." I devoted all the time I could spare to this
work from the inevitable duties of receptions, séances,
and lectures, all of which pressed in upon me with ever-
increasing urgency.

Having completed my great literary undertaking, and
settled my dear mother in a pleasant home under charge
of my good sister and her husband, I prepared myself for
my next transit to America, with a view of publishing my
book in the land and amongst the people most interested
in the important record.

Prior to undertaking this new departure, however, I
agreed to accept an engagement that had been long
pressed upon me, namely, to visit Scotland, and deliver
three lectures in Glasgow. As the circumstances attending this engagement were of a somewhat remarkable
character, I will here pause upon a brief description of
their procedure.

The lectures were to take place in the Merchants'
Hall, Glasgow, and although one or two other speakers
had already appeared there in the capacity of Spiritual
Missionaries, the field was not deemed a very favourable
one, and it was only at the kind solicitation of Mr. Hay
Nesbitt, by whose family I was most hospitably entertained,

that I consented to break ground in Glasgow City, still in some measure dominated by the stern Presbyterian opinions of John Knox. My engagement was for three week-evening lectures, and although they seemed to me to be coldly listened to and received, they were deemed by my kind allies so unprecedentedly successful—especially the last one, when a committee of the audience chose the subject—that I was entreated to stay over the Sunday and speak in a free open meeting in the afternoon. I know there were many amongst my warmest supporters who deemed this experiment a somewhat dangerous one, and, for my own part, I had heard so much about the conservatism of a city where, even in their grandest old church, the use of an organ was forbidden, and the Sundays were generally observed as days of Sabbatarian penance, that I was scared at the mere thought of a woman and a Spiritualist getting up to preach on a Glasgow Sabbath. "Never fear," said one of my committee, "there will be at least five thousand of the population drunk in the streets on Saturday night, and it is quite doubtful if they will be sufficiently recovered by Sunday afternoon to get up a row." For the truth of the first part of this consoling speech I can certainly answer, as Mr. and Mrs. Nesbitt took me a drive through the city on Saturday evening, and even then, before nine o'clock, I don't think I ever saw so many intoxicated people reeling through the streets as I saw on that one occasion.

Another thing that I saw was the announcements of my own Sunday lecture in what I deemed to be unnecessarily large letters, and my only hope was that the rain, which had been long threatening, would fall in sufficient torrents to wash them away. Contrary to expectation, however, the day was fine, and when the cab with myself and friends drove up to the short street in which Merchants' Hall was situated, the crowd was so great that we had to drive round to another street, and enter the building by a back way.

In the ante-room I found my committee assembled, all of them looking very grave, and one or two decidedly pale as well as anxious.

Already a committee of the audience had been formed, and a subject chosen before I took my place on the platform. The subject chosen was, " What are the proofs of man's immortality ? "

The scene which met my eyes as I first stood on the platform was certainly an unparalleled one in my experience. The hall was crowded to suffocation, and, with the exception only of *three* women, that vast assemblage was all composed of men, and these offering me the greatest insult they could by every one wearing their hat. The platform was as crowded as the auditorium, but it was by my kind committee, who stood, with uncovered heads, *close* around me.

I took the hymn book, and after naming the hymn and calling attention to the fact that there were numbers of hymn books scattered on the seats, I said, in a firm voice, so composed as to become an astonishment to myself, "The audience will join in singing each verse as I read it." I then read out the first verse, and Mr. Logan, a young gentleman standing by my side, sang in a clear and beautiful tenor voice, the first verse of the hymn through *alone.* I then read out the second verse, when two or three rather quavering voices joined Mr. Logan, the singers being distinguishable by taking off their hats. Repeating my previous formula, "The audience will ALL join in singing," etc., I read out the third verse. There was a rustle as of the soughing wind, when every one in that immense audience rose to their feet, every hat went off, and they sang ! aye, sang such a strain as must have gone straight up to Heaven. The fourth verse was read, in a voice no longer firm, but broken with emotion. The singing was even more powerful and heartfelt than before, and this, followed by a fervent invocation, and, as I believe, one of the best lectures I had ever been the instrument of giving, completed the victory.

All was done and won. A large company of men, *bareheaded*, and formed into a sort of improvised procession, accompanied our carriage, now at the FRONT door, to the end of the street, and took leave of me, as I leaned from the window, with waving hats, and many a murmured "God bless you."

I must now ask my readers for a few minutes to step behind the scenes and go back with me, in a mental flight, to the Saturday afternoon prior to this memorable Sunday.

About four o'clock I had retired to the room assigned me in Mrs. Nesbitt's hospitable dwelling, on the pretext of seeking a little rest after receiving visitors, but, in reality, in the effort to shake off by quiet reflection the terrible crowd of apprehensions that filled my mind concerning the trial that awaited me on the next day.

I recalled the scenes of wild impulse and violence I had read of in Scottish history; the characteristics of John Knox and his stern influence upon his followers, many of whom still held the same religious opinions in Glasgow.

Turning from the window through which I had been gazing into the street, and fixing my eyes upon my bedroom fire, I beheld seated in the rocking-chair, which was placed before the hearth (for the month was November), my Indian spirit friend "Arrowhead." He seemed always impressed to come to me upon momentous occasions, or before periods of apprehended danger. Sometimes he would stand over me, waving his war hatchet above my head, as if in the attitude of protection. Sometimes he would dash his tomahawk in the air, as if in the act of striking an enemy. On the present occasion his gigantic form seemed to be resting peacefully in that chair, whilst his war hatchet was laid, as if unused, across his knees. His head was bound with a glittering band, on which were the words "*Arrowhead the Terrible*," but his noble face was turned towards me, overspread with a kindly smile. In an instant all my fears of the to-morrow were dispelled, and I felt as if he had repeated my spirit sailor brother's constant phrase, that "*if a park of artillery were brought against me it could not harm me.*"

As I stood gazing upon that splendid apparition a knock came at my door, and, by invitation to enter, my kind hostess, Mrs. Nesbitt, came in, her face anxious in sympathy with her guest. Advancing towards the rocking-chair she laid her hand on the back, and then suddenly withdrew it as if it had come in contact with something startling. Then she said, "Come in and have a cup of tea, dear; it will cheer you up." The spirit nodded, and I said I would. As I passed him he turned his magnificent head and smiling face towards me, and I felt that all was well.

We had not been seated more than ten minutes in Mrs. Nesbitt's sitting-room, with some though not all the family around me, when the youngest girl, Georgina, entered the room, and, addressing an elder sister, she said, "Ellen, will you please fetch my boots to go out in? They are in the cupboard in Mrs. Hardinge's room."

"Fetch them yourself, Georgie," replied the sister.

"Oh, I darena," answered the child in her pretty Scotch way. "I saw Mrs. Hardinge's room door open, and the fire burning brightly, and I thought I would go in and warm mysel'. I was just about to seat mysel' in the rocking chair before the fire when—oh my! there rose up from that chair a figure as tall as the ceiling; oh, such a grand creature! but all dressed—oh, I don't know how! and so awful he was that I darena go there again for my life."

I mention this simply to quote the corroborative but unsolicited testimony of these Glasgow friends to the fact of the Spirit surroundings and protection with which I was environed.   I have simply to add that the tremendous power that sustained me on my Sunday's platform, when even some of my bravest and most devoted friends looked pale and anxious, was the vision of " Arrowhead the Terrible," standing during my lecture in front of me with his war hatchet upraised above my head.   I may add, that on the Monday following I spoke again to a crowded audience on " Inspiration."   On the Tuesday a private party at Mr. Nesbitt's introduced me to the wonderful painting medium David Duguid, and on Thursday I took part, by special invitation, in a public meeting held at the Glasgow City Hall in honour of and sympathy with Garibaldi, the Italian patriot.   In a speech, which the continued cries of " Go on, go on!" extended to over an hour, I was privileged to show to several thousands of the Glasgow population that women can still be patriots, public speakers, and women at the same time.

The scene of special interest that I have next to notice was my return to America in the ill-fated ship the *City of Boston.*

I had finished my voluminous history of " Modern American Spiritualism."   It was assuredly the desire of wise spirits no less than by my own sense of reason, that this work should help to form a part of the Bible of the future.   It was to be published in America, however, the all too narrow spirit of national egotism rendering even the record of Spiritualism's *birthplace* unwelcome in any other land.

I embarked on the *City of Boston* in the fall of 1869. On the voyage I thus made, Captain Halcro, the commander, had just returned to the post of duty after a suspension of his engagement with the Inman Line company of six months, for causes of which I was not informed.

The passage was a very stormy one, and I, in company with all the other passengers, received the kindest and most courteous attention from the captain and all his officers. When we were within twenty-four hours' sail of New York the storms that had beset our entire voyage increased so violently that we were informed our good captain was *on the bridge*—the look-out point of all large steamships—and had declared he would not quit it until we got within sight of New York. Then it was that some of the passengers, whom I knew to be friends and partisans of poor Captain Halcro, asked me, as a journalist and ready writer, to pen down a testimonial to the worth and kindness of the captain. I readily agreed to do so, but the writing was executed under stupendous difficulties amidst the raging of the storm. However, we managed its completion, and it was at once signed by all the passengers. This done, the paper had to be carried and presented to the good captain as he stood, like the very genius of the storm, on the bridge, which he refused to leave for a single instant.

For the purpose of conveying this cheering document to our brave commander I and Dr. Brandreth—known throughout the States as the inventor and dispenser of " Brandreth's celebrated pills "—were chosen as a delegation to carry the aforesaid testimonial and present it to the captain. After the doctor's hat, coat, and all movable parts of his garments had been 'bound up by strings, and mine ditto by scarfs, we struggled up to the deck, and, arm in arm, staggered along, on the night before our expected landing, guided by a lantern tied on to a pole carried in my hand, until we reached the bridge.

The captain had been apprised of our coming, and crowds of such of the crew as were able to be spared stood around us.

The storm howled, and our lantern rocked in rhythm with the tossing ship. Reading was impossible, but I gave the substance of the paper I had to present in a hoarse shout, chorussed by the bellowing of the winds, after which, and when about a dozen strong arms had pushed me half way up the steps of the bridge, there was a sudden and temporary lull, and a great glare of white moonlight came out and shone full in the face of the captain, over which big tears were running. He took the paper from my hands, put it in his breast, and said a few words of deep and pathetic thankfulness, ending with this well-remembered sentence—"To you and our friends all, Mrs. Hardinge, I say, this paper shall never leave me more, whether I am drifting on to my next station in Heaven or in hell." "Captain," I replied, "wherever your *next* station may be, you and I will yet talk over this scene and that paper together in the ports of Heaven when our several courses on earth are ended."

I never spoke with Captain Halcro more, and, after landing the next day in New York, never saw him again.

I heard that some of the experts of the company to which the *City of Boston* belonged, declared, when she was about to proceed on her return voyage, that the vessel was unseaworthy. In reply to this statement, report alleges that Captain Halcro had said, in his unceremonious phraseology, he " would take that ship into Liverpool or hell." A few days later I saw a vision of a large broken-up dismantled hulk of a ship far out at sea. The evening sun seemed to be sinking red and angrily amidst banks of piled-up black clouds, broken from time to time into massy rifts by flashes of forked lightning. In the midst of the bare black hulk I saw the form of Captain Halcro standing alone, with folded arms, and a despair as black as the pitiless scene around him on his ashy face. He seemed, in vision, to see me, and made as if speaking, but his words were lost amidst terrific peals of thunder until the awful scene faded from my eyes.

"*The City of Boston* is lost; she will never be heard from more."

These were the ominous words that constantly burst from my lips when the fate of this doomed ship was mentioned in my presence. All too surely have those unpremeditated words been realised, "*The City of Boston*" *has never been heard from more*, and never will be except in the archives of eternity. And yet in the ages that shall be I still anticipate that Captain Halcro and I will meet again when both of us are found good enough to enter and greet each other in the ports of Heaven.

My "Modern American Spiritualism" was published amidst the same struggles and trials that have ever beset my onerous way. Once more I rushed from point to point of the mighty West, returning to New York and to the house of my very dear friends, Mr. and Mrs. Jackson (now both saints in Heaven) in time to give my hand in marriage on the eleventh of October, 1870, to my best beloved, the kindest, truest, and dearest of husbands, with whom I shortly after returned to England in the *City of Abyssinia*, and to-day live ever to bless the time and act which converted me from Emma Hardinge into Emma Hardinge Britten.

CHAPTER XIX.

" Know well, my soul, God's hand controls
Whate'er thou fearest."

As my sole object in writing, and, as I earnestly hope, in ultimately publishing these autobiographical memoirs, is to perpetuate the remembrance of the notable personages and events that marked the early days of Modern Spiritualism, rather than to egotistically thrust myself—a mere instrument in the mighty movement—into prominent notice ; so I shall recall only such of my own personal experiences as may seem essential to the best understanding of the great cause with which I have been for so many years publicly identified.

After my marriage with Mr. Britten, in October, 1870, my good husband and I having returned to England to fetch my dear mother back to America, we established ourselves in a pleasant country home near Boston, where I determined to study medical electricity, both as a practice for myself and my husband, and with a view of superseding the necessity of my leaving home for distant lecturing engagements.

As my sister, Mrs. Margaret Wilkinson, soon after joined us for the purpose of studying medical electricity, and our practice became widely extended and successful, we ultimately moved into and settled in Boston.

As I could not be reconciled to abandon my long and highly appreciated public advocacy of the cause of Spiritualism, my husband hired " New Era Hall " in Boston, where I continued to give Spiritual lectures every Sunday evening.

As my sister, Mrs. Wilkinson, after being with us some time, at length felt obliged to return to England to rejoin her husband, who was unable to leave his engagement there, and our dear and now aged mother required the quiet and seclusion of home, we finally broke up our Boston practice, and took our beloved mother to England, there to rest and live peacefully with my sister and her husband.

After parting with these dear ones my husband and I ultimately returned to Boston, and from thence proceeded to fill an engagement that had long pressed upon me to lecture to promote the honoured cause of Spiritualism in Australia, our only condition being, that, in passing through the United States and embarking at California, we should remain in each section of the country we traversed as long as we deemed beneficial to the movement we had so dearly at heart.

During an extended course of lectures in California my husband managed my meetings, the former kind and unitary association of pure Spiritualism being unhappily broken up into divided cliques and parties.

During our overland journey to California, we stopped by special invitation from the so-called Gentiles of the Salt Lake City, Utah, where I gave a course of lectures for the large body of seceders from Mormonism, many of whom had become warm Spiritualists.

I could, indeed, unfold a harrowing tale of the wrong and heart-break, and often mysterious deaths which befel the wretched women who came out to that land of horrors on the vague but false representation, that they were going to a Kingdom of Heaven upon earth. If there be any philosophy concealed in the old classic fable "that the foundations of Heaven are laid in the depths of Hell," then the victims of man's licentiousness lured out to the Hell of Salt Lake City, as I knew it in more than one early visit to its romantic precincts, must assuredly be the steps by which many a hapless woman with bleeding feet and broken heart has reached the gates of Paradise.

It was on January 21st, 1878, that my husband and I
embarked from California in the steamship *City of
Sydney*, for Australia. After a rough passage and short
visit to the Sandwich Islands and New Zealand, we landed
at Sydney, New South Wales, February 19th, 1878.

At Sydney we were met and welcomed by many warm
friends of Spiritualism, prominent among whom I note
with ever-grateful remembrance good Dr. Bowie Wilson,
now a dweller of the higher life, Mr. Henry Gale, and
many others devoted to the work I came to perform. At
the request of these good friends I agreed to remain with
them for two or three weeks before proceeding to
Melbourne.

Our friends aided my husband in hiring halls and
organising a short course of highly successful lectures,
after which, with a promise to return for a more extended
period, we took leave of our warm-hearted Sydney friends,
and re-embarking, made our way to Melbourne, in the
Province of Victoria.

We arrived at Melbourne, as it seemed, at an auspicious
juncture. Mr. Thomas Walker, a young Englishman, who
in the absence of more polished missionaries, had been
distinguishing himself in the Colonies as a trance speaker,
had been challenged to debate with a Mr. Green, a clergyman, an adherent of one of the hundreds of sects ranged
under the standard of Christianity, and, like most of his
profession, a devout believer in *Ancient* Spiritualism, and
a no less fierce opponent of Modern Spiritualism. The
evening of our arrival at Melbourne was the third occasion
on which this debate had been continued, and our friends,
deeming we should be interested listeners to the proceedings, pressed us to attend the meeting.

There was a very large gathering in the hall, and it had
been announced that the debate was to terminate that
evening. The interest excited by the subject discussed,

and the ability of the orators on both sides was so great, however, that when Mr. Green asked for an adjournment of two more nights, the proposition was carried with acclamation.

The fourth night of this debate and the second of our attendance at the hall, Mr. Green was evidently prepared to deliver some closing remarks, the anticipation of which seemed to preface the impending defeat alike of Mr. Walker and his supporters.

The expected blow, however, was reserved for the last portion of the evening, when Mr. Green, commencing his peroration with many comments on the ability of his opponent, and his own regret at being obliged to *crush to the earth* an antagonist at once so earnest and able in defence of what he believed to be " divine truth," added, that for the sake alike of religion, good morals, and good citizenship, he felt obliged to read a letter, a copy of which he had received in print. The letter came, he said, from New York, itself the birthplace of Spiritualism, and the land in which thousands of Spiritualists flourished, in comparison to the tens of any other country.

He added that the letter he was about to read came from a learned and educated physician of high standing in New York City, one who had been at one time an adherent of Spiritualism, but who had felt obliged to relinquish that cause from the fact of its being associated with abominations, alike ruinous to morality, decency, honour, and good citizenship. Not waiting to listen to the universal gasp of horror which this peroration excited, the gentleman went on to read a letter in which all the above-named accusations were preferred against the mass generally, though not against the personalities of the Spiritualists. He (the writer) declared that nearly all the Spiritual teachers, preachers, and Mediums, were living in infamy with other wives and husbands than their own ;

were often known to sit in *nude* circles, and were so generally infamous, as to be shunned by every decent citizen.

The letter was signed by a well-known certain M.D., of New York, but with no other address.

The reading of this document from a doctor, one who claimed to be of "high standing," and that from New York, the focus and centre of the New World's Spiritualism, produced such an astounding effect upon the audience, that an awful sort of paralysis fell upon the whole assembly, striking them into dead silence, and preventing the utterance of a word or sound. After the first shock of surprise and horror had subsided Mr. Green sat down, seeming overpowered, and covering his face with his hand. After a few minutes more of deep and ominous silence, Mr. Walker arose, with a countenance of ashy paleness.

He said he had just come from England, where Spiritualism was as popular amongst the nobility and best classes of society as Christianity; that he himself had never been to America and knew nothing of America, its people, habits, or customs; furthermore, as he was entirely unprepared for the nature of the letter that had been read that night, he must ask permission to defer making his answer until the following evening, when the debate was to close.

A very informal and muttered sort of acquiescence being accorded to this request, the meeting closed, and that in a terribly ominous and disconcerted fashion.

On that same day my husband and I had been invited by Mr. Watson, of Yarra Grange, Melbourne, to come to his house and spend two or three weeks with him, his dear wife, and charming family. (I here interrupt the conclusion of my narrative to say our two or three weeks visit extended to the entire period of our first residence in Melbourne—namely, ten months, during which we often

pleaded to be permitted to relieve our dear host and
hostess of their visitors, but they themselves, and their
sweet children all raised such a terrible rebellion against
our proposed departure, that perforce we had to stay.)

To return, however, to the matter in hand, namely, Mr.
Green's tremendous thunderbolt of a letter above alluded
to. Having explained in full to our friends at home how
the case really stood, I asked permission to spend the
night in writing a statement, the sum of which was as
follows :—

I spoke in the first instance of a young country girl who,
at fifteen years of age, had been discovered by Professor
Mapes, of New York, to be one of the finest trance mediums
of the day. By aid of some other distinguished scientists
interested in Spiritualism, this young girl was introduced
to the public of New York, where her wonderful trance
addresses were the astonishment and delight of all who
heard her. Pretty soon this young and beautiful girl,
being, of course, a highly susceptible psychological subject,
was found by an old crafty and experienced magnetiser of
over fifty years of age, and by him was easily coaxed into
becoming his wife, under the assurance that with *his*
management he could soon put her in possession of a large
fortune. This man took her about from place to place,
acting the part of her showman, charging exorbitant prices
for the *show*, but keeping her so hard at work that the
poor girl was frequently compelled to appear in public
when she was fairly sinking with fatigue and indisposition.

But this was not all. Whether this man had any legal
right or not to the title of Doctor which he assumed,
certain it was that he was known in New York as a man
of notoriously bad character, the associate of courtesans,
and a worthless adventurer.

Soon after the unfortunate girl's ill-starred marriage
with this wretch, reports began to be circulated of his

brutal treatment of his victim.   How far these reports
were borne out by direct testimony may be shown in the
following incident:—

A gentleman, travelling on professional business, was
one night detained at New Haven, Connecticut, and went
to the principal hotel, the Tontine House, to stay over-
night. Whilst he was reading in the coffee-room he heard
an unusual sound of voices in the passage outside, in which
a seemingly distressed female voice took part.   On going
out to enquire what was the matter, he found the landlady
of the hotel in colloquy with a very interesting young
woman who, with many tears, was beseeching permission
to obtain shelter in the hotel that night, and protection
against a brutal husband, from whom she had just made
her escape, and from whose violence she considered her
life to be in danger.   When the gentleman enquired
further into the matter he found that the unfortunate
pleader was none other than Mrs. Cora Hatch, the wife of
the Spiritualist showman, as he was called, and it was at
the gentleman's urgent entreaty that the unhappy victim
was that night sheltered and kindly protected at the New
Haven Tontine House.   As the gentleman who thus
mercifully intervened to save a delicate young wife from
the fury of a brute was none other than Dr. Britten, the
husband of the present writer, the audience who will be
called upon to-night to listen to the reading of this paper,
can question Dr. Britten at their leisure as to the truth or
error of the statement above set down.

It is enough to add that the wrongs, cruelty, and priva-
tions to which the unfortunate wife was subjected at
length aroused public indignation to such an extent, that
Professor Mapes, Judge Edmonds, Drs. Gray and Hallock,
and several other leading Spiritualists, first insisted upon
the poor young woman being placed under proper prote-
tion, and then summoning her monster of a husband

to appear in the Divorce Court. The pleadings on the poor wife's account were sustained by many witnesses with such abundant evidences of wrong and ill usage, that a decree of divorce was granted instantly, and the man's name became at once branded with the infamy of his all too well known practices.

Being still in possession of the thousands of dollars the unfortunate ex-wife had coined for him, the fellow endeavoured to wreak his vengeance against the whole cult of Spiritualism by spending her money in writing, publishing, and scattering broadcast tracts defaming the cause in such *un-personal* attacks as no *individual* could take hold of as a case for prosecution, and it was one of these infamous and cowardly documents that Mr. Green thought proper to read out as an authoritative representation of Spiritualism ; while *his eminent New York physician* was none other than the notorious and hoary sinner— branded with infamy in the Divorce Court of New York— called " Dr. Hatch," once the husband of poor Cora Scott.

For the truth of these revelations, I added that I was willing to refer to the Judge of the Divorce Court, and any twelve of the most respectable citizens of New York. As to the generally high moral tone, respectability, and unblemished character of all the known Spiritualists of New York I would be willing to seek the sworn testimony of the present Mayor, and any number of persons holding office in New York City whom it might be deemed desirable to apply to.

This statement I signed, adding thereto, by Mr. Watson's permission, his address. I also expressed my willingness to testify to this statement on oath before any magistrate or other selected authority of Melbourne.

Immediately after breakfast on the morning which saw this paper completed we, that is, Mr. Watson, my husband, and I, drove over to the house in which Mr. Walker was quartered.

Ushered into his presence I at once read out to him the statement I had written. Mr. Walker, who was a young and apparently somewhat impulsive personage, nearly jumped up as high as the ceiling with delight at the evidence thus furnished him, and eagerly took the paper for the purpose of copying it out in his own hand-writing prior to the evening meeting.

That night the attendance at the debate was greater than ever ; in fact, large crowds gathered round the door, unable even to obtain standing room. Whether for the purpose of seeing the Spiritualists' final defeat I am unable to say. I should think this idea was the prevalent one, as my husband had strictly charged Mr. Walker not to breathe a word about the intended disclosures to any human being. As Mr. Walker had never been to America, and we had only met him for the first time that morning, it certainly seemed as if our arrival in Melbourne had been equally providential and well-timed for him and the cause he was defending.

When the debate was opened it seemed as if both parties assumed an unusually quiet, not to say humble, tone.

Mr. Green displayed all the magnanimity of a generous victor, one who was too sure and too well aware of his triumph to press his poor beaten adversary any farther ; whilst Mr. Walker, with more policy than we could have given him credit for, seemed, in his quiet and subdued manner, to acquiesce in his defeat. It was only when Mr. Green had concluded a long speech, in which he claimed that the terrible letter of the previous evening was only read by him *as a clergyman* and the champion of public virtue, that Mr. Walker, in a very mild tone, in his reply, announced that he too had a letter to read, one that he had received from a party who up to that morning had been a total stranger to him; still the letter, he said, would speak for itself. He then proceeded in a firm, clear voice, which rang powerfully throughout that packed assembly, to read out the letter, the substance of which I have given above.

As the reading went on, Mr. Walker was interrupted by occasional murmurs of "Oh!" and other tokens of both sympathy and indignation. These deepened as the reading advanced, until at its close, and after the offer of references, etc., which I had made were read out, such a storm of shouts, clapping, and cheers, renewed again and again, rang through that building, as I, in all my public life, had never before listened to. When at length, and with great difficulty, silence had been obtained, Mr. Green arose with a face as pale as death, and said, in a thick and husky voice: "And pray, who and where is the writer of that letter?"

"Here!" cried my husband, giving me his hand to rise, and rising with me. "You ask who is the writer of that letter? She is the speaker of next Sunday evening at the Prince's Opera House. You ask where is she? She is here to answer for herself."

"And to say," I added, "that if this audience will nominate a committee of enquiry into the truth of the statements made in that letter, I will afford them every facility for that enquiry, and not attempt to leave this city until the answers are returned."

More shouts, more cheers, and three special cheers now for "Emma Hardinge Britten," and now for "Thomas Walker" followed, and it was long, very long before all the efforts of the two platform committees could still the clamour.

When at length silence was obtained, Mr. Green rose, and in a very brief but manly and graceful speech, said: "He was, like his friend Mr. Walker, entirely unacquainted with America or American doings except by report; that

the letter that had been put into *his* hands had been given
to him, and read by him, in all good faith; that he did not
deem that a committee of enquiry was necessary, as the
writer of Mr. Walker's letter was present, and the circumstances she had narrated spoke for themselves, as did her
candid offer of abundant reference.   Under these circumstances, he, Mr. Green, was willing to acknowledge the
letter he had quoted as unproved, and to consider that as
both of the disputants had acted in perfect good faith,
their best course was to shake hands, in token of mutual
goodwill, and close the debate then and there."

I cannot say that this speech was received with any
demonstrations of enthusiasm, nor even when the late
opponents shook hands, whilst the two parties who acted
on their behalf as chairmen of their committees exchanged
complimentary remarks on their several clients, did the
close of the debate seem to re-awaken any of its past
interest ; in truth, to speak candidly, the whole thing
seemed to fall far more flat at its close than during its
continuance.   Not so the kind greeting that awaited me,
my husband, and party of friends.   As we left the hall, a
perfect crowd of congratulators addressed us, assuring me
my letter had been the best possible advertisement that
could have been given for my opening meeting on the
following Sunday.

CHAPTER XX.

"And ever the truth comes uppermost,
And ever is justice done."

AFTER the scene related in the last chapter, I remained in Melbourne some ten months from the period of my first landing in the city, lecturing every Sunday evening in the Prince's Opera House, to audiences often numbering two thousand persons, whilst one or more week evening lectures were given in other halls of the city. Besides my Melbourne lectures, I frequently spoke at St. Kilda, Gippsland, Ballarat, Geelong, Sandhurst, and other places accessible from Melbourne.

Mr. Terry and the Victorian Association rendered us all the assistance they could, consistently with their own business duties; the chief part of the work of organising and conducting these meetings, however, devolved upon Dr. Britten, whilst I was called upon to devote almost every spare hour in writing answers to antagonistic press correspondents, which answers I am bound to say the various Victorian journals always courteously inserted.

Passing over any detailed notice of my ordinary round of professional duties, in which darkness and light, storm and sunshine, each by turns, played as conspicuous a part as the same changes ever do in the physical atmosphere, I shall only refer to the few events which bore any direct influence on the cause I was engaged in advocating.

The first notable case worth mentioning occurred thus: After I had been lecturing some six months in Melbourne with invariable success and to immense audiences, we were visited by a gentleman who announced himself as a collector for the Melbourne Hospital, and his

ostensible object in calling was, if possible, to induce me
to give a benefit lecture for the funds of that excellent
institution.

He represented the great need of financial aid, the
heavy debts with which the hospital was burdened, and
the necessity of assistance to carry out the beneficent work
for which he pleaded.   He added that he had himself
attended one of my lectures recently, and observing the
very large attendance on that occasion, he could not
forbear from calling in the hope that I would devote my
"wonderful powers of attraction," as he phrased it, in
behalf of so noble a cause as the maintenance of the
Melbourne Hospital.

Both Dr. Britten and I assured our visitor that nothing
would afford us greater pleasure than to give one or more,
if necessary, benefit lectures in aid of the hospital, but we
then repeated, and that in presence of friends who vouched
for the truth of what we had to relate, how the Spiritualists,
on the occasion of a certain Hospital Sunday collection,
before our arrival, had sent the sum of eight pounds from
their own association in aid of the hospital funds, and how
that donation had been contemptuously returned by the
wife of Bishop Perry, one of the hospital trustees, with the
insulting remark that they declined to accept any assistance
from such infidel sources as the Spiritualists.

Some of our friends present at this interview added, that
though the righteous Bishop and his lady had disdained
the help of a body of as good people and good religionists
as any in the city, they were not above accepting two
benefit entertainments from parties of *Negro Minstrels*,
and had instituted a grand *ball* in aid of the hospital
funds, at which several hundreds of pounds were collected,
the entire mass of which (with the exception of twenty
pounds donated to the hospital) was spent in decorations,
lights, rent, and banqueting.

All this the poor collector admitted, but at the same time he urged that the management of the hospital was now in more liberal hands, that the need of the institution was urgent, and he felt confident from the nature of my teachings that I should not refuse the aid which I could so readily accord.

I laughingly replied to him that as long as I should not be required to black my face, play the bones or banjo, or see the entrance fees devoted to dancing and feasting, I should be most happy to give such free service as I could render, to the aid of the Melbourne Hospital. As one of our most esteemed personal friends, Dr. Motherwell, was himself intimately connected with the hospital arrangements, we soon learned that our visitor, the collector, was severely censured for inviting me to lecture for the hospital without the authority of the committee; next, that whilst the majority of the said committee were in favour of accepting my offer, the minority, who were especially ruled by their chairman, declined, on the ground that they were not going to make the Melbourne Hospital a "stalking horse" for the advertisement of Mrs. Britten's lectures.

As it was well known in Melbourne that my lectures *fully* advertised themselves, and that they needed no benefit lectures to be used as a "stalking horse" to advertise them, the letter of rude rejection we received, refusing my services, Dr. Britten took at once to the *Melbourne Age,* one of the most liberal journals of the city. This, together with a written statement from myself of the entire story, from beginning to end, was published, not only in the *Age* but in other journals also, and the hospital directors at last *were moved,* I cannot say whether by shame, or by what other impulse, into sending me—as I imperatively required—a written apology, and request to give the lecture as proposed, for the benefit of the hospital.

This I at once agreed to do, and as the best minds of the city were aroused by the injustice attempted to be practised against me, the result more than answered our expectations.

The various city journals commented in uncompromising terms on the treatment we had received, and inserted our announcements of the hospital benefit lecture free of charge.

Our kind printers contributed cards and notices, and when Dr. Britten and our friend Mr. Dempster called on the Mayor and represented the need of the hospital committee for assistance, he generously remitted the usual charge of twenty pounds rent, for the use of the great town hall in which I was to lecture, and one of the finest musicians of the city gave his services to perform on the grand organ for an hour before the commencement of the address.

I must add that instead of making the "Melbourne Hospital a stalking horse for the announcement of my Spiritual lecture," I purposely selected for this special occasion one of the most approved of the physiological lectures which I had been accustomed to give when studying as a student of physiology and electrical science.

The lecture was enthusiastically received. The vast hall was filled to overflowing, and the admission fees realised over two hundred pounds, all of which was handed over to the hospital committee without one penny's deduction.

According to the laws of that institution, these sums of money donated to the hospital entitled my husband and myself to become life governors, the recorded papers of which are in our possession to this day, signed by the very party who first insultingly rejected our assistance.

The second event of note I have to record is the publication of a small volume of my writing, which has had a circulation of many thousands, and is entitled, "The Faiths, Facts, and Frauds of Religious History."

The circumstances which called for the publication of this work were these: After my first few inaugural lectures explaining the history, principles, and philosophy of Spiritualism, the audiences were called upon to nominate a committee of five gentlemen from amongst those present, who, according to my usual custom, were allowed to select the subject for the ensuing lecture. For many weeks following on this arrangement, the subjects chosen were invariably either upon, or in connection with, the origin of different ancient faiths and their relations to the later doctrines and claims set up for Christianity and its Founder. In view of the startling revelations thus brought before the public mind, the former adherents of a certain "*Reverend* gentleman," whose congregations had sensibly diminished since the Prince's Opera House Sunday meetings commenced, was urged to answer, even to debate with and confound, the infidel lecturer's iconoclastic assertions. At first the said reverend scoffed at the idea of noticing, much less *debating* with a female preacher, contenting himself with quoting Paul's famous charge for women to *keep silence in meeting*, etc. When, however, the *Curator* of souls found his people not to be silenced by the Pauline logic of two thousand years ago, or willing to remain his adherents any longer than he could convince them that the daring infidel female preacher was *wrong* as well as *daring*, the learned gentleman put forth a pamphlet, in which he acknowledged the historical announcements of the various "Messiahs," "Avatars," "Sons of God," and "Christs," that were all *said to have preceded the appearance of Jesus of Nazareth*, and the wonderful *similarities of their histories and teachings with those of the Nazarene.* BUT WHAT OF THAT? All these *Heathen Messiahs,* he alleged, were *myths*, all "expectations," or, in other words, *prophecies of the last but only* REAL *and original Christ* and Jesus of Nazareth (even if he was the last of all), was the special one to be worshipped AS " THE ONLY BEGOTTEN SON OF GOD."

For the present I have no other comments to make on this curious style of argument and *historical accuracy*, except to say that to my certain knowledge a great many people did not believe it, and that, happily, the ingenious " Reverend" has found in a certain city of Christian England, namely, Manchester, a more trusting and easily satisfied congregation of believers than the shrewd Colonists afforded him.

The result of the above circumstances, however, was the publication of my " Faiths, Facts, and Frauds of Religious History," printed in Melbourne, and in conformity with the following introductory words :—

"Prompted by the obvious tendency of popular feeling, the author's lectures were necessarily directed towards analytical researches into the origin of religious beliefs, their nature, authenticity, and the evidences which ecclesiasticism could bring to prove its right to dominate over the human mind. The propositions thus called forth involved many startling and revolutionary assertions, and as the limit of extemporaneous addresses scarcely permitted the quotation of numerous authoritative witnesses, the author realised the duty of providing for her many trusting listeners some compendious and accessible definitions of the chief points contained in her theological lectures, together with such a mass of corroborative testimony, and references to acknowledged authorities, as would place the means of verification at each reader's command. . . . As far as possible the most available means of referring to the authors quoted from have been clearly pointed out, and although but a tithe of the matter worthy of the true thinker's study has been touched upon, the author feels confident that the sum of what has already been given will suffice to point the way to the realisation of purer FAITHS and more enduring FACTS than religious history can ever furnish to mankind under the specious garb of clerical authority, and the tremendous shroud of that mystery which is the stronghold of priestly FRAUD and ecclesiastical imposture."

I must not omit to mention that we had our full share of experience in travelling through the Australian bush, as well as in the busy cities. Prior to our second visit to Sydney, Mr. Wilson, a gentleman of means, and a devoted Spiritualist, urged us strongly to make our journey overland instead of by water, pleading also that I would stop to give lectures at six different bush towns he mentioned, all the arrangements for which, as well as expenses, he engaged to meet, besides paying me fairly for my services. As there were no means of travelling through the districts he had selected, except in heavy old American stage-coaches, over dreadful roads, beaten down or cut into by waggons, oxen, and sheep drivers, or the celebrated bushranging brigands; as every ditch or water hole through which the coach and five horses had to drag us, was full of snakes, and the renowned Kelly band of brigands particularly affected the ranges through which we had to pass, the prospect, however romantic, opened up one of the most daring adventures I think I ever took part in. Looking back now upon the dangers of our wild journeys and the indescribable fatigues we had to encounter, I can truthfully allege, I wonder that we both lived to go through with it. Our last stopping place was Albury, where we met and were most kindly entertained by Mr. Phillippi, an extensive grape grower and wine manufacturer, and a gentleman of high Spiritual culture. In this as in all our preceding stopping places we were well received, cheered by excellent audiences, and often thrilled by the narration of the weird and wild experiences with which these remote regions seemed to be rife.

Some of the haunting earth-bound Spirits of the untamed aborigines, the wild bushrangers, or the, as yet undeveloped spirits of convict criminals, I encountered many times, and their presence afforded me good reason to realise the truth of my wise Spirit friends' assertions to the effect that the Spirit world is here ; that it is the rarified, sublimated, æther realm of being permeating this planet and stretching away in zones and belts until it impinges on the Spirit spheres of its neighbour planets in space.

Thus I had no difficulty in accounting for the flood of savage and criminal Spirits that haunted these Australian mountains, ranges and bush scenes, all filled with the special parts of the Spirit spheres inhabited by the earth-bound souls of those who had once been (like roots or plants) dwellers in these particular regions.

From Albury we had to proceed by a ninety miles dreadful stage-coach journey, to Wagga Wagga, the station from which we expected to take a train to Sydney.

It was a terrible journey this. We heard of more than one traveller whose brains had been dashed out against the roof of the coaches as they were plunged into, or dragged out of the water holes that beset the frightful road.

The *via dolorosa* came to an end at last, and when we reached the rude, wild station called Wagga Wagga, the great cattle-trading depôt of that district, our tired limbs and weary heads found shelter in an hotel which exactly faced a street in which was the memorable house, with closed-up doors and shuttered windows of a shop, over which was inscribed in large painted letters " ARTHUR ORTON, BUTCHER."

This house, our landlord informed us, was deserted. Its evil reputation was obtained as having been the residence and place of business of that Arthur Orton, a man of low origin, whom the people of that district, most familiar with his character, *believe* to have palmed himself off on the English public as Sir Roger Tichborne.

The deeper we inquired into this story the worse it seemed, and it would be difficult to persuade the inhabitants of Wagga Wagga, that the real Sir Roger Tichborne, over whom this Arthur Orton was known to have acquired a strong influence, did not experience sooner or later his Australian attendant's skill in his butcher's trade, leaving Mr. Orton to personate his identity as THE CLAIMANT.

From that lone, desolate spot, the scene of so much that was repulsive alike in association and surroundings, we soon departed, taking the train that bore us to Sydney.

Here we again alternated between any amount of professional hard work with occasional excursions—now to the orange groves of Paramatta or some of the lovely spots up the beautiful bay of Sydney, and now to the desolate, lonely beach with the one house *only* upon it, overlooking a restless tossing sea, and a country extending far away from the beach up to green places so covered with wild flowers as to have earned for that remote spot its celebrated but ominous name of Botany Bay. Let it be understood, however, that this place was never, as erroneously reported, a convict settlement. The one house of public entertainment for visitors now found upon its shores, was the only erection put up there, and that is of modern date. The actual site of the penal station was six miles distant. It was formerly called Port Jackson, a name too odious to be endured after it ceased to be a convict settlement, and therefore it has been altered to its present title of Sydney. From this fair city we finally departed amidst outstretched hands, not a few tearful faces, and the murmured blessings of dear and ever remembered friends, to fill my next and last engagement at Melbourne.

Once again I entered upon the scenes of restless mental strife and conflict which must ever attend the pioneers of a new, and especially an unpopular, reform. I can now calmly but still solemnly declare the scenes amidst which

I and my active, energetic, but still deeply sensitive
husband had to pass could never have been endured
without sacrifice of health, spirits, or life itself, had we not
both been constantly upheld, advised, and sustained by
the ever present good cheer, wise counsel, and strong
helping hands of our beloved Spirit friends.

"ALL'S WELL THAT ENDS WELL!"   All my faithful,
sincere, and true friends rallied round me in the same
force as ever ; the audiences were just as enthusiastic as
before, and my closing and farewell meeting in the city
was graced by the presentation to me of a splendid emu
egg stand, with the most elaborate silver carved work and
ornaments, and a rich gold pencilcase to my husband, both
noble testimonials being given by a dear lady—Miss
Ricketts—a great and good philanthropist, better known
by her private charities than by her public works.

Many of the esteemed friends who served to make my
colonial visit a series of public triumphs and social friend-
ships, have passed on to the higher life.   Our beloved
friends Dr. Bowie Wilson, Mr. S. G. Watson (of Yarra
Grange), Dr. Motherwell, several of Mr. Hugh Junor
Brown's sweet children, besides many another prized
friend, are amongst the vanished faces that the colonial
world will miss.   Mr. W. H. Terry is still the indefatigable
worker for the cause he has done so much to found and
uphold; whilst Mr. H. Junor Brown, with his beloved
wife and his remaining family, give their noble testimony
and honoured names to uphold the grand cause by their
personal influence and fine literary contributions.

It must suffice to say that on Tuesday, April 8th, 1879,
my husband and I embarked on the steamboat *Albion*,
and, surrounded by a large group of kind and sympathetic
friends, we bade a loving farewell to them and the shores
of Australia for ever on earth, as we sailed away to the
paradise of the Southern Seas—New Zealand.

CHAPTER XXI.

"And broad and bright on either hand,
Stretched the green slopes of fairy land."

LANDED on the shores of fair New Zealand, and conveyed up eight miles from our port of debarkation to Dunedin, the principal city of the three islands, and the point from which our professional correspondence came, we found, as before, in our colonial wanderings, that all our work, whether of temporary home settlement or the organisation of our public meetings, had to depend upon our own energy and personal endeavours. Unlike the well-arranged methods of the good American societies, there was no speaker's home provided, no hall engaged, public announcements made, or any preliminary means of helpfulness devised. All these steps had to be taken by my indefatigable husband, and that on strange ground.

A few kind Spiritualistic friends met and advised us at what hotel to stop, and what prospects there *might* be of success in Sunday meetings, but a hall had to be found and a boarding place arranged by Dr. Britten himself before a step in advance could be taken.

Later on we found many friends whom we grew to highly appreciate in Dunedin, but our first entrance was a lonely and sorrowful one, and we thought longingly of the warm-hearted and energetic friends five or six thousand miles away in New York or Boston, with many a sigh of regret.

Rising then, as ever, to the situation, Dr. Britten hired the Princess's Theatre for my opening Sunday evening lectures, got the announcements made, the bills printed, a pleasant boarding place provided, and with an ever-increasing circle of what at last became valued friends, I lectured for some months on Sunday evenings at Dunedin to large and enthusiastic audiences, and on week nights at other accessible places.

Spiritualism was by no means a strange belief in New Zealand.   Mr. Peebles and Mr. Charles Bright had both lectured in Dunedin to good acceptance, and one of the most popular Scotch settlers of that city (mostly inhabited by Scotch emigrants), Mr. John Logan, who was not only a popular citizen but a rich landowner of the place, had gone through a curious experience there, the details of which I shall step aside from the narration of my own special experiences, to give a brief account of by quoting from my "Nineteenth Century Miracles."

"Among the earliest investigators in the islands was Mr. John Logan, a wealthy and influential settler in Dunedin.   This gentleman, although holding a high and dignified position in the first Presbyterian Church in the city, had not only dared to attend the Spiritual circles instituted amongst many other respectable enquirers, but report spoke of him as having become an excellent Medium for Spiritual communications in his own person. . . .

"On the 19th of March, 1873, Mr. Logan was summoned to appear before the Church Convocation to be held for the purpose of trying his case, and, if necessary, dealing with his grave delinquency.

"Up to this time the accused gentleman's noble wife had not followed him in his Spiritual researches.

"Now in the hour of trial she was by his side, and listened attentively to the conduct of the high-handed procedure of which he was the victim.

"The farce of a modern 'Star Chamber' trial ended, as might have been expected, by Mr. Logan's conviction, and excommunication from the heavenly benefits and hopes of which the Presbyterian Synod claimed to be the appointed dispensers.   Before the breaking up of this most fraternal assembly of Christians,

Mrs. Logan, moved by those tender feminine impulses which rendered the severance of once cherished ties of friendship and religious communion very painful to her, rose up, and with all the dignity and earnestness which marks this estimable lady she asked in thrilling tones *if there was no one there to speak for John Logan?*

"No voice responded. Of all the former friends and associates who had been bound to John Logan by ties of gratitude, as well as companionship in a foreign land, not one held out a hand to sustain him, not one breathed a word to mitigate the insensate tyranny of the sentence pronounced upon him! It seemed as if the ice bolts of a hard and savage theology had shut humanity out of the hearts of those present, even as they would have shut a good man out of Heaven for daring to follow the dictates of his conscience.

"Again and yet again the sweet voice of the brave lady rang through the stillness of that guilty crowd in the pathetic question: 'Is there no one here to speak a word for John Logan?'

"When it was fully shown that not one recreant present dared to break that solemn silence, the devoted wife, taking her husband's arm, passed out from amongst them, saying as she went, in her own touching tones, 'This is no place for us; let us go hence.' And thus they went forth, that good John Logan and his noble wife—out from the stifling atmosphere of man-made sectarianism into the free air of spiritual life, light, and reason—out from the night of bigotry into the sunlight of God's truth—never more to return, but, still better, never more to tread separate paths in life again. From that hour Mrs. Logan resolved to enquire into the faith that had enabled her husband to withstand the multitude, and prove how one man in a good cause is mightier than a host.

"Struck with the base ingratitude of those who had deserted him, and ashamed of the faith which thus disgraced its members in attempting to disgrace their friend, Mrs. Logan sought and found the source of her brave companion's strength, and not only found it to be true and good, but she herself came to be a minister of its divine afflatus, and when I visited Dunedin in 1879 I found

Mrs. Logan not only firm in the faith of Spiritualism, but one of its most marked evidences in her own beautiful and convincing phases of Mediumship.　.　.　."

I may add that it is equally my pride and happiness to remember that it was in Mr. and Mrs. Logan's residence, and delightful family circle, that some of our happiest hours were spent in Dunedin.

In this place the good, true-hearted, and energetic Scotch element prevails largely; hence the remarkable steady growth of Dunedin, the neatness of its residences and gardens, and the astonishing industry with which its mountains are graded with fine roads and adorned with palatial dwellings.

As I have before stated, Dr. Britten had to manage for me alone; to bear the brunt of all the expenses, the risk of every undertaking, and the· entire conduct of our meetings, with very few exceptions. Kind friends were ever ready to tender service, but it was not of that well-practised nature which grows out of experience, and lacked all the strength of associative action.

When it is remembered that we had to pay enormous prices for halls, hirelings, advertisements, tickets, bills, and stickers, board, lodging, washing, and fabulous sums for travelling expenses; when all this is taken into consideration, and with it the fact that we felt obliged to follow the custom of our predecessors, and charge in general such nominal fees at our Sunday evening meetings as threepence, sixpence, and one shilling, my readers may guess that my magnificent two thousand audiences could not go very far in exceeding all the demands made upon us. When every expense is to be met by the attractions of the speaker, and that at the most inconsiderable possible entrance fees; when that speaker comes a stranger, too, to the customs of the place, and that from countries where associated numbers assume all the responsibilities, the urgent necessity for organised aid for foreign missionaries will be at once apparent.

I must now once more introduce our *Christian friend, Mr. Green,* to my reader's notice.

I had not been many days in Dunedin before I discovered that this irrepressible minister of the "Church of Christ," as he called the noisy and totally un-Christ like set of low people, that he managed to gather together wherever he went, had inflicted himself upon Dunedin, and by the aid of his *noble* followers was as rampant in thrusting his doctrines upon the public and denouncing every other form of belief but his own, as when I found him out first in Melbourne in debate with Thomas Walker.

Just as I arrived at Dunedin this same Mr. Green, who had not been long settled there, had published a series of scandalous lectures on the fruits of Spiritualism, and in proof of his theory of "Satanic Agency" drew the entire of his charges from the lives, writings, opinions and practices of those worthless novelty-seekers, or adventurers of all classes, who thrust themselves into our ranks ; and although merely the camp followers or vultures who are ever to be found on the skirts of every great army of reform, are too often and injuriously classed as "Spiritualists."

The course I finally adopted under the advice and guidance of good and wise friends from the shores beyond, was as follows :—

We procured the largest and best hall in Dunedin. The Hon. Robert Stout, our honoured and talented Attorney-General, was my chairman, and to a mob of howling Christian followers of my reverend opponent, and surrounded by a jammed and almost frantic crowd of excited people, I gave the following definitions of my religion and faith in Spiritualism.

1st.—Spiritualism proves by a set of obviously supermundane phenomena, that a world of invisible intelligence is communicating with us.

2nd.—It demonstrates by an immense array of test facts given all over the world, under circumstances that forbid the possibility of collusion or human contrivance, that the communicating intelligences are identical with the souls of mortals who once lived on earth.

3rd.—It shows by universal coincidence in the communications, that every living soul is in judgment for the deeds done in the body, and reaps the fruits of its good or evil life on earth, in happiness or suffering hereafter.

4th.—All the communicating spirits coincide in declaring that the life succeeding mortal dissolution is not a final state, but one which manifests innumerable conditions of progress; and these four propositions I emphatically protest are *the all* of Spiritual facts we know, the all that are absolutely proved, or upon which all the immense varieties of persons that make up the ranks of Spiritualism, can absolutely agree.

The whole of my lecture, printed under the title of "Spiritualism Vindicated and Clerical Slanders Refuted," is now in the hands of thousands of colonists, and bitter as the occasion was that demanded it, I thank the Great Spirit, whose instrumentality called forth so trenchant a plea for a cause so eminently worthy as Spiritualism.

During my course of Dunedin lectures, the Hon. Robert Stout, the Attorney-General and member for Dunedin, deemed himself called upon to oppose with all his widespread influence the introduction of the Bible in the public schools as a necessary element of education. The partisans of this movement had been strenuous in their efforts to effect such an introduction.

The opponents, headed by their popular leader, Mr. Stout (now Sir Robert Stout), had been equally persistent in their opposition, and it was in this state of divided opinion that the committee of the "Free-thought Association," of whom Mr. Stout was the president, solicited me to give a lecture on the subject.

The attendance on this occasion was overwhelming. The question under consideration was, of course, treated from the Liberalists' standpoint, but the main feature of the occasion was the citation of the Bible itself, *as its own witness.* This was done by the simple presentation of about seventy or eighty quotations, in which the character and consistency of the Jewish Jehovah, the morality and humanity of the commands issued, and the agreement of the passages cited with science and chronology were fully displayed, and that on biblical testimony alone, without comment or criticism. At the close of the lecture it was determined to print and circulate gratuitously, ten thousand copies of the biblical quotations, and this was done without any other notice of the texts presented than the simple headings which the extracts illustrated. The sensation produced by this procedure increased the effect of the newspaper and rostrum discussions, and when we were finally compelled to quit Dunedin to fill other engagements, the ladies who had been my most staunch friends and supporters, organised a farewell meeting, at which they presented me with a splendid set of ornaments formed from the jade, or "green stone," so highly prized by the natives as to be deemed "sacred," set in pure New Zealand gold.

Resisting the appeals of many warm friends to make our home in Dunedin, and even the tempting offer of a house and land in that fair city, we at length took leave of the many well-remembered and much prized friends we met there, and passed on our way northwards towards the equator, to the North Island.

We stopped for some weeks at Nelson, Wellington, and Auckland, in each place conducting the same efforts of missionary labour with more or less of the same kind and friendly sympathy from the numerous Spiritualists we met, and encountered the same conflicts with the opponents of our cause.

It was on the last day of the year, 1879, that we once again set foot on the' soil of the United States, landing from the *City of New York* at San Francisco, after a voyage so tempestuous and perilous, that we were unable to land the usual mails and passengers at Honolulu, bringing on also the pilot who breasted the furious storm to reach and warn us off the shore, and losing his boat, with five splendid young Kanakas, swept off in the ebb of boiling waters, which in all human probability proved their grave.

It was then two years since we had set sail for those lands which a few centuries ago were deemed the " nethermost parts of the earth ; " the grave of the mystic Sun God ; the realms of fire, perdition, and every horror which the fevered imaginings of superstitious ignorance could depict. Amongst the fair cities and warm-hearted inhabitants of that once dreaded *terra incognita* we had spent two and twenty of the most eventful months of my career as a messenger of Spiritual glad tidings, and a warrior rather than a propagandist, in the mighty warfare of a faith founded on truth and proven fact, in place of one derived from the myths, legends, and theories of the dark ages two thousand years ago.

The day we landed again at San Francisco we were greeted by our esteemed friends Mr. and Mrs. Foye. From them we learned that little if any favourable change had taken place amongst the broken ranks of the Californian Spiritualists.

Belief in the communion of Spirits and mortals could not fail to be on the rapid increase in a district phenomenally instructed by such an inimitable Medium as Ada Foye, to say nothing of the many others who, with different phases of power, were exercising their gifts in the direction of public tests. As for the religious and philosophic side of the movement, our friends sorrowfully acknowledged that it was at a lower ebb than ever.

Broken up into petty cliques and opposing parties, it seemed as if my mere appearance on the scene only sufficed to unite the discordant elements sufficiently to determine them if they could not engage me in their partisan service, they would at least unite to oppose me. It was in view of this pitiful spirit of "rule or ruin," that dear Ada Foye proposed that we should jointly aid in giving a higher and nobler impulse to the cause by holding meetings in a good hall. I should conduct Sunday services morning and evening, together with certain week-evening meetings for answering questions and holding conferences. At the latter, also on Sunday evenings, Mrs. Foye, then as ever, the best test Medium of the age, agreed to give short test séances. These arrangements were soon concluded between us, and I may here anticipate their results by saying that they were carried on for some months with unwavering success, and the most heartfelt gratification to all concerned, whether as chief actors, managers, or audiences.

We had now been absent from my dear and aged mother over two years, and besides being weary of wandering, longing for home, rest, and anxious for a re-union with my few remaining kindred ties on earth, I deemed it most desirable also that my good husband should be relieved from the incessant toil which the nature of my last series of engagements had imposed upon him. As we were always unanimous in our views of future action, we steadily declined the offers that were pressed upon us to settle in California, or at least to remain there for an extended period of time.

After a final parting with our esteemed friends, we took passage over the Pacific Railway, only stopping to fill brief engagements at Salt Lake City, Nebraska, Rock Island, and the various large cities *en route* from the North West to New York, from whence it was our fixed purpose to embark early in the ensuing year of 1881.

As I am now closing up all my records of foreign travel, and have but little to say of the far more limited scenes of effort which home Spiritualism supplies, I may with propriety devote a few words of introduction to another character in my busy life's drama, who for many months from the time I am writing of had played his constant part in all the scenes we had passed through. This, our invariable attendant everywhere, and on all occasions, was no other than an Australian bird, a splendid specimen of the Corilla, a bird of the parrot species, but white as milk, with a beautiful collar of crimson feathers round his neck, and a large circle of azure round his beautiful black eyes. We bought this bird at a Melbourne Town Hall show of all the wonderful varieties of the Australian feathered tribes, and we were principally moved to do so to please our aged mother, who had always expressed an earnest desire to have the companionship of a fine talking bird. Besides the remarkable conversational powers of my new friend Joe—or, as he chose to call himself, "poor Joey"—we both became warmly attached to him from his remarkable intelligence and his passionate attachment to us. True, we had with him all the discomforts of continual changes, far and wide travel, stormy ocean voyages, and the perils of stage coach bush travelling, but our darling accompanied us joyously. He became acquainted with all the sailors, coachmen, guards, and waiters we encountered, and often called them by name. He was a universal favourite, an excellent dancer, fond of music, to which he moved and danced in capital time—in short, if that creature had not a soul capable of growth and aspiration, an intellect susceptible of cultivation, and a heart full of tender emotions, even to worship of his protectors, neither do any of these glorious attributes, as exhibited in man, constitute claims to immortality. My husband had bought Joe to please me, I had desired to have him to please the dear old mother at home, but both of us soon learned to love and cherish him for his own bright self. Still, in the midst of a constant succession of perils and difficulties attendant upon carrying about this bird, his large cage, and a larder-box, it was a continual comfort to us to hear the good Spirits' invariable assurance that "Joe should go home to mother in England." This promise was especially cheering to me during our last few stormy voyages. During our last passage from New Zealand to San Franciso, out of sixty beautiful Australian birds brought on shipboard, only one survived the stormy and tempestuous twenty days' tossing, and that one was our Joe. True it is that Dr. Britten constantly descended to the hold where he and the rest of the poor birds were kept, to feed, talk to, and comfort him, but even then I should never have expected him to survive the other fifty-nine but for the reiterated assurance of the good Spirits. When all the trials and tribulations of our different journeyings were at length fairly ended, and we were established in a New York boarding-house, a still greater trial awaited our feathered friend. Our landlords and landladies grumbled at poor Joe's clatter. He had learned to imitate ducks, fowls, dogs, and make all sorts of noises on his own account. My dear husband was in very ill health, and no matter how worn out or indisposed he was, Joe and his large cage had to be carried about everywhere. Crowds would gather round us at stations or on steamboats to hear and see him, and reporters called to see and write of him.

We could not leave him when we went hither and thither, and as Dr. Britten's health grew more and more feeble, I not only felt as if poor Joe was killing his kind master, but I contemplated the future difficulties of the ocean passage back to England, with this terrible encumbrance on an invalid, with perfect terror. In this dilemma, I called on Mr. Bergh, the noble and justly

celebrated animals' friend, and the founder of the animal
protection societies, which in New York have rendered his
good name immortal.   Mr. Bergh listened most kindly to
my story, and in answer to my petition that he would find
my feathered darling a good home, he promised to do so
at once, especially as he knew of a lady who had just lost
a bird on which she doated.   She was his dear friend,
would give Joe a splendid home, and was just the best
person in the world to entrust him to.

The interview closed with Mr. Bergh's promise to write
to me as soon as he could see his friend, and arrange for
the transfer, as the lady lived sixty miles away up the
Hudson River.

My dear husband was too ill to remonstrate with me on
my informing him of the arrangement I had made with
Mr. Bergh.   At length, however, the letter came which
apprised me that the next day, the future owner of my
darling would come down from her home to fetch her new
friend.   Mr. Bergh, who was, as it seemed to me, a quiet
but determined man of business, added, in his letter, that
I was to pack up all my bird's belongings, write out his
history, what he could say, and bring him in his cage
to the Hudson River railway station the next day by
three p.m. precisely.   He, Mr. Bergh, would be there
with the lady to meet us.   The next day I packed up my
bird's larder box, wrote out his history, and my husband,
ill as he was, insisting on taking him (knowing too,
perhaps that the parting would half kill me), took a cab,
and placing Joe and his baggage within it, drove off in
time for the appointment.

When my loving and beloved friend of the last two toilsome years was gone, when the cheerful cry of "Emma!
Emma!" was hushed, the merry voice silent, and the
creature that would climb up my dress, sit on my shoulder,
and kiss me again and again was gone, a great still hideous
silence fell on me.

I thought what a coward I had been to banish the thing that so loved me, because he had troubled us. For one hour I walked the *silent, silent* room, in a deep and unmitigated agony of self-reproach.

All of a sudden, and for the first time for some days, I remembered the Spirits' words, so often repeated: "Joe shall go home to mother in England." The remembrance of these words—perhaps more than all else—aggravated the bitterness of the hour, and in that inextinguishable pain the thought that the Spirits had deceived me was the keenest pang of all.

In my intemperate grief and anguish, as I paced that room I stamped my rebellious foot and cried (thinking only of the false Spirit promise), "Liars!" It was at that very moment that I heard the well-known sound of my bird's voice, shouting on the stairs—"Emma! Emma!" To rush to the door, open it, and meet my pale dispirited-looking husband, toiling up the stairs with Joe and his cage in his hand, to snatch that cage back, open it, and clasp my darling to my lips, was all the work of a single minute. Then turning to my still more precious companion, I asked, "How is this?" "Mr. Bergh never came," he replied, "and here I have been waiting for him nearly an hour, with a crowd round me, talking to poor Joe, and admiring him at the Haarlem River Railway Station.

"The *Haarlem River!*" I cried, "That's the wrong side of the station. It's the *Hudson River* at which Mr. Bergh was to meet you—the other side of the station, and a quarter of a mile away."

It was all true; my husband had mistaken my instructions, and gone to the wrong side of the immense Vanderbilt Station, and, as we afterwards found, Mr. Bergh and his friend had been waiting for me a quarter of a mile away, whilst my husband and Joe had been vainly waiting for him at another side of the meeting place.

Again and yet again we asked each other, Was this all
mere accident? Was this all chance? The very moanings
of the winds, the voices of nature, the choral cries of the
mighty city—all answered, NO! The low but never to be
mistaken whispers of angel friends from the life beyond
answered, " NO !" The tender caresses of my recovered
pet syllabled, " NO"! And my own trembling, distrustful
soul was fain to join in the universal chorale of intelligence
around me, and affirm that the seemingly accidental
mistake, was the providential outworking of the inspired
poet's dictum that

> " There's a divinity that shapes our ends,
> Rough-hew them how we will."

That same day, after my treasure had been restored to
me, a friend called, who, finding that by a rare chance I
was disengaged that evening, asked me if I would oblige
him by taking his place as a reporter at the Masonic Hall,
where a conjuror or prestidigitateur was to exhibit for the
first time, an occasion which our friend had promised to
report. I agreed to do this, and about eight o'clock, Dr.
Britten and I entered the great Masonic Hall.

There were scarcely more than twenty people there, and
after we had taken our seats I asked Dr. Britten to go
back to the door and get me a programme. Just as he
left me, some one tapped me on the shoulder, and looking
up, I saw to my astonishment, Mr. Bergh. I should not
have been surprised at his presence anywhere, as every
public building or place of meeting was free and open to
this beneficent and celebrated reformer, but to see him
there, on that *night*, and at the very time when my
husband and I had been planning how best we could
excuse ourselves to him on the following day, for failing
in our appointment—all this, and the singularity of my visit
to such a place, as if on purpose to meet him, so completely

took me by surprise, that all my prepared excuses were
thrown to the winds, and I poured out my whole story to
him at once, and without reserve, winding up with my
involuntary but uncontrollable declaration that the "good
angels had sent my darling back to me."

"I believe you," replied my tall, grave companion, on
whose face I now saw the tears of sympathy falling fast
and thick; then, in a voice broken by emotion, he added:
"I don't know what brought me in here to-night, except,
I suppose, to see you, and tell you that Joe belongs to you.
Keep him until the wise disposer of events calls him hence.
And now, good night."

I have kept him, kept him for twelve years longer, first
"*taking him home to mother.*"

Very soon after our return, that blessed mother found
a higher and sweeter rest than any our love could provide
for her on earth, and as to the fair white pet we brought
her—his cheery voice is hushed in death, and his
crumbling dead form reposes beneath our garden bushes.

But now for the conclusion of this seemingly irrelevant
episode; and yet I write of it because I feel that it involves
some ideas which are indelibly fixed in my mind concerning the philosophy of life here and hereafter. Thus I shall
trespass on my readers' patience by quoting two pages'
from my own magazine, "The Unseen Universe" (No. 10),
pages 528 and 529. Writing of the remarkable intelligence
of my pet bird I had occasion to say: "This creature's love
for me, like his singular intelligence, knew no bounds. He
would follow me about like a dog wherever I went. His
favourite station was on my shoulder, where he would sit
for hours, crooning soft words to me whilst I wrote. I am
not ashamed to say I fully reciprocated his affection, and
and on more occasions than one incurred the *anathema
maranatha* of some of my pious acquaintances by declaring
that no place hereafter would be heaven to me unless I

could meet Joe there." Mr. Colville, in our occasional interviews in America and this country, had formed Joe's acquaintance, and more than once had been invited by the said Joe to "have a cup of tea" with him.

On Sunday, September 18th, 1893, my precious pet terminated his earthly career, nestled in the place he loved best—my arms.

I must state that, for reasons of my own, I never mentioned my loss, either by word of mouth or writing, to any one but my most intimate friends, and none but these have heard of the matter before this writing. For the first time I believe in my acquaintance with him, Mr. Colville wrote to me two or three weeks after I had lost my pet. His letter was dated from Michigan, and though he could not give me any settled address just then where to write to him, he was most anxious to know where and from whence those sounds, so like my old remembered bird's voice, came from. Early in October my darling Joey came fluttering around him, and the names of "Emma" and "Joey" were again and again impressed upon his ear. "He seemed," said Mr. Colville, "as truly with me in my house in Pembroke Street, and again in Baltimore, as when I last saw him with you. What does this mean?" It was not till the November afterwards that Mr. Colville went to New York, and there met Mrs. Wallace, just after her return from England. Mr. Colville mentioned to her the curious and irresistible impression he had of my poor bird's visits, when Mrs. Wallace informed him, *for the first time*, of his departure, as I believe, and think *I know, to another and a higher sphere of being than earth*. I should not care to dwell thus long upon a mere personal episode were it not that I find amongst a large number of educated persons—and that not Spiritualists alone—a strong belief gaining ground of the perpetuity of Spirit being, even in the humblest forms grown on earth.

But little, at least of wide travel or interest, remains for me to say, and perhaps 'nothing that would be worth narrating of my past few years of life passed in England. Under the resistless influence of my ever wise and loving Spirit friends, I and my good husband returned to this land in time to cheer and comfort the last days of my good and faithful mother's life ere its close in her 94th year; yet for special family reasons, though by no means as a matter of personal choice, we resolved to spend the succeeding years of our own fast-fading lives in Manchester, England, the home of the very few scattered relatives that remained to me. On re-visiting London—my own native city—I found that many of the bravest, best, and most eminent of the early pioneers of the Spiritual cause in England had finished their earthly career and passed on higher, leaving few indeed to fill their honoured places.

However, as my future seemed to me to be a solemn duty to carry on the record of the wonderful Spiritual movement everywhere, I determined, as Manchester must be my present sphere of residence, to remain there until released. The last, and as I trust, the final, record in my later life's memorial notices, being the most sad and sorrowful, will also be my last. It reads thus:—

In Memoriam.

Dr. William Britten passed away from his home, The Lindens, Humphrey Street, Cheetham Hill, Manchester, England, and entered the higher life after a long and painful illness of over two years, on November 24th, 1894.

Dr. Britten's ill health, caused by heart disease, though greatly aggravated by lung and liver difficulties, was borne with his usual patience by the uncomplaining sufferer, and none but his medical attendant, Dr. Leslie Jones, and his desolate heart-broken wife—she who now pens these sad lines—ever knew of the weary nights, and days of anguish, the patient suffered and endured.

When at last the bitter end came, good John Lamont, of Liverpool, came to officiate at the usual Spiritual service, and though the earnest friends that passed in were but few of them Spiritualists, all the throng there assembled were deeply touched by the beauty and deep religious significance of the service given. I may venture to say, during our twenty-four years of married life, we had but one heart, soul, purse, or purpose, nor can I recal a word of difference or unkindness that ever passed between us.

Dr. Britten was a widely travelled man. He spoke and wrote in many foreign languages, and was an accomplished scientist in almost every department of earthly knowledge.

As for me, his forsaken earth companion, I can but wait and watch for the echoes of his beloved Spirit voice, still cheering, still guiding me, and longing to join him, when the great Dispenser of eternal law permits, in the land where the parted loved ones rejoin their lamented vanished ones, and where the old adage's hopes will be realised, that " The wicked cease from troubling, and the weary are at rest."

Or, still again, where, with yet nobler realisations of Divine Providence, the struggling souls of earth take their next step in the land of light, and their approach to the spheres of eternal progress.

EMMA HARDINGE BRITTEN.

VALEDICTORY.

In presenting the foregoing pages of the autobiography of my dearly beloved sister, Mrs. Emma Hardinge Britten, to the Spiritualists of the whole world, I have no apology to offer.

The entire history, in every particular, was written and arranged by her during the latter years of her life, and I have (in copying for the benefit of the printers) scrupulously respected her wishes, namely, that nothing should be added to, or taken from, the original manuscript. There is much more of interest and wonderful adventure in her life that could have been told, but she has deemed that what has been given to the public is sufficient to bring before the notice of those interested in the movement of Modern Spiritualism, the wonderful guidance and power, exercised over her during the many years of continuous arduous work and missionary propagandism, through which she has passed.

She sacredly deputed me to complete the work she contemplated undertaking herself before she passed over to the Spirit world, where she still earnestly and faithfully carries on her mission by teaching and preaching to the enfranchised Spirits who have been, from one cause or other, prevented from fulfilling all their earthly career.

The latter part of her life was a sad and suffering one, and more especially so, as her active brain and spirit still wished to do the work she had been accustomed to, and the poor enfeebled frame and worn-out constitution prevented her carrying out her desires. The writings treat more especially of her American experiences, and introduce the names of the early workers in the cause; those, who, like herself, went through scenes and trials (happily now unlikely to be re-enacted) which would deter many of the present workers from entering upon the task of propagating the truths of Spiritualism.

Mrs. E. H. Britten's English experiences are before the world, and in the memory of nearly all now living, and there is so little of incident in them, that she has not thought fit to introduce them into this work. I have, however, in my possession, a vast amount of literary and press notices, which are most valuable and interesting, and may, at some favourable opportunity, be collated and formed into a pamphlet, if it be deemed advisable to do so.

I now send forth the book on its voyage, and trust that it will sail gently but surely to the port at which it has been originally intended to land.

To the many friends who have in my hour of bereavement and trial, sent out their kind and loving sympathy to me, I take this opportunity of presenting my lasting and grateful acknowledgment, and though I may never meet many of them on this side, I shall meet and recognise them on the shores of eternal progress; till then, farewell.

MARGARET WILKINSON.

APPENDIX.

At the request of some of the friends and workers in the Spiritual movement, I have annexed to these auto-biographical sketches a few extracts from a small pamphlet published after Mrs. E. H. Britten's decease.

Margaret Wilkinson.

In Memoriam.

We give her back to Thee, who hast in Thy wisdom given her to us for so long.

Her voice, hushed upon the lower planes of physical being, shall now with sweet cadence awaken the echoes of the empyrean spheres to which she has been called.

No longer shall she tread these earthly paths with weary feet; no longer shall she wander to and fro in eager haste to spread the glad tidings upon this plane of the living. Now in the realms of more exalted matter she shall tread the shining ways of everlasting peace—ever and anon returning in angelic splendour to bless this world for which she laboured with some more sublime revelation of that which is to be.

No longer do we see her in the flesh; but, with exalted countenance lighted by radiant glory, she still stands to bless us with the benediction of her thoughts. And, like a lovely chain of pearls, those thoughts stretch over the border line, linking our hearts to hers.

Emancipated from the wasting sickness, the weariness of the body, the jars and discords of earth-strife, she stands above them now, triumphant in the glory of the new revelation which bursts upon her enraptured soul, as the sunlight breaks upon the countenance of the miner emerging from the bowels of the earth, where, toiling in subterranean passages, amid the shadows cast by his flickering candle, he has been shut off from the greater, brighter, broader beneficence of the sun's life-giving forces.

Oh! sing for the glory which has come to her. Take up your harps, ye earth toilers, and join in the glory-song of those who have greeted her in their midst.

She goes to them as a conqueror from the battlefield. She has slain her tens-of-thousands of errors and superstitions. She has met her opponent by the way and vanquished him.

Now to the clash of arms succeeds the martial note of triumph and the joyous song of praise. The heavens hold for her the glories she has stored.

Ah! they waited long to meet her. From far and near they came to greet her rising soul; as, snapped at last, the feeble cord gave way, and rising free, no longer bound to the body which had ceased to be of service, she emerged into the full waking realisation of the glory she had often dimly seen.

From north, south, east, and west they gathered, waiting for that momentous period when she, who had declared to them the gospel, she who had toiled over prairie and mountain, across river and plain, she who had overcome all kinds of obstacles that she may preach to those in darkness, should step from the barque which had carried her over the tide of earth-life on the mainland of the new country, the spirit-world.

Rough miner and burly ranch-man join in the throng with the cultured of the world. The countess knows no title now save that she earned by toil and love; the duke, the lawyer, the physician; all, all earth's children represented here in this vast concourse which steps forth to greet her; and as she lands, heaven's artillery rends the air in pealing salvoes, and cheer upon cheer ascends from a thousand throats for the joy which comes to the souls who have watched and waited for her coming ever since the thought was passed around that she was near the portal.

All there—no, not all. Some whom she had fondly hoped to see have not yet reached that sphere whence they could join in the welcome-home; but they will be there.

She lives to work, not to rest in idle ease.

Already her active mind is planning new enterprises, and looking forward with great zest to when, shortly, she shall again commence her labours where the failure of her earth-instrument bid her cease for awhile.

And now she speaks to us: "Be of good cheer, the work before you is hard, the way is steep, the dangers are many. Consolidate your forces, strive to organise your strength, let jealousies give place to love and selfishness to sincerity. The path of spiritual knowledge has been but in small part trodden. Go on to greater achievements, grander conquests, more sublime realities.

"In the morning tide the bud of promise hangs decked with diamonds of dew which sparkle in the growing sunlight; the birds carol their brightest lays; the sky is o'erclouded with the haze of promise for a bright and radiant day. On the distant shore you can hear the surf beating, the waves of opposition, cruelty and oppression. The storm is o'er, and these waves gradually grow less and less. Even as we gaze the white crests of the waves are disappearing, and by and by the peaceful calm of a fulfilment shall settle on the scene of erstwhile theological strife.

"Be courageous! It is only so that you can be victors in the world's warfare. Be bold! It is only so you can expect to overcome. Be strong! It is only so you can bear the burden and heat of the day, and help in your time to forward the car of progress, and assist men towards the attainment of their most promising ideals.

"Oh! for the strong man, the resolute woman, not resolute in selfishness and strong in the attainment of personal aggrandisement; but mighty in the championship of right against might, and pertinacious in the advancement of purity and justice.

"Men and women, the call is to you to-day. The spring-time is yours in which to sow. The gathering-time is for your children, who shall reap the harvest of your sowing.

"Fathers and mothers, toil! labour! pray! that ye may be strengthened to help and bless the rising humanity which is slowly marching up 'the steep of time.'

"My day is done—I have striven for the Cause. Humanity has been my congregation, and the world has truly been my parish. From point to point on the globe have I wandered, speaking, organising, working. With those I loved, I laboured to bring to men the 'glad tidings of great joy' of that new birth of spirit revelation; and now my earthly lips are sealed for ever, and my eye of flesh no longer beholds the audience of the earth; but being arisen, yet I speak, and with voice of trumpet tone I would urge you onward and upward toward the realisation of the brightest hopes of the oldest pioneers of Modern Spiritualism."

Let us listen to her message as it is wafted to us from beyond the border. Let us remember her noble life, her continuous endeavours. Let us recal her perseverance in the propagation of the truth, and her bold enterprise in spiritualistically unexplored regions.

Gifted with such an energy as hers, with such a determination as she possessed, our movement should progress as it never yet has done.

Let us use the legacy which she has left to us. Before us lie our possibilities, an unexplored country. What wonders may be revealed to us; what good we may accomplish; what sorrow we may alleviate; what strife we may subdue.

From the Summerland she calls. Shall we heed that call? Shall we be pioneers in the great campaign? Yes! Then come, Spiritualists of all countries, climes, and colours, let her passing on be the signal for a new effort, a determined endeavour, and the commencement of a struggle into which we shall enter with all we possess—our talents, time, and wealth for the good of humanity and the glory of God.

WILL PHILLIPS.

Mrs. Britten's last public efforts for the cause she had done so much to found, and which she loved so dearly, were the opening of the Jubilee Bazaar and the unveiling of a stained-glass window in the Salford Spiritual Church. The following extracts are also from the pamphlet referred to :—

At the Jubilee Bazaar Mrs. Britten threw aside the oncoming weakness, and appeared upon the platform to open the bazaar on the first day. She was greeted with the warmest marks of appreciation, and her appearance evoked the enthusiasm of the great crowd which had assembled.

Loved and respected by all who knew her, she retains in our hearts a place of honour. She laboured for a cause which was all in all to her ; for by its wondrous revelations she had found the shining path of truth ; and having her own spiritual wants relieved, she strove her utmost to meet the necessities of her fellowmen.

The last public ceremony which she performed was the unveiling of a stained-glass window in the Salford Spiritual Church, when she also made her last public appearance. Her wondrous strength and power were again manifested there, for, although weak and feeble, she rose to the occasion, and with much of her old accustomed vigour she spoke of the possibilities and progress of Spiritualism.

This last public act had in it a touch of deep significance. She found Spiritualism in the throes of its arduous birth struggle, and watched it and laboured for it through her life, beholding its steady growth with the intense interest of a parent for her child ; and then, when her time was nearly come, her unveiling of the beautiful stained-glass window was a sign that Spiritualism was consolidating its forces, that gradually it was realising the full dignity of its position, and that it was commencing to bestir itself for a greater effort, which should appeal to the outer world, and answer its great need by providing a beautiful setting for the more lovely jewel of the Gospel of Spiritualism.

Funeral Rites.

The first part of the funeral service was conducted in the house, and only a few of the close personal friends of Mrs. Britten joined her relatives in her study, where, hushed by the icy hand of death, her body lay in calm repose, encased in a neat coffin of polished elm.

The face was calm and reposeful, bearing no trace of the suffering she had undergone. Age only had left its mark; her years numbered only 76, but into her active life she had crowded many times the number of experiences falling to the lot of the ordinary man or woman.

Mr. John Lamont, brave old pioneer, performed the funeral rites. Mrs. Britten always wished him to place away the casket of flesh, as he had done those of her mother and her husband; and before commencing the service he said :—

"It is indeed a privilege to take part on such an occasion as this in performing the last rites for so noble a woman, whose inspirations have instructed and blessed the hearts of men and women the wide world over. Thirty years ago I heard Mrs. Hardinge speak in Hope Hall. Six subjects were chosen by non-Spiritualists, each subject to be given without previous notice. I was asked what I thought of the effort? I said, a most extraordinary woman; but the question of spirits must be set aside. However, having had hundreds of opportunities since, both public and private, of making this noble soul's acquaintance, all those quibbles, for they were quibbles, were dissipated. Revering the honest character with which this lady has raised the flag of reform, we are here to-day meeting on a joyous occasion, not a sorrowful one. Released from that form which has served her so well, and which has been fading away until her desire to be with her loved ones is to-day fulfilled. We here meet with each other, and with those invisible beings with whom we rejoice at the entrance of our sister from weakness into power. The life which now is, and the life which is to be, are closely allied. And now, when the greeting with old friends has been accomplished, what a joyful meeting it must be, and what a welcome she must have had from those whom she had known and loved here—such a welcome as has seldom been accorded to such an illustrious worker. Emma Hardinge Britten, a living sentient soul to-day, is not the woman to remain idle ; she enters upon a work of a more noble and far-reaching character even than that which she has left."

The hymn, " We do not die, we cannot die," was then sung, after which Mr. John Lamont read a short funeral service, with comments. Speaking of the natural body and the spiritual body, he said that " truly the spiritual body which was now hers was as natural as that decaying form which they there beheld. Both physical and spiritual bodies had their glories ; and who, having looked upon the noble bearing and commanding presence of their sister, her face lighted up with the beauty of divine inspiration, could refuse to believe that there was a glory of the physical body ? "

Then, amid a profound silence, broken only by the voice of the speaker, Mr. Lamont said : " Dear sister, we see and recognise you now in your radiant, celestial body, putting that away which you have left. We rejoice on this occasion that we have an opportunity of congratulating you upon your entrance into the higher and brighter life, of which you have so often spoken. We recognise you, not as an influence afar off, but as a living, sentient spirit in our midst, with a large number who have congratulated you on your second birth and entrance into the higher life, where you are surrounded by hundreds who received messages of love and liberty from your lips. We consider it our privilege to enter into the sacred circle of visible and invisible friends who have met together ; and we earnestly pray that in some measure we may be able to follow in the steps of the noble reformers who have gone before. May the Holy Spirit bless us with light, and liberty, and goodness, now and ever. Amen."

Mr. J. J. Morse, president of the National Conference and the British Lyceum Union, then delivered a brief but impressive oration. He said : " My esteemed friends and fellow-workers, I consider it an honour and a privilege just to add a few feeble words of my own to the feeling and eloquent testimony that our venerable senior, Mr. John Lamont, has just offered. Earth has been made the richer by Mrs. Emma Hardinge Britten having lived upon it. Thousands of men and women have had their souls touched and the divine spirit kindled to brighter beauty by the eloquence which has flowed from her lips. Not only her eloquence but the intelligence uttered in those rich reverberating tones echo in our hearts to-day. I treasure as a beautiful and precious possession that I, as a young man, was stimulated to greater and more arduous toil by having had her hand-clasp and encouragement to urge me on. If I can offer no more on the altar of her memory than my esteem for her because of this, I can offer no better nor richer treasure. She fainted not nor spared herself. Consistent and earnest at all times and in all places; in the new life of a new country, and amid the polish of the great cities in the civilised world. Speaking bravely, living earnestly, she never held back to gain a favour, nor for fear of any living mortal. No one has done more to rationalise, to strengthen, and to beautify our Spiritualism than she. She is with us to-day, and the spirit of her life will, I am sure, linger in our minds and in our souls as long as Reason holds her throne and Memory retains her power. I will only say, 'God bless her for her work, and may the echo of her voice ever resound in our inmost beings, causing us to look higher and to be even more zealous than she, if that be possible.' If her life does this for us it will have preached the best sermon that has ever been given to us even through her noble inspiration. Let us remember these things; but let us also remember the sister who has to live for awhile without the personal presence that we, too, loved. We know that death is not death, that our dear sister lives; but there is that sense of personal loss that *must* come to us; and the tears must flow to give relief to our overburdened souls. Looking beyond, we shall each of us come to that time when we shall be able to clasp her hand again, and say 'God bless you,' to her whom we all loved and honoured for her life and for her work."

Mr. Walter Howell said he could scarcely add anything to what had already been said, but they all of them felt that day that their meeting together was not a gathering of mourners, and although tears would come to the eyes, and the darkness of earthly sorrow would for a time intercept the sunlight for them, there was still the consciousness that behind the tears and the cloud of their sadness the sunlight of an immortal spirit smiled. The very tears and cloud which hung in the sky wove the rainbow which spoke to them of the time and state where all tears should be wiped away, and when they should receive their welcome home to that great house of their Heavenly Father. He, too, well remembered listening to the oratorical ability and marvellous inspiration of their risen sister, and having followed humbly over the wide tracts of country where her feet had trod, and had heard the words of praise of those who had heard her voice pleading for the slave, black and white, religious and secular, he could not help recognising that her emancipation had come, and that the chains which had bound her so long had at last been snapped, and that the soul had gone out into the sun-kissed landscape, where father, mother, husband, and brother, had given her a welcome home. And, by and by, when their work was done and their labour ended, may they receive the " well done " as conscientiously as she had received it.

This concluded the ceremonial in the house, and then the coffin was borne amid the lines of assembled friends to the hearse.

The funeral *cortège* was a long one, and contained representatives from all parts of the country. The Yorkshire Union was represented by the following : Messrs. Burchell (President), Whittaker (vice-president), Parker, Collins, and Sutcliffe.

First came a wreath-car, covered with lovely floral emblems, and then the hearse, also loaded with beautiful wreaths, which literally hid the coffin from sight. Punctually at two o'clock the *cortège* left the house, and passing through the heart of Manchester attracted widespread attention. The line of carriages was so extended that when the wreath-car was well out of Albert-square into Cross-street the last conveyance was just entering the square at the other end. Beside the Yorkshire Union, *Light*, the London Spiritualists' Alliance, and The *Two Worlds* Company were represented ; but it would be invidious to attempt to record the names of the societies represented, for from far and near all had united to pay one vast tribute to the memory of our sister's noble work.

From the entrance of the cemetery to the graveside the pathway was lined with Lyceumists, clothed in white, having been arranged in their places by Mr. J. B. Longstaff, ably assisted by Messrs. T. Taylor and Stafford. Mr. A. Rocke conducted the singing.

Around the grave there speedily gathered a great concourse of people. The Lyceum children were in the centre.

Mr. John Lamont gave out a hymn, which was heartily sung, and Mr. J. J. Morse offered an impressive invocation, after which Mr. Lamont spoke briefly in committing the coffin to the grave. He said : " We have not met to bury a woman, but to do honour to a woman who has been resurrected to the spiritual realm of life. She bore the holy flag of reform for many years unsullied and with bravery unexampled. We can here congratulate our sister on her resurrection. Here, standing over these remains, we simply say we are here to give back to nature the physical form through which our sister appeared, while she has arisen to wear the wreath which she wove by her earnest work and loving endeavour."

Mr. E. W. Wallis, as representing the London Spiritualists' Alliance, said they had rendered the last offices which love could render to the mortal form which once enshrined the spirit they had learned to esteem and love. No other cause could have gathered together a more representative body than was there assembled. Knowing, as she did, from the frequent out-pourings of the influence of those wise, teaching spirits, the reality of that life after death, she would feel with them then, she being there and sensing their feelings of gratitude for her noble life. They were standing on sacred ground, for there the two worlds were wedded into one. He trusted that by her noble example they should all be urged more than ever to live their Spiritualism.

Another hymn having been sung, " Tell me not in mournful numbers," Mr. Lamont pronounced a closing benediction, and the assembled crowd surged toward the grave to take a last look at the coffin besprinkled with lovely flowers.

And thus we left her body amid the silence and the stillness of the field of graves.

Soon the crowd had dispersed, although there could be seen many little knots of friends talking over old times and the proceedings of the day.

Throughout the country references were made to the great event of the week, and many resolutions and votes of sympathy and condolence with those left behind were passed in the Societies throughout the length and breadth of the land.